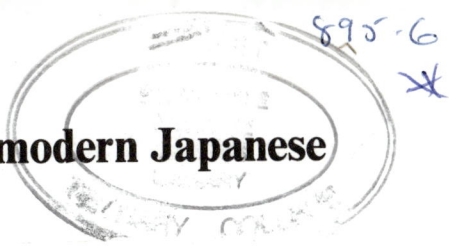

The fantastic in modern Japanese literature

The fantastic brings out the repressed anxieties, fears and hopes of modern Japan. Susan J. Napier's exploration of fantasy in literature, film and comics puts the dark side of Japanese society under the spotlight. She argues that the fantastic reveals the ambivalence felt by many Japanese toward the modernization, economic success and Westernization of Japan in the twentieth century. The bizarre creations of the fantasists produce radically different visions of contemporary Japan from those that stress Japan's success story.

Susan J. Napier brings under scrutiny a rich seam of writers, film-makers and artists: many are discussed here in English for the first time; some are neglected by critics in Japan. Her hunting ground takes in both "high" and "popular" culture. Her discussion of fantasy women embraces the enchantresses created by Izumi Kyōka at the turn of the century and the grotesque and comic sex fantasies of recent science fiction writer Tsutsui Yasutaka. This book introduces the extraordinary range of Japanese fantasy; it also explores the role of fantasy as a cross-cultural genre.

Susan J. Napier is Associate Professor of Japanese Literature and Culture at the University of Texas at Austin.

The Nissan Institute/Routledge Japanese Studies Series

Other titles in the series:

The Myth of Japanese Uniqueness, *Peter Dale*

The Emperor's Adviser: Saionji Kinmochi and Pre-war Japanese Politics, *Lesley Connors*

A History of Japanese Economic Thought, *Tessa Morris-Suzuki*

The Establishment of the Japanese Constitutional System, *Junji Banno, translated by J. A. A. Stockwin*

Industrial Relations in Japan: the Peripheral Workforce, *Norma Chalmers*

Banking Policy in Japan: American Efforts at Reform during the Occupation, *William M. Tsutsui*

Education Reform in Japan, *Leonard Schoppa*

How the Japanese Learn to Work, *Ronald P. Dore and Mari Sako*

Japanese Economic Development: Theory and Practice, *Penelope Francks*

Japan and Protection: the Growth of Protectionist Sentiment and the Japanese Response, *Syed Javed Maswood*

The Soil, by Nagatsuka Takashi: a Portrait of Rural Life in Meiji Japan, *translated and with an introduction by Ann Waswo*

Biotechnology in Japan, *Malcolm Brock*

Britain's Educational Reform: a Comparison with Japan, *Mike Howarth*

Language and the Modern State: the Reform of Written Japanese, *Nanette Twine*

Industrial Harmony in Modern Japan: the Invention of a Tradition, *W. Dean Kinzley*

Japanese Science Fiction: a View of a Changing Society, *Robert Matthew*

The Japanese Numbers Game: the Use and Understanding of Numbers in Modern Japan, *Thomas Crump*

Ideology and Practice in Modern Japan, *Roger Goodman and Kirsten Refsing*

Technology and Industrial Development in Pre-War Japan, *Yukiko Fukasaku*

Japan's Early Parliaments 1890–1905, *Andrew Fraser, R. H. P. Mason and Philip Mitchell*

Japan's Foreign Aid Challenge, *Alan Rix*

Emperor Hirohito and Showa Japan, *Stephen S. Large*

Japan: Beyond the End of History, *David Williams*

Ceremony and Ritual in Japan: Religious Practices in an Industrialized Society, *Jan van Breman and D. P. Martinez*

Understanding Japanese Society: Second Edition, *Joy Hendry*

Militarization and Demilitarization in Contemporary Japan, *Glenn D. Hook*

The fantastic in modern Japanese literature

The subversion of modernity

Susan J. Napier

London and New York

First published 1996
by Routledge
11 New Fetter Lane, London EC4P 4EE

Simultaneously published in the USA and Canada
by Routledge
29 West 35th Street, New York, NY 10001

Typeset in Times by Datix International Limited, Bungay, Suffolk
Printed and bound in Great Britain by
Mackays of Chatham PLC, Chatham, Kent

British Library Cataloguing in Publication Data
A catalogue record for this book is available from the British Library

Library of Congress Cataloguing in Publication Data
A catalogue record for this book has been requested

ISBN   0–415–12457–3 (hbk)
ISBN   0–415–12458–1 (pbk)

To my parents, Julia and Reginald Phelps,
who opened the magic casements

Contents

Series editor's preface

It remains unfortunately true, halfway through the 1990s, that Japan is an underreported country. Despite significant increases in the amount of information available, it is still the case that few aspects of Japan and its people are discussed in comparable depth, or with similar assumptions about familiarity, to discussion of the United States, Britain or other major countries. Differences of language and culture of course constitute a barrier, though less so than in the past. As the patterns of our post-cold-war world gradually consolidate, it is clearer than ever that the regional and global importance of Japan is increasing, often in ways more subtle than blatant. To borrow a phrase from Ronald Dore, we really should start "taking Japan seriously."

The Nissan Institute/Routledge Japanese Studies Series seeks to foster an informed and balanced, but not uncritical, understanding of Japan. One aim of the series is to show the depth and variety of Japanese institutions, practices and ideas. Another is, by using comparison, to see what lessons, positive and negative, can be drawn for other countries. The tendency in commentary on Japan to resort to outdated, ill-informed or sensational stereotypes still remains, and needs to be combated.

The year 1995 began with a devastating earthquake in and around the city of Kōbe, in western Japan, killing over 5,000 people. A little later in the year, the underground railway system of Tokyo was disrupted by the deliberate spilling of toxic chemicals. Several people died and thousands became seriously ill. In the aftermath of this incident, police and media attention focused on a strange new religious sect which dealt in occult beliefs and engaged in bizarre practices. In a sense these events symbolized the unpredictable and turbulent undercurrents beneath the normal day-to-day existence of supermodern Japan. Unsurprisingly, the constant tensions of Japanese life have created a fantasy literature of great richness and diversity. If a people's literature is a mirror of its society, then its fantasy literature reflects, and diffracts through the medium of imagination, the neuroses and tensions of that society. Susan Napier's book introduces us to a world of literary fantasy that, while bearing comparison with much fantasy literature elsewhere, testifies intriguingly to the salient dichotomies of Japan: order with turbulence, delicacy with ugliness, belief in progress with neurotic despair, the assumption of formality in human inter-action with the search for freer and wilder worlds.

J. A. A. Stockwin

Acknowledgements

Many people have helped over the nine (!) years that it took to complete this book. First and foremost I would like to thank my two most important mentors, Professor Howard Hibbett of Harvard University and Professor Asai Kiyoshi of Ochanomizu Womens' University. Proffesor Hibbett remained a gracious and supportive resource throughout the long process. Professor Asai not only gave encouragement but offered considerable time and energy in helping me track down all kinds of interesting and novel sources. I am profoundly grateful to both of them.

Professor Earl Miner of Princeton encouraged me while I was there to teach a graduate seminar on the fantastic in Japanese literature. It was the success of that seminar which made me see the potential for this book. I would also like to thank all the students who participated in that seminar for their interest and industriousness.

The Fulbright Foundation provided the grant for me to carry out my initial research. I cannot thank them enough. Caroline Yang, director of the Japanese Fulbright office at that time, was particularly helpful and inspiring.

My former colleagues at the School of Oriental and African Studies at the University of Texas were also extremely helpful. I would particularly like to thank Dr. Lola Martinez who helped with anthropological sources. Two of my students at SOAS also deserve special mention: Isolde Standish who wrote a brilliant paper on Murakami Haruki's *Hard Boiled Wonderland and the End of the World*, and Paul Hulbert whose fascinating paper on Yumeno Kyūsaku piqued my interest in this regrettably little-known writer.

My interest in Izumi Kyōka was further developed, thanks to Charles Inouye of Tufts University, whose panel on Kyōka prompted me to do further research on Kyōka's masterpiece *Kōya hijiri*. Three other friends who deserve very special gratitude are Joel Cohn of the xii *Acknowledgements*

University of Hawaii, Mary Ellen Mori of Santa Clara University and John Treat of The University of Washington. Their suggestions for improving the manuscript were incredibly thorough and helpful, well above and beyond the call of duty. I also owe John Treat another vote of thanks for helping to promote my interest in Japanese *manga*, especially *Akira*. I am also grateful to Professor Arthur Stockwin of the Nissan Institute at Oxford for his kind words and support of the project.

My editors at Routledge were all wonderful to work with. I would especially like to thank Gordon Smith, who "discovered" the manuscript and shepherded it through its first stages, and Victoria Smith and Diane Stafford who had the arduous job of helping me stay on track through the final stages. I would also like to thank Professor Robert Luskin of the University of Texas whose editing suggestions were extremely helpful.

Finally, I would like to thank Dr. Rodney Moag, my former chairman at the Department of Oriental and African Languages at the University of Texas. Dr. Moag allowed me a semester's leave to complete this project and I am very grateful.

Susan J. Napier,
Austin, Texas.

A note on the text

Not all the works discussed in this book are available in English, although the number of good literary translations from Japanese is increasing, aided by events such as Ōe Kenzaburō recently winning the Nobel Prize for literature. Where a work is available in translation this is clearly indicated and the title and date of the translation are given as well as the Japanese title and original publication date. In these cases any page numbers quoted refer to the translation. Where a work is not available in translation an English approximation of the title is given when the work is first mentioned. For ease of reference the bibliography is divided into works in English and works in Japanese.

1 Introduction

Fantasies are never ideologically "innocent."
(Rosemary Jackson, *Fantasy: The Literature of Subversion*)

In 1908 Natsume Sōseki,[1] perhaps the greatest of modern Japanese writers, published an eerie fantasy called *Yume jūya* (trans. *Ten Nights of Dream* (1974)) consisting of ten short visionary stories purporting to be dreams. In the haunting "Dream of the Sixth Night" the dreaming "I" watches absorbedly as Unkei, a master sculptor from the thirteenth century, carves immense "guardian gods" on the gate of a Tokyo temple. Inspired by Unkei's brilliance, the protagonist returns home to try to carve gods out of the wooden logs in his garden. His attempt is a failure. As he relates it:

> I chose the largest log and began to carve with great spirit. But unfortunately, I found no god within it. . . . I dug through every log in the woodpile, one after another, but nary a one contained a guardian god. And finally it dawned on me that guardian gods were not, after all, buried in trees of this present age [Meiji period in the original]; and thus I came to understand why Unkei is living to this day.
>
> (p. 48)

I begin a discussion of the fantastic in Japanese literature with this dream because it foregrounds a number of the most important aspects of the modern Japanese fantastic, including the contradictory presence of the Japanese past. "Dream of the Sixth Night" is suffused with a nostalgia for a purer, richer past, a past which is increasingly inaccessible to the modernizing Japan of the Meiji period (1868–1912) during which Sōseki wrote.

The narrative strategies Sōseki uses to describe this inaccessibility are far from traditional, however. Indeed, *Ten Nights of Dream* is so different from premodern fantasy literature that one critic has stated that "modern Japanese fantasy begins with *Ten Nights of Dream*."[2] In its effective development of a surreal atmosphere of Otherness, combined with its imaginative use of the notion of dream itself, the work creates a liminal literary world which is clearly that of the twentieth century. It is a world which Freud or Jung would certainly have recognized in terms of its suffocating representation of such peculiarly modern anxieties as crises of identity and free-floating guilt, expressed through archetypal imagery.

But *Ten Nights of Dream* does more than reflect a generalized modern angst. Although the ten dreams use such universal fantastic strategies as dreams, metamorphoses, magical women, and magical other worlds, the work is also highly culturally specific to modern Japan. In this ability to be universally accessible yet culturally specific it shares some of the aspects of another, more famous, non-Western version of the fantastic, the magic realism of Latin America.

Latin American magic realism produces compelling archetypal fantasy while expressing the complex and tragic history of Latin America. Similarly, Sōseki and other writers of Japanese fantasy created works that appeal to non-Japanese readers at the same time as they used specifically Japanese elements to portray concerns particular to modern Japan. In the case of Sōseki's *Ten Nights of Dream*, his ten short fantasies problematize in a memorably original fashion the question of what it is to be a modern Japanese, trapped in a world where the "guardian gods" have disappeared.

Sōseki's fantastic dreams are also peculiarly apt representations of their period, the late Meiji, a time of enormous change in Japanese society. This period is typically viewed as the first chapter in Japan's extraordinary success story, but Sōseki's works deal with the dark side of the Meiji success. These darker elements include the increasing oppressiveness of technology, the isolation of the individual, and the seemingly permanent identity crisis suffered by the Japanese *vis-à-vis* the West.

Turning to the 1990s, such concerns may initially seem outmoded. If anything, the history of Japan since the Second World War has been a success story of even more impressive proportions. Indeed, post-war Japan itself has become something of a myth if not a full-blown fantasy.

In both Japan and other countries, the nation was seen by economists and sociologists as a "phoenix from the ashes", rising from the defeat and devastation of the 1940s and early 1950s to become the

"Japan as Number One" of the 1970s. To its own people, and to many non-Japanese observers as well, Japan seemed to embody both the dreams and nightmares of the twentieth century. The "dream" side of a stable, harmonious, and prosperous society was perhaps best represented when Ezra Vogel's 1978 book *Japan as Number One* (subtitled *Lessons for America*) became a bestseller in Japan while achieving the rank of required reading on numerous American university courses.

On the nightmare side, we might consider Ridley Scott's 1982 dystopian film *Blade Runner*, whose dark opening scene is dominated by clearly Japanese images. The film portrays its down-and-out protagonist, a twenty-first-century detective, eating sushi in a bleak urban cityscape that is technically Los Angeles. But this is a Los Angeles in which, as Giulana Bruno describes it, "[t]he explosive Orient dominates, the Orient of yesterday incorporating the Orient of today. Overlooking the city is the 'Japanese simulacrum', the huge advertisement which alternates a seductive Japanese face and a Coca-Cola sign."[3]

In *Blade Runner* the "Orient," especially Japan, is seen in a dual role, as both "explosive" and "seductive." In William Gibson's (1984) classic cyberpunk novel, *Neuromancer*, in contrast, the seductive side is lost. The reader follows the opening adventures of its computer-hacker protagonist through the high-tech wasteland of twenty-first-century Chiba, an industrial city outside of Tokyo. In Gibson's vision this mazelike international city becomes a metaphor for the bleak postmodern culture his protagonist inhabits.

Other media visions of Japan are less international, although indubitably fantastic. A 1992 *Newsweek* article on Japan's economic threat included a quotation referring to the Japanese as a potential race of "economic terminators."[4] The reference was to the American movie *Terminator*, about a high-tech monster that continuously comes back from the dead to crush its opponents, but the tone was parochial rather than cosmopolitan.

The Japanese themselves have created memorably bleak fantasy scenarios about their future. From the turn of the century Japanese readers and writers eagerly embraced the science fiction genre, but science fiction celebrations of Japanese modernization are few. Instead, dystopian visions of technology run amok and social and psychological collapse have been a consistent thread throughout twentieth-century Japanese science fiction.[5]

This trend has been even more obvious in film. In 1989, for example, just when Japan seemed to be riding high with its unprecedented bubble economy, the brilliant dystopian animation film *Akira* became the highest-grossing film in Japan. A few years later, with Japan mired in an apparently endless recession, *Akira* became a major cult favorite both in America and in England, its success due both to its exuberant postmodern celebrations of vivid metamorphoses and its remarkably well-realized vision of a grim twenty-first-century Japan.

Both internally and externally, then, images of Japan seem destined to be flavored with fantastic associations. Furthermore, these associations are both positive and negative. They range from the image of Japan as a Utopian world, in which modernity actually works, to the forbidding image of Japan as dystopian high-tech nightmare.

Modern Japan has also had a long and important tradition of mimetic fiction which has delved into the contradictory complexities of modern Japanese society. Even many of the writers discussed in this book are best-known for their works of realism. The realistic tradition in Japanese literature has already been widely studied, however, both in Japan and in the West. Furthermore, as I hope the above examples hint, it is my contention that it is the fantastic genre in the Japanese arts, from Sōseki's brief, disturbing *Ten Nights of Dream* to *Akira*'s apocalyptic vision, that best encapsulates the contradictory state of modern Japan, in which capitalist success on an unprecedented scale clashes with a still unburied traditional culture.

This is not to say that every Japanese fantasy tells the same story. Although many works contain important common elements, there is also an immense and fascinating variety to the modern Japanese fantastic. In its strategies, its techniques, and finally in its messages the fantastic is multivalent. It also changes dramatically depending on the period.

Thus, while Sōseki's "Dream of the Sixth Night" is an appropriate representative for Meiji Japan, perhaps the archetypal fantasy for contemporary Japan is Murakami Haruki's *Sekai no owari to hādoboirudo wandārando* (1985) (trans. *Hard Boiled Wonderland and the End of the World* (1991)). Told in a style that mixes Raymond Chandler with *The Forbidden Planet* (and thus a splendid reflection of the assimilation of Western influences on modern Japanese culture), the book portrays a future Japan which has, again, been abandoned by any sort of guardian spirit. But, unlike the implicit decision to continue living in the abandoned modern world expressed by the "I" of Sōseki's work, the "I" in *Hard Boiled Wonderland and the End of the World* ultimately decides to leave the outer high-tech world of modern late twentieth-century Japan to retreat into a fantasy Utopia inside his own mind.

When his other self in shadow form attempts to reason with him about this decision, the "I" explains: "I have responsibilities ... I cannot forsake the people and places and things I have created. . . . This is my world." In this late-twentieth-century world the protagonist feels that his responsibilities are to himself, not to a wider society or history.

Between these two poles, Sōseki's dreamer who digs ever more frantically into wooden logs to carve out an ultimately unattainable past and resignedly accepts living in his present period, and Murakami's bifurcated "I" who consciously abandons his present age to carve his own world inside his brain, lies close to a century of modern Japanese history. This has been a history arguably more psychically tumultuous than that of any other nation. Despite the recent developments in China, it is still Japan which stands alone at the nexus of modernization and Westernization, still the only non-Western country to be counted as an equal by the Western powers.

In its own way the idea of Japan itself is at the convergence of Utopian and fantastic traditions, a country whose economic success has defamiliarized the very notion of capitalist development by allowing the West to see itself through a glass darkly. The changes in Japan over the twentieth century have both echoed and amended the developments of the West, from the militarism of Meiji Japan to the imperialism of Taishō and early Shōwa. In the postwar period Japan (and Western observers) have seen the dawning and eventual triumph of a careerist, materialist consumer culture so widespread as to seem almost a parody of capitalism's ultimate goal. Finally, in the 1990s with the rise of marginalized and subversive elements in Japanese society, the consumer dream seems now to contain elements of the dystopian nightmare such as the recent slaying of little girls by a young man supposedly inspired by his enormous video collection.

DEFINITIONS AND FUNCTIONS OF THE FANTASTIC

Given this extraordinary history it seems appropriate that the fantastic should be the vehicle most suited for understanding modern Japan. It is important, however, to understand more specifically how the fantastic works and its differences from mimetic or realistic fiction. Perhaps the most important difference is one of degree. While all fiction inherently defamiliarizes the "real," the very *raison d'être* of fantastic fiction is its existence in contrast to the "real."

The works discussed in this book all maintain a diverse, complex, and fascinating relationship to the "real", in this case the "real" of twentieth-century Japan, its history, its society, and its official ideology.

Occasionally they confirm the official world-view, even celebrate it. More frequently, their relationship is oppositional, but in a subtle and indirect fashion. In some cases these works escape from or compensate for the real in an implicit form of subversion. In other cases, however, they resist it, transgress it, and ultimately attempt explicitly to subvert it. The works discussed here vary greatly from one to the other but they all belong to the problematic and fascinating genre of the fantastic.

What is the fantastic? In writing this book I came across innumerable definitions. Many tend to equate it with wish-fulfillment fantasy and see the genre primarily as one of escape. David Hartwell, in an essay in the *New York Times Book Review*, puts it bluntly:

> Fantasy promises escape from reality. It is characteristic of fantasy stories that they take the readers out of the real world of hard facts, hard objects and hard decisions into a world of wonders and enchantments.[6]

Hartwell is the descendant of a long line of critics on fantasy (often fantasy writers themselves) who not only see fantasy as escape but also applaud that particular function. One of the most famous of these writers is J.R.R. Tolkien, who asserts,

> Why should a man be scorned if, finding himself in prison, he tries to get out and go home? Or, if and when he cannot do so, he thinks and talks about other topics than jailers and prison-walls? The world outside has not become any less real because the prisoner cannot see it.[7]

Tolkien's notion of fantasy is a traditional, indeed moralistic one, but the function of the fantastic as wish-fulfillment is an important one in many of the Japanese works discussed here. Tolkien's implicit notion of some transcendent "home" located, one presumes, within the fantastic, versus the "prison-like world outside" that seems to embody Tolkien's vision of reality is a concept that is echoed in the works of many Japanese writers, especially those of earlier periods such as Tanizaki and Kawabata.

For some critics, fantasy, especially popular fantasy, is a dangerous instrument of control, subtly propounding a consensual world view that allows for but ultimately contains any thoughts of escape or rebellion. In this view fantasy is akin to a drug, "an agent of stasis", as Peter Kramer says of psychotherapy and anti-depressants.[8] This kind of palliative function of fantasy, what Jameson describes as the "legitimation of the existing order,"[9] is also very much part of

Japanese popular culture. Notable examples include such popular science fiction as the *Gundam* series, which is essentially a celebration of advanced technology and hegemonic warfare, or the *Warau sērusman* (Laughing Salesman) comics which use fantasies to drive home conservative messages.

Other critics completely ignore the ideological and moral implications of the fantastic, preferring to concentrate on its formal aspects as a genre. Of these more formalistic interpretations, the most well known and compelling is Tzvetan Todorov's definition in his book *The Fantastic: A Structural Approach to a Literary Genre* (1975). In Todorov's theory, the fantastic is a limited genre marked by a moment of hesitation on the part of the reader, and often the characters, as to how to explain a particular event or occurrence which appears to be impossible. The explanations distill down into two types: the impossible event really happens, in which case we are in the realm of the supernatural, or the event can be explained by some rational determination, as an hallucination, perhaps, or a trick. For Todorov, however, it is not the explanation, but the moment of hesitation before the explanation, when the reader/protagonist waits in suspenseful anticipation for the final resolution, that constitutes the true fantastic.

As many critics of Todorov have pointed out, his theory, although brilliant, is an extremely limiting one. Few works can actually maintain the fantastic hesitation throughout the entire text. Interestingly, however, Japanese literature contains some superb examples of this type, such as Akutagawa's "Yabu no naka" (1921) (trans. "In a Grove" (1952)), Ōe Kenzaburō's "Sora no kaibutsu Aguii" (1964) (trans. "Agwhee the Sky Monster" (1977)), and Endō Shūsaku's *Sukyandaru* (1986) (trans. *Scandal* (1988)). Even if we prefer a broader definition, however, Todorov's structuralist and reader-response based theory brings up some important implications.

The first is the implication that the fantastic is a genre based on uncertainties. Unlike the presumed purpose of "Realism", the fantastic is specifically not trying scientifically to observe and represent the world as we know it, because the fantastic implies that we cannot know the world. This is also in important contrast to what W. R. Irwin distinguishes as the genre of traditional "fantasy", or wish-fulfillment. As he explains it:

> The writer of fantasy avoids prompting those hesitations, uncertainties and perceptions of ambiguity that Todorov takes to be essential in the experiencing of *litterature fantastique*. In successful fantasy all is clarity and certainty, as far as presentation goes. Thus fantasy,

though often using the same material, moves in a direction opposite to that of *litterature fantastique*.[10]

Pure "fantasy" literature, then, is an escape, not so much from reality, or not entirely at least, as an escape from uncertainty. Tolkien's own trilogy, *The Lord of the Rings*, whose last book is significantly titled *The Return of the King*, is an example of the resolution of uncertainty that Todorov's fantastic would not allow.

And yet, if we widen our definition to include both the marvellous or wish-fulfilling and the Todorovian fantastic, we find that the fantastic is, as Rosemary Jackson argues, a paradoxical genre.[11] Constituted on uncertainties, it seeks to resolve them, and it is this constant, unfulfilled quest of desire which gives impetus to much of the genre, from wish-fulfillment to a limited Todorovian "fantastic." In an oft-quoted passage Jackson explains that "fantasy" (which she uses interchangeably with "the fantastic," a practice which this book also adopts),

> characteristically attempts to compensate for a lack resulting from cultural constraints: it is a literature of desire which seeks that which is experienced as absence and loss.[12]

She later adds:

> The fantastic traces the unsaid and the unseen of culture: that which has been silenced, made invisible, covered over and made "absent."[13]

Jackson's interpretation returns us to the realm of ideological criticism. Her description of the fantastic as a literature of desire leads naturally to her more general point, which is that fantasy is most importantly a literature of subversion. She examines this aspect of fantasy in relation to the rise of the realistic novel with its vision of "unity" in the nineteenth-century West and concludes that, "[s]ubverting this unitary vision, the fantastic introduces confusion and alternatives; in the nineteenth century this meant an opposition to bourgeois ideology upheld through the 'realistic' novel."[14]

In my own research on the Japanese fantastic I have increasingly come to agree with Jackson. Despite the popular culture celebrations, most Japanese fantasy exists as a counter-discourse to the modern, even when it seems most blatantly escapist. For I would like to emphasize that even escapist fantasy can be subversive. An escapist dream can comment subversively on the reality from which the dreamer wishes to escape, as was clear in Tolkien's emotional defense of the emancipating powers of fantasy. Furthermore, in generic terms the existence of a fantastic genre itself is a comment upon the "real," since it exists in contrast to it.

Other well-known definitions of fantasy or the fantastic are worth considering. Eric Rabkin's *Fantastic in Literature* (1976) concerns itself largely with subject matter. The work begins with an analysis of Alice's astonished reaction to the talking plants in Lewis Carroll's *Through the Looking Glass*. Rabkin argues that the fantastic mode is established through the reversal of the ground rules: as he says, "One of the key distinguishing marks of the fantastic is that the perspectives enforced by the ground rules of the narrative world must be diametrically contradicted."[15] Important ways in which ground rules are contradicted are through the common themes of fantasy such as talking beasts, magic mirrors, dreams, journeys to other worlds, metamorphoses, and doubling, all of which occur frequently in Japanese fantasy.

Rabkin's work is less concerned with the extraliterary dimensions of fantasy than Jackson's book. Looking for a definition that would better encompass the multivalent aspects of the fantastic, I finally chose the widest possible one, based on Kathryn Hume's definition in *Fantasy and Mimesis: Responses to Reality in Western Literature* (1984), which is that "*Fantasy is any departure from consensus reality*"[16] (Hume's italics). Such a broad definition will render this book liable to criticisms of its being too all-inclusive. However, given that there are, as yet, no other studies of the fantastic in modern Japanese literature, I feel that broadness is actually a virtue.

In that regard, I would amend Hume's definition slightly to add that, "fantasy is any *conscious* departure from consensus reality," since I am also concerned with the motivations behind the writer's decision to write in the fantastic mode. By choosing to use the fantastic the author guarantees that the story will be received differently from one written in a conventional realistic mode. Indeed, for many years to write in the fantastic genre in Japan was implicitly to marginalize oneself compared to the mainstream genre of Naturalism.

This was true in the West as well since, for much of the twentieth century, the fantastic has been looked down upon as a marginal genre in relation to the "serious" genre of realism.[17] Paradoxically, in both the West and Japan such marginalization could be liberating to some writers. The turn-of-the-century writer Izumi Kyōka (1873–1939),[18] for example, wrote powerful fantasies in which traditional Japan in the form of its most fantastic denizens consistently revenged itself on modernity and its representatives.

In recent years, however, the perception of the fantastic as nonserious has changed radically as the fantastic has become a genre whose importance is increasingly recognized in current literary theory. One of the most obvious reasons behind this change is simply the increased number of fantastic texts now available. As Marguerite Alexander puts it in *Flights from Realism: Themes and Strategies in Postmodernist British and American Fiction* (1990), "The late twentieth century ... has seen a revival of the fantastic on a scale unprecedented since the Middle Ages."[19] Alexander's work refers mainly to the ever-increasing number of "anti-realist" postmodernist texts, but it is worthwhile to remember how important the fantastic has been in popular culture as well, as even a cursory glance at the average airport bookstore will show.

Why do contemporary authors choose to write in an anti-realist mode? As Hume, and many other critics argue, traditional realism no longer seems to satisfy or give meaning in an increasingly complex world. The fantastic, whether it subverts the search for meaning through postmodernist deconstructive form, or provides alternative ways to search for meaning through the reactionary popular forms of sword and sorcery, at least seems to inherently recognize that complexity and unknowability.

Japanese writers seem to be recognizing that unknowability even more than their Western counterparts. It is not surprising therefore, that some of the most interesting and often most popular of Japanese writers today, such as Murakami Haruki, Kurahashi Yumiko, and Tsutsui Yasutaka routinely depart from consensus reality in their works. The fantastic, ranging from the complex parodies of Kurahashi Yumiko to the immensely popular *manga* (comics) of Takahashi Rumiko and Ōtomo Katsuhiro, is a firmly entrenched part of Japanese culture. Most large bookstores nowadays not only routinely have a science fiction section but a fantasy section as well, and Japanese critics write a considerable amount on both Western and domestic fantasy.

Needless to say, Japan is not unique among non-Western countries in possessing an important tradition of fantastic literature. Indeed, the fantastic mode is perhaps one of the most universal of literary forms, encompassing such classics as the *1001 Nights* of the Arabic world or the Chinese magical quest saga, *The Journey to the West*.

Outside of Europe and North America, however, the most well-known and studied anti-realist tradition has been the "magic realism" of Latin America. The Latin American magic realists share some significant commonalities with Japanese fantasists. The most important of these is their shared problematic relationship to the "real," a real that for many years was constituted in terms of the dominant Western discourse.[20] By the late nineteenth century, "realism" as it was understood in the Western realist tradition, as an attempt to represent empirical reality, was held up as the ideal literary mode in both Japan and Latin America. Attempts to write in this approved realistic fashion often led to important and successful works, but frequently also led to a conscious belittling of the indigenous literary tradition.

For twentieth-century writers of both Japanese and Latin American literature, then, the decision to write in the fantastic mode was, almost inherently, a subversive one. It was a decision to choose an alternative, consciously non-Western way of representing the world. Or as Lois Zamora says of ghosts, one of the key elements of magical realist fiction (and, as we shall see, an important element of the Japanese fantastic as well):

> [The ghosts'] presence in magical realist fiction is inherently oppositional, because they represent an assault on the basic scientific and materialist assumptions of western modernity: that reality is knowable, predictable, controllable.[21]

Ghosts, androgynes, metamorphoses, and mirror images abound in Japanese fantasy, inherently questioning the notion of a single "real." Moreover, just as Latin American writers went back to their indigenous folk traditions to draw inspiration for contemporary fantasies, a number of Japanese writers, from Izumi Kyōka to Ōe Kenzaburō and Nakagami Kenji, go back to rural myth to revitalize their own visionary works. We might suggest that the Latin American and Japanese impulse toward the fantastic is a literal rediscovery of a lost imaginary, the world that in Lacan's theories constitutes the womb, the place of union before the law of the father forces the infant into the world of the Symbolic. In the case of Japan and Latin America, the law of the father is clearly the discourse of the West. It is perhaps not a coincidence, therefore, that imagery of the womb is extremely important in the Japanese fantastic while the father, virtually a staple in pre-war Japanese realism, is notable for his absence.

THE FANTASTIC IN JAPANESE LITERATURE

At the same time, however, major differences do remain between the fantastic literatures of Latin America and Japan; in fact, between Japan and any other non-Western nation. Perhaps the most important one is that, paradoxically, it is Japan in the 1990s, rather than Latin America for all its Western roots, which is unequivocally a "First

World" nation. The fact that it is also the only non-Western nation to be so accepted only makes the position of the fantastic in its literature all the more complicated and interesting. For Japanese fantasy does not only look back to indigenous myth, it also creates its own worlds, worlds which are totally "modern" at the same time as they are "Japanese."

Thus, Japanese fantasy does not always celebrate the inability to control the real that is part of the pleasure in magic realism. Bound far more tightly to the technological modern world of the twentieth century, the Japanese fantasy writer often depicts characters in desperate search of some form of "knowability" or certainty, only to find that even the search itself is simply an illusion.

What the fantastic is subverting in modern Japanese literature, then, is not so much "Westernization" as modernity itself, a modernity in which Japan has participated at least as fully and wholeheartedly as any Western country. To study the fantastic in modern Japanese literature is, therefore, to find a kind of mirror image of modern Japanese history, the reverse side of the myths of constant progress, economic miracle, and social harmony; stereotypes which have dominated the thinking not only of those outside Japan but among the Japanese themselves.

This myth is omnipresent throughout Japanese society and culture, starting before the twentieth century, in fact, with the stunning success of the Meiji Restoration in 1868. Although literally an attempt to "restore" the emperor, the Restoration was in actuality closer to a revolution, ushering in a floodtide of change in which Japanese society attempted to both "modernize" and "Westernize" to a degree and with a success yet to be equalled by any other non-Western country. This program of development was carried out under government auspices, but the deep-seated response of the citizenry was also notably enthusiastic.

Carol Gluck in *Japan's Modern Myths: Ideology in the Late Meiji Period* (1985) discusses the importance of such beliefs as progress, often symbolized by the image of the locomotive, and material success in general, as the foundation on which Japan's modernity was conceived.[22] Indeed, Gluck suggests that, more than the state or the imperial house, it was the word "modernity" itself which held a strange appeal for the late-nineteenth-and twentieth-century Japanese. At the same time, however, modernization was not a seamless process and the costs, both social and psychological, were many.

Japanese literature, whether mimetic or fantastic, has often explored these costs in a variety of important and evocative works. It is my view, however, that it is the fantastic that has shown both the positive and negative sides of modernity on the deepest and most archetypal level. On the positive side, the fantastic was particularly suited for treating such images of progress as the locomotive which becomes a "night train to the stars" in the works of Miyazawa Kenji or a train back to rural identity in Inoue Hisashi's *Kirikirijin* (The People of Kirikiri)(1981).

More often, however, the fantastic has revealed the dark depths of modernity in extraordinary and memorable images, such as the lunatic asylums and hospitals of Akutagawa and Yumeno Kyūsaku, the out-of-control technology of Abe and Ōe, or in the sustained and vivid attacks on evolution by such disparate writers as Izumi Kyōka and Tsutsui Yasutaka. Alternatively, the Japanese fantastic, at least in the pre-war period, also proffered images of escape, often inscribed in the figure of a fantasy woman, whose luminous maternality in the pages of a Tanizaki novel or a Kyōka story offered a refuge from the turmoil of the real world.

Even in its images of escape, however, the Japanese fantastic inherently questioned the dominant ideology of progress and modernity, raising the issue of why such an escape should be necessary. Even at its most wish-fulfilling, then, the Japanese fantastic has had a stimulating function rather than an opiate one. As Tom Moylan puts it, "[f]antasy links the unconscious with consciousness, dreams with reality, and preserves the tabooed images of freedom."[23] Rather than accepting stasis, the fantastic has undermined and resisted it, often in ways which forced readers to question or at least investigate their identity as modern Japanese.

This brings me to another aim of this study, which is to discover if there is in fact such a thing as a purely "Japanese" fantastic. Writers such as Miyoshi Masao (1991) and Edward Fowler (1988) have pointed out that the Japanese view of the "real" in general and literary realism in particular is markedly different from that of the West, even when Japanese writers were supposedly "copying" Western realism, especially the Naturalist tradition. They point to the importance of the *shishōsetsu* (loosely translatable as autobiographical or confessional novel), which privileges "lived experience" and "sincerity" over the supposedly artificial constructs of Western realism. Fowler points out that the Japanese writer "never had the faith in the authority of representation that his Western counterpart had"[24] and that in Japan "the notion of what is real or authentic is traditionally limited to personal observations and experiences."[25]

If the Japanese attitude toward the "real" is so different, then is it possible to find the equivalent of the Western fantastic in Japan? Indeed, is my search for a "Japanese equivalent" an inherently hegemonic or reductive one, suggesting that Japan "needs" Western equivalents? Obviously I would not have written such a book had I thought the answer to be yes, but the question is still an important one.

Once again I turn to Hume for a broad enough theory that will not reduce Japanese fantasy to simply a lower form of its Western counterpart. As Hume puts it in a discussion of the fantastic impulse in general, "the impulse to depart from consensus reality is present for as long as we have had literature."[26]

We may, of course, argue that the Japanese version of "consensus reality" is different from that of the West, but I would still assert that there at least exists a consensus reality in Japan from which writers have consciously departed throughout Japanese history. As Hume argues, "consensus reality" is "verifiable reality," and she presents Greek myths as some of the earliest Western forms of "departure." In Japan, mythmaking occurs at least as early as the *Kojiki* (Record of Ancient Matters (*circa* AD 712)), which is the most important text of Japanese Shinto. In the *Kojiki* the dead return to life, heroes slay dragons, and a male and a female god create the Japanese archipelago. It may be that none of these occurrences was considered impossible by premodern Japanese but they were, at least, unverifiable.

Satire has also often been linked to the fantastic impulse, and we can find early examples of what could be called fantastic satire in the animal scrolls of the Heian period, grotesque parodies of contemporary noblemen and clerics. Moving to a later but still premodern period in Japanese history, we find that the plays and fiction of the pleasure quarters in the Tokugawa period (1600–1868) contained a large number of admittedly impossible occurrences and events. Furthermore, Tokugawa fiction also often mixes the fantastic with the satiric.

It should be noted, however, that this sort of obviously fictional writing was looked down upon as vulgar by the elite. Fowler explains that Tokugawa writing was divided into "two distinct strains: 'refined' nonfiction literature that commented seriously on life and 'vulgar' nonliterary fiction that burlesqued life."[27] This general condemnation of fiction continued until the late nineteenth century and the onset of Westernization with its overwhelmingly influential doctrines of realism and Naturalism.

It was such popular but serious writers as Natsume Sōseki and Akutagawa Ryūnosuke who helped to give *junbungaku* (pure literature) a good name. Both writers were avid students of Western literature, although both also possessed strong backgrounds in Japanese and

Chinese classics. Intriguingly, Akutagawa and Sōseki were among the most vociferous critics of the *shishōsetsu* (although Akutagawa would come closer to the genre toward the end of his life) and wrote a number of works that could be classified as fantastic. Akutagawa, in particular, is known in both Japan and the West for his imaginative and often surprising fantasies which incorporate both "impossible" situations with an attitude toward the real that is fascinatingly ambivalent. Perhaps the best example of this is Akutagawa's famous short story, "In a Grove" (familiar to many Westerners in Kurosawa's 1953 film version, *Rashōmon*).

Based on a tenth-century story from the *Konjaku monogatari*, "In a Grove" illustrates one of Akutagawa's primary techniques, the use of the fantastic to inject a further note of uncertainty into an already unknowable world. In this work, Akutagawa uses a mystery-story format, specifically a trial scene in which victims and perpetrators of a crime are gathered together to ascertain the actual truth of a rape-murder of an aristocratic woman and her husband.[28] Each of the participants left alive gives a startlingly different account of the incident until finally the woman's murdered husband is summoned from the dead. In a traditional ghost/mystery story, this introduction of the supernatural would lead to the final unravelling of the mystery. In "In a Grove," however, Akutagawa's final twist is simply one more turn of the screw: the ghost gives a completely different, but obviously prejudiced version of the events and the final truth is never discovered.

Akutagawa's use of the fantastic as a means to a final awareness of unknowability, rather than an end to a final truth, is almost postmodern in its narrative effect, but the ambiguous nature of truth, reality, and fantasy is an aspect that many Japanese writers work with. Tanizaki and Abe in particular are writers whose enjoyment of narrative uncertainty has created some distinctively memorable fantasies. More recently, Endō Shūsaku's *Scandal* problematizes the notion of the *doppelgänger* as the narrative follows a well-known Christian author who may or may not have a double who is committing sexual crimes.

Other writers use the fantastic in a more conventional form. Sōseki, for example, perhaps the most "Western" of the great Japanese writers, in 1906 – early in his career – created a fantasy, "Maboroshi no tate" (The Shield of Illusion), which is almost startlingly Western in style and content. The story of two young lovers, "William" and "Clara," in medieval Europe, "Maboroshi no tate" traces their increasingly frenzied attempts to escape a war at home that promises to separate them forever. In the final moments of battle, however, William turns to his magic shield and, together with Clara, enters into "a world beyond the shield," "a Southern land whereof the troubadours sing" (my translation).

"Maboroshi no tate" is not Sōseki's greatest fantasy but it is fascinating in its total adherence to late-nineteenth-century European fantastic conventions. This more conventional form of fantasy is also one that would have important descendants in twentieth-century Japanese literature. Murakami's *Hard Boiled Wonderland and the End of the World*, for example, consciously and brilliantly mixes generic fantasy elements with motifs from Western science fiction and the detective story.

Sōseki's "Maboroshi no tate" is also interesting for another reason, however: its title. The characters for "Maboroshi" can also be read "*genei*," a word meaning "phantom," and which is connected to the word "*gensō*" or fantasy. Like "*genei*," "*gensō*" and "*gensō bungaku*" (fantasy literature) incorporate the notion of illusion, often positive but sometimes nightmarish. Sōseki's fantasy work shows both aspects of illusions, as do most of the works discussed in this book.

Perhaps the greatest "illusion" of all is the myth of modern Japan as a continuous success story. The works discussed in this book show the different ways in which that illusion is amended, contradicted, and finally subverted. This book offers a compendium of alternatives to that fairly seamless myth. We begin with a discussion of the fantasy woman, a departure from consensus reality whose nature changes sharply from prewar to postwar Japanese fiction. Women in prewar texts are generally seen as an alternative to modernity but in postwar literature they become a threatening part of modernity itself. The book then moves on to another form of departure, the alien, a disturbing alternative being whose presence directly interrogates such basic contemporary Japanese myths as the notion of Japan as a harmonious and homogeneous society. The book ends with a discussion of the broadest form of departures from consensus reality, the alternative worlds encapsulated in the varied forms of Utopias and dystopias which critique both the wishes and the fears which the Japanese have entertained toward their own society.

As with my definition of the fantastic, my aims in this book are broad ones: to annotate and analyze some of the most significant varieties of the fantastic in twentieth-century Japanese literature to see how they have critiqued, rejected, or subverted the most important myths of Japanese modernity. If there is a theme to this book, it is the theme of the fantastic itself and how it interacts with the supposed "real" of twentieth-century Japan.

Claude Brémond has summed up the function of the theme as

something which "takes an abstract entity and makes it the point of departure for a series of concrete variations."[29] This is precisely what the broad range of the fantastic does. By looking at a number of variations of the fantastic, I hope to trace both its function and its manifestation in modern Japanese literature.

In addition, the book examines what might be called a kind of Ur-theme of the fantastic, the search for home or identity, a notion which is part of all literature but which the fantastic is particularly suited for. As Moylan explains it, "the romance or the fantastic, including Utopia, focuses on a quest for what has been repressed or denied, for *Heimat* ... that sense of home which includes happiness and fulfillment".[30] Moylan's summary echoes Jackson's idea of fantasy as a literature of ever-seeking desire. It is not surprising, therefore, that virtually all the works discussed here include some form of movement, often in the form of quest, as their narrative subtext.

At this point, having described what the book is about, it might be strategic to mention what it is not about, namely, it is not a formal history of the fantastic in modern Japanese literature. Eminently useful though such a book might be, it is not where my particular interests, which are more in the nexus of literature, psychology and culture, lie. Although in each chapter I try to give some historical background for the particular subject under discussion, my focus is more on the dynamics between theme and Japanese history than on detailed chronological development.

I do try and relate certain developments of the Japanese fantastic to events in modern Japanese history. It is useful therefore to be aware of modern Japan's historical periods, Meiji (1868–1912), Taishō (1912–1926) and Shōwa (1926–1989). The current era, Heisei, only began in 1989 so I usually refer to works written in this period and in late Shōwa as "contemporary writings." Overreliance on period-ization can be reductive but it is clear that the fantastic does change over time and a work from the Taishō period often has quite different concerns and literary strategies than a novel from the postwar era.

The Fantastic in Japanese Literature is not an encyclopedia of the Japanese fantastic, again, despite such a work's usefulness. Although I do on occasion discuss films, art, science fiction, and popular comic books, I am not attempting an encyclopedic treatment of the enormous variety of manifestations of the fantastic in Japanese culture, or even in Japanese literature. This means that, unfortunately, I have not been able to treat all the fantastic writers in twentieth-century Japan, although I have tried to deal with as many of the most important ones as possible.

Inevitably, some omissions will occur. When I have had to decide which writers to include I have been guided by three principles: the availability of their works in translation, the writer's importance in relation to Japanese literature in general, and the particular work's relevance to the themes I am discussing. On these counts, such fascinating writers as Uchida Hyakken, Edogawa Ranpo or Takahashi Takako[31] have been reluctantly excluded in preference for writers who, if not known primarily for their fantastic literature (the most obvious examples being Sōseki and Kawabata), are of major importance in Japanese literature overall. Fortunately, a number of writers who qualify on all of the above counts, such as Akutagawa, Abe and Murakami, do exist and are treated extensively.

I have made some major exceptions to the above rule of available translations, and these include works by the writers Izumi Kyōka, Ōe Kenzaburō, Inoue Hisashi, Kurahashi Yumiko, and Ishikawa Jun. Ōe's work has been relatively well served by translators, but his monumental Utopian work, *Dōjidai gēmu* (The Game of Contemporaneity)(1979), is still unavailable in English. The last three writers also appear in my chapter on Utopias, and their writings, although regrettably untranslated, are of crucial importance to an understanding of the Japanese Utopian imagination.

Kyōka is a slightly different case. Although his work has recently begun to be translated, these translations are still hard to obtain. Kyōka is such a towering figure in modern Japanese fantasy, however, that I could not exclude him. Rather than try to deal comprehensively with his enormous output, though, I have decided to concentrate on his masterpiece written in 1900, *Kōya hijiri* (The Priest of Mount Kōya)(1981), unfortunately still difficult to obtain in translation, but of immense literary importance.

Even with the exclusion of a number of worthy candidates, this book treats a large number of modern Japanese writers. Although I hope their importance and qualities will be become apparent in the textual discussions themselves, I also include a brief appendix at the end of book for the reader's reference.

In the long run, however, it is less the individual writer, fascinating though each one is, than the extraordinary sweep and variety of the Japanese fantastic which I hope will remain in the reader's memory. Furthermore, by examining what has heretofore been considered marginal or populist, I hope to present an overall picture of modern Japan that is both broader and deeper than would be possible by exploring only the mainstream literature. By examining the role of the anti-real, paradoxically, the "real" Japan may actually become clearer.

NOTES

1 Although Natsume is the family name, I will follow Japanese convention and refer to him by his pen name, Sōseki, throughout the discussion.
2 Oka Yasuo, Kasahara Nobo and Soya Shinpei, 1979, p. 14 (my translation).
3 G. Bruno, 1990, p. 186.
4 B. Powell, 1992, p. 48.
5 Exceptions to this grim picture do exist, most notably the lighthearted short stories of Hoshi Shinichi. For a detailed description of some of the most important themes of Japanese science fiction see R. Matthew, 1989.
6 D. G. Hartwell, 1990, p. 1.
7 J. R. R. Tolkien, 1966, p. 60.
8 P. Kramer, 1993, p. 272.
9 F. Jameson, 1990, p. 30.
10 W. R. Irwin, 1976, p. 55.
11 In fact, Jackson suggests that it may be more useful to call the fantastic a mode rather than a genre (R. Jackson, 1981, p. 32).
12 Jackson, 1981, p. 3.
13 Jackson, 1981, p. 4.
14 Jackson, 1981, p. 35.
15 E. Rabkin, 1976, p. 8.
16 K. Hume, 1984, p. 21.
17 Ann Swinfen sums up the typical attitude toward realism as "an attitude which suggests that the so-called 'realist' mode of writing is somehow more profound, more morally committed, more involved with 'real' human concerns than a mode of writing which employs the marvellous" (A. Swinfen, 1984, pp. 10–11).
18 Although Izumi is the family name, I will follow Japanese convention and refer to him by his pen name, Kyōka, throughout the discussion.
19 M. Alexander, 1990, p. 13.
20 Not just fiction but the entire profession of literary criticism was essentially a Western import. Or, as Masao Miyoshi puts it, "[l]iterature as a discipline is a historical product of European colonialism and nationalism" (M. Miyoshi, 1991, p. 17). Fiction has had an important ideological function in the West as well. As Jochen Schulte-Sasse points out concerning the time of the rise of the novel in the West, "with the development of the bourgeois public realm and of public interaction, a need arose for a medium that could develop norms and could regulate interaction within the social realm" (J. Schulte-Sasse, 1988, p. 209).
21 L. Zamora, 1994, p. 33.
22 C. Gluck, 1985. See especially p. 101 and 261 for discussions of the image of railroads as "engines of civilization."
23 T. Moylan, 1986, p. 25.
24 E. Fowler, 1988, p. xxiii.
25 Fowler, 1988, p. 5.
26 Hume, 1984, p. 30.
27 Fowler, 1988, p. 23.
28 Just as in the West, modern fantasy and horror were initially strongly linked with the mystery story format; the immensely popular writer

Edogawa Ranpo (whose name itself suggests an explicit homage to Edgar Allan Poe) wrote stories which combined elements of mystery, fantasy and science fiction. Besides, Edogawa, Akutagawa, Tanizaki, Abe and Murakami all frequently employ mystery-story motifs in their work. "In a Grove" is the most famous example but Abe's *Moetsukita chizu* (1967) (trans. *Ruined Map* (1980)) is essentially an existential detective story. Sōseki himself employed the detective motif in his mimetic novel *Gubijinso* (The Poppy) (1907) and in real life was known for having a paranoid fear of detectives. For more on the relation between mystery, fantasy, and SF in Japanese literature see Sano and Komatsu, 1975, pp. 5–29.

29   C. Brémond, 1993, p. 47.
30   Moyland, 1986, p. 34.
31   Uchida Hyakken is virtually unknown among English-language translators and scholars, but Edogawa and Takahashi have been somewhat better served. A number of Edogawa's stories are available in translation, while Takahashi is the subject of a paper, "Transgression and Self-Transformation in the Fantasy Fiction of Takahashi Takako" by Mary Ellen Mori (1994).

2 Woman found

Encounters with supernatural women in prewar Japanese fantasy

Between 1885 and 1887 the journalist Shiba Shirō (1852–1922) published serially his novel *Kajin no kigū* (Chance Encounters with Beautiful Women). The work became an instant success, even though, despite its titillating title, it is actually a *seiji shōsetsu* (political novel), one of many didactic works on contemporary world society and politics that appeared in the Meiji period. *Kajin no kigū* attempts to educate its readers on such historically important topics as the American Revolution, the political crisis in Ireland, and Japanese interests in Korea. As for the "women" of the title, they are indeed beautiful and exotic (one of them, Crimson Lotus, possesses long yellow hair and green eyes), but they are essentially one-dimensional mouthpieces, existing largely as attractive conveyors of information on international subjects. For example, the book's male protagonist, known only as "the Wanderer," meets the yellow-haired lady at Valley Forge and she uses this opportunity to relate Ireland's oppression at the hands of the English.

Kajin no kigū, despite its exotic Western setting, is in many ways a paradoxically conservative work. Through its Western female characters it instructs its readers to respect the traditions of Japan, lest it, too, be overrun by foreigners, as was the case with Ireland and England. Furthermore, by using one of the stock images of modernization (and one that was used frequently in mimetic fiction), the young Japanese male wandering the West in search of enlightenment, it enforces a conservative message.

Kajin no kigū may thus be seen as heralding a new unease with modernity, an unease that was growing throughout Japanese society. As Chieko Mulhern sums up,

> [W]esternization was encouraged and promoted by the government in an effort to present a more modern image of Japan so as to facilitate favorable treaty revisions with foreign nations. But at the

same time, in preparation for the 1896 promulgation of the constitution and in support of its subsequent enforcement, the government was carefully cultivating a nationalism reinforced by the absolute monarchy and a revival of Confucian ethics, both distinctly non-modern policies.[1]

It was not only the government which was turning toward a more conservative vision of Japan. What Donald Shively has described as the "Japanization of the mid-Meiji"[2] was occurring throughout society during this period, as increasing numbers of Japanese began to feel a growing unease toward the West and toward modernity in general, and to feel a concomitant resurgence of pride in being Japanese.

The "consensus reality" of this period, then, was a complex one. Modernization, at least in terms of technological change and industrialization, was generally accepted, but without the parallel enthusiasm which had characterized the initial, heady stages of Westernization. This chapter explores this complex side of prewar Japan, a period in which "progress" and "Civilization and Enlightenment" were still accepted and propounded in some quarters, while in other areas they were regarded with at best ambivalence, and occasionally outright distaste. The vehicle for this exploration will be female characters in their connection with fantasy.

This connection is in important contrast to the women of *Kajin no kigū*, whose characters and teachings attempt to represent the new historical reality of the nineteenth-century world. Despite their exotic beauty, Crimson Lotus, Mysterious Orchid, and the host of other beauties whom the Wanderer encounters are clearly not "supernatural" in any sense except their link with the still mysterious Western Other.

Subverting this prosaic view of history and womanhood are the female characters of the fantastic who are associated with a very different world, in which the notion of an inevitable march of modernity is openly called into question. *Kajin no kigū* clearly represents the Enlightenment spirit of Meiji, part of a vast nation-wide project to glean new information and to disseminate it to the Japanese citizenry as broadly as possible. The other world of the fantastic problematizes this project on a variety of levels, and particularly through its female characters who often hark back to premodern female archetypes.

Unlike the earnest one-dimensional characters of *Kajin no kigū*, these premodern archetypes are notable for their passionate intensity. Furthermore, although positive characterizations of womanly virtue do exist, such as Genji's wife Murasaki in the tenth-century *Genji*

Monogatari (trans. *The Tale of Genji* (1976)), the most memorable female characters in premodern literature tend to be those associated with the negative, even with the demonic. Thus, more than the good-hearted Murasaki, the most famous female character in *The Tale of Genji* is probably Lady Rokujo whose jealous spirit haunts and kills Genji's lovers both when she is alive and after she is dead.

The association of women with ghosts and metamorphosis is also an important part of Japanese tradition, encompassing everything from the Nō and kabuki theaters to the woodblock prints of the early nineteenth century and even the post-Restoration era. In premodern literature and prints beautiful women turned into serpents, metamorphosed into mountain witches (the so-called *yamauba*) and, most frequently, transformed into horrific and vengeful ghosts, wreaking revenge against their (usually male) oppressor with a success that their real-life counterparts could never have achieved. After the Restoration, however, such melodramatic depictions of women and the supernatural were increasingly regarded as old-fashioned or vulgar, although the depiction of demonic women remained a favorite subject of popular artists and journals. Even more importantly, the avenging demonic woman was a popular icon in fantastic literature as well.

Another kind of female character was also becoming important in Meiji and Taishō literature. This type might be called the "oasis woman," a woman linked to a space outside of the real which offers comfort and revitalization to the weary male. This paradigm also exists in realistic fiction as well, particularly in the mimetic works of Sōseki and to some extent in Tanizaki. Intriguingly, the oasis woman and the avenging woman can also be combined, most obviously in the works of Izumi Kyōka.

Whether combined or separate, the oasis woman and the avenging woman in prewar literature tend to operate in similar ways as repositories of tradition, "symbols of cultural retrenchment," as Auerbach puts it.[3] This female role has been an important one in virtually all modernizing cultures, including those of the West.

Thus, the fantastic women characters are linked not only to an alternative to consensus reality but also to an alternative which frequently embraces traditional Japan. Furthermore, the fantasy woman often encapsulates the most literal form of fantasy, that of wish-fulfillment. In all the fantasies discussed in this chapter we see a clear dynamic: the male characters wish intensely for an escape from the reality of the modern world through the discovery or at times the creation of a woman linked to a non-modern world.

Women characters also act in a more complex way than simply as

"repositories" of tradition or objects of male wish-fulfillment, however. They can function both as textual signifiers of male anxiety
toward the changes going on around them, and also offer potential
solutions to the problems arising from these changes. As Carolyn Heilbrun says, "some of the most interesting writers of the past have pro-
jected culturally repressed values onto 'outside' female characters in
order to criticize the established order."[4]

This privileged positioning of women characters as implicit critical
commentary is of course true of mimetic Japanese fiction as well. It is
particularly fascinatingly represented in fantastic fiction, however, as
women and the supernatural come to form a nexus of resistance
toward the still amorphous but steadily building consensus reality of
modernizing Japan. What Heilbrun calls "the ambivalence of women
as signifier"[5] allows female characters a kind of flexibility denied to
the male characters. Women characters, especially in their role of demonic avenger, have a kind of creative energy that allows for more
narrative creativity and excitement than in many realistic texts. Liberated from the constraints of realist representation on the one hand
and, conversely, by the very Otherness and unknowability of female
characters on the other, writers could not only mine a more diverse
literary vein but also allow both their dreams and nightmares freer
play within that vein.

The flexible role of female characters in fantasy differs sharply from
that of *Kajin no kigū* female characters, who were unproblematic
representations of useful learning. It also differs importantly from the
role of female characters in much early modern mimetic fiction, who
were often secondary compared to realist literature's main theme of a
young man discovering himself, usually through a break with the
father. In comparison to these female representations, the women in
Japanese fantasies of the prewar period are far more powerful, complex, and disturbing.

Thus, in 1890, three years after *Kajin no kigū* was serialized,
Kōda Rohan (1867–1947), a writer who had in fact been inspired to
write by Shiba's novel, published another and very different form of
encounter with a beautiful woman, the unearthly fantasy *Taidokuro*
(Encounter with a Skull)(1890). Although Rohan too was concerned
about improving Japan, *Taidokuro* is a far cry from the didactic,
fiction-wrapped history which comprises *Kajin no kigū*. A
romantic writer, steeped in both contemporary literature and premodern Chinese and Japanese tradition, Rohan produces in *Taidokuro* a
memorable blend of eroticism, horror, and the metaphysical: a young
man lost in the mountains takes shelter in a small hut with an eerily

beautiful woman who invites him to share the single bed. In order to stay awake and, we presume, to resist the woman's blandishments, he asks her to tell her story, which concerns an accursed family fate which she has not been able to escape. As the morning sunlight comes in, the house and woman disappear and the young man finds himself alone in a field with a single white skull. Later on, he discovers that a crazed leper woman had vanished in the mountains some time previously and realizes both who the woman was and what her accursed fate must have been.

As is obvious from this brief retelling, *Taidokuro* gives a very different picture of womanhood from that provided by *Kajin no kigū*. As opposed to women as exemplary vehicles of education and enlightenment, albeit of a conservative nature, Rohan's woman is maternal, erotic, mysterious, and ultimately terrifying, a *memento mori* wrapped in a beautiful physical package. The work harks back to a premodern supernatural tradition such as that of Ueda Akinari, or of the Nō plays. Indeed, as Donald Keene points out, Rohan seems "almost untouched by the work of his contemporaries."[6] At the same time it is important to remember that his early works such as *Taidokuro* were immensely popular, hinting at a public taste that yearned more for eerie entertainment than for the didactic fiction of Shiba.

The association of women, the past (even if it is in the form of a family curse), and death is an important one in most of the prewar fantasies to be examined in this chapter. Paradoxically, however, these associations are often surprisingly positive. Moreover, frequently it is the woman who has supernatural control over life, death, and the connection with the past. This is particularly true in the fantasies of Izumi Kyōka, whose powerful enchantress figures are the gatekeepers to a lost Japanese tradition, in which premodern legends come alive. They open the gates only to a few chosen men, however, and destroy the men whom they deem unworthy.

In other prewar fantasies the dead women return to life, sometimes through the result of male manipulation. Whether in control of or controlled by men, fantasy women are usually associated with some transcendent absolute, and one that is often inscribed in terms of traditional Japanese culture. Kyōka's heroines, for example, seem to represent both the Otherness and fundamental indestructibility of traditional culture as they war against the reality of modern Japan using their supernatural powers. Similarly, the revenant woman restored through male power becomes an example of successful defiance, a gesture of male resistance against the onrushing tide of modernity.

The male characters in prewar fantasy are often on quests, whether conscious or not. In these wish-fulfillment quests they go in search of a fantasy female, often of a maternal type. Clearly, this quest relates to the desire for *Heimat* which lies at the basis of much fantasy fiction. What is more surprising, however, is that this quest motif takes a very different turn in postwar fantasy. Where once men were looking for a woman, in the fiction from the 1960s to the present the quest is now one away from the female. To understand these surprising differences this chapter explores the search for a woman-based *Heimat* in pre- and immediate postwar fiction, while Chapter 3 examines the contrasting quest modes of more recent Japanese fiction.

THE AVENGER AND THE OASIS: WOMEN IN KYŌKA, TANIZAKI AND SŌSEKI

Fantastic fiction of the prewar period reveals perhaps even more strongly than realistic fiction some of the fears and anxieties attendant on modernization. Interestingly, however, fantastic fiction of the prewar period also operated to compensate for these insecurities, offering solutions, at least on a wish-fulfillment level, to the complexities and anxieties expressed in realist fiction. The two female paradigms mentioned above, woman as oasis and woman as avenger, are the most important examples of this kind of compensation.

The Doomsday Woman: Izumi Kyōka's avenging females

I will discuss first the paradigm of woman as avenger, focusing primarily on the writings of Izumi Kyōka, arguably the greatest of Japanese fantasy writers, and certainly the greatest chronicler of fantastic females in Japanese literature. One of the most self-consciously traditional of post-Meiji writers, Kyōka produced a great volume of romantic plays, novels, and short stories, virtually all of which abound in such premodern figures as geisha, travelling artists, and mendicant priests. Although Kyōka's subjects were not always fantastic, his works do contain a memorable variety of ghosts, demons, and monsters. As Donald Keene sums up, "About half of Kyōka's enormous literary production – more than three hundred stories and plays – deal with the supernatural."[7]

Kyōka's choice of subject, therefore, immediately placed him outside of mainstream mimetic currents. Furthermore, even his non-fantastic works were written in a lush prose style, evocative of traditional premodern fiction, an aspect which also set Kyōka apart from the Naturalist movement. So different were Kyōka's topics and style, in fact, that his literary reputation was long shadowed because it contrasted so greatly with the prevailing literary currents of his day.

Throughout his career Kyōka was strongly aware of the shadow of Naturalism and what he perceived as the oppressive influence of modernization in general on the traditional culture of Japan. To counter these threats, Kyōka created a brilliant variety of memorable female characters all of whom were deeply associated with old Japan and many of whom are strongly connected with the supernatural. Although some, usually in his more realistic works, are victims, in the mold of the all-sacrificing geisha type of his play *Nihonbashi*, many others are powerful, even frightening characters.

These powerful females usually attain their power through fantastic sources such as witchcraft, or through simply being associated with the supernatural world. Many of them, such as the characters in his 1913 play *Yashagaike* (Demon Pond)(1913), and the 1917 *Tenshu monogatari* (The Castle Tower)(1982), are in fact supernatural themselves, demonesses who confront, attack and sometimes vanquish the world of reality. The princess who dwells beneath the "demon pond" in Kyōka's play *Yashagaike*, for example, calls down a flood upon the hapless villagers who have refused to believe in her existence. Even more shocking are the man-eating demonnesses of *Tenshu monogatari* who show only pleasure as they entrap and devour their foolish male victims.

In many ways these strong, vengeful women are associated with the *yamauba*, the premodern "mountain witch" who lived in the wilds and consumed unwary travellers especially men and children. In recent years Japanese women writers have reappropriated the *yamauba* archetype for their own subversive use, as we will see in the next chapter, but Kyōka's women too can clearly be seen as figures of resistance. They may have even earlier archetypes as well, such as the premodern shamaness, a central figure in Japanese folklore, as Fujimoto Tokuaki points out.[8]

Perhaps the most memorable and affecting of these mysteriously powerful female characters is the heroine of Kyōka's masterpiece *Kōya hijiri* (The Priest of Mount Kōya)(1981). This novella, written in 1900, encapsulates most of Kyōka's important themes in a richly evocative manner and is fully deserving of the enormous amount of critical attention that has been lavished on it over the last decades. This critical attention is explainable partly because Kyōka's own literary star has recently been in the ascendant, as Japanese critics have rediscovered in his romantic themes and ornate prose style a refreshing contrast to much of modern Japanese literature. It is also due to the density and richness of the novella itself, full of images which are often intriguingly resonant, both of premodern Japanese folklore and mythology and of more general psychoanalytic archetypes as well. For our purposes, *Kōya hijiri* is important not only for its fascinating heroine, but also for its striking presentation of an erotic landscape which is linked not only to changing conceptions of Japan but also to the quest motif.

Kōya hijiri may be seen as exemplifying a kind of quest narrative in which the protagonist is forced to endure a variety of dangers before symbolically dying and finally achieving a symbolic rebirth. The narrative, therefore, is an intricate one, detailing the increasingly fantastic and subliminally erotic encounters of a young monk from the temple complex on Mount Kōya as he wanders in the mountains in the remote Hida district of Japan. Although the narrative is framed by an opening story in which an anonymous narrator encounters the now aged monk on a train journey, the real story belongs to the monk himself.

He begins with a description of his younger self lost in a landscape of blankness, consulting a map on a mountain road while the sun beats down fiercely. As the blank landscape suggests, the young monk is truly "lost" to the rational world of the symbolic and his journey from this point on is one into the world of the imaginary. The monk's journey consists of a variety of significant meetings with the human, natural, and supernatural worlds, culminating in a climactic encounter with a mysterious and beautiful woman.

The monk's first encounter is with the opposite of everything beautiful and mysterious, however; it is with a disagreeably vulgar medicine peddler to whom the monk takes an immediate dislike. This dislike is perhaps due to the fact that the peddler and the equally vulgar maid at an inn where he has stopped make fun of him for his cowardice in not drinking the river water because of his fear that it may be contaminated. The monk is glad when the peddler passes him on the road. His relief soon changes to concern, however, when he finds that the "old road" that the peddler has chosen is a lonely and dangerous one. Prompted by what he believes to be guilt, the monk follows the peddler onto the "old road" in hopes of warning him. He never sees the peddler in human form again.

Technically, the monk's "quest" is to find the medicine peddler, but it is also a quest to rise above his own cowardice, because the old road is a genuinely frightening prospect to him. For, as we shall see, his quest ultimately takes the monk on a journey into his own personal "heart of darkness." Upon entering the road, the monk leaves the world of everyday reality and enters not only the realm of the fantastic, but also the realm of his own mind, a world which contains both the things he most fears and the things he most desires.

At first, his fears take concrete shape in the form of a number of huge snakes which cross his path and of which he admits to "having an innate hatred." He treats the largest snake politely, however, acknowledging its position as a mountain deity in the Shinto faith and taking care not to tread on it. Soon afterwards he enters a dark and overgrown forest.

This forest, perhaps a symbol of the psyche and of the libido, turns out to be filled with huge leeches which suck his blood to the point of unconsciousness. As Rosemary Jackson points out on the subject of vampires, the leeches' ability to penetrate and suck has both masculine and feminine connotations, evoking both intercourse and the infant's sucking of blood in the womb and its later sucking at the breast. These actions, Jackson argues, thus become an "extreme attempt to negate, or reverse, the subject's insertion into the symbolic."[9]

Before the escape from the symbolic and the rebirth into the imaginary comes death. It is in the leech forest, Togo Katsumi argues, that the monk dies symbolically, rendered unconscious by the pain and intensity of the leech attack.[10] Interestingly, it is at this moment that the monk has a bizarre vision of the end of the world. Almost hallucinating, the monk imagines the trees of the forest turning into leeches and the leeches vomiting the blood they had sucked from humans until the entire area has become a "great swamp of mud and blood." At this point he imagines:

> It may be that when humanity perishes it will not be that the earth's thin crust cracks and fire falls from the sky or that a great sea will cover the world. But rather, Doomsday will begin with the forests of Hida turning tree by tree into leeches and in the end everything will be blood and mud with black veined insects swimming therein.
>
> (p. 85; my translation)

Initially, this extraordinary apocalyptic vision may seem out of place for a story so firmly grounded in the elements of the traditional Japanese folk tale. Structurally, however, this horrific landscape occurs at the appropriate narrative moment, the beginning of the monk's overtly fantastic, almost mythic, adventures. As Girard says, following Lévi-Strauss, "a primordial absence of order . . . prevails at the beginning of most myths."[11] Girard adds that this disorder is usually a violent one, which is certainly the case in the monk's bizarre illusion. It is a chaos in which order, rationality, and learning, the world of the Symbolic, and of "Civilization and Enlightenment," have no place.

The vision is also, at least subliminally, an erotic one. As Eric Rabkin notes, "visions of the end of the world . . . often involve violence. . . . And typically they involve sex."[12] The images of primordial chaos involving the phallic leeches swimming in a womblike bloody swamp suggest both sexuality and rebirth on a personal and a suprapersonal level. In the monk's case this rebirth is mediated by a mysterious woman who is capable both of creating chaos and controlling it.

It is only after the monk stumbles out of the forest and away from the terror of his hallucinatory visions that he finds the womblike place wherein he enacts a spiritual rebirth, one that takes him back into the imaginary order where the pre-verbal infant still feels at one with the mother. This takes place in the remote valley which the monk discovers beyond the leech forest. In the valley, he finds a lonely house which at first seems to be solely inhabited by an idiot with a distended navel who can only babble meaninglessly. As Togo points out, the idiot, who is actually the husband of the enigmatic woman whom the monk next encounters, is also a distorted mirror image of what the monk has symbolically become, a pre-linguistic infant.[13]

As for the woman herself, her initial appearance is particularly troubling since she, like her husband, seems to occupy a liminal state, in this case between serpent and human. When the monk first sees her he imagines that he sees scales on her neck and even a tail, although he quickly decides that his eyes were mistaken. All the same, the impression of hidden metamorphic powers lingers.

The woman's seemingly liminal state suggests what Auerbach calls "the myth of [woman's] disruptive capacity for boundless transformations,"[14] but, unlike the Victorian females whom Auerbach is describing, this metamorphic capacity is only threatening to those men who do not appreciate her or who presume upon her sexually. Thus, the woman is the epitome of maternal tenderness both to her idiot husband and, initially at least, to the monk, whose wounds from the leech forest she offers to salve by taking him to bathe in a nearby spring.

In the actual bathing scene, however, she encapsulates a continuum of feminine archetypes, from nurturing mother to sexual temptress, the embodiment of what both the leeches and the snakes in the previous encounters seem to have been forecasting. In this scene, water, which is clearly associated with the feminine, subtextually enacts the many roles that the woman herself plays.[15] The spring itself, which is reached by going through a dense forest and finally crossing a narrow log bridge, evokes the physical configuration of the womb, while its waters are said to be remarkable for their healing (i.e. nurturing) powers. At the same time, however, the waters have erotic connotations as well, since moisture has been associated consistently with sexuality from the earliest periods of Japanese literature, particularly in *waka* poetry.

These erotic connotations become increasingly apparent as the woman has the monk strip while she herself disrobes and, when he stiffens in embarrassment at her touch, she whispers persuasively that "no one is watching" (p. 103). Caught between sexual excitement and the pleasure of being taken care of like an infant by its mother, the monk feels as if he were encased in flower petals, while simultaneously feeling his blood "coursing hotly" within him. Just when he and the woman are about to admit their mutual attraction, they are frustrated by the sudden arrival of two strange animals, a huge bat which flies out at them, and a monkey which clings to the woman and covers her nakedness.

Just as water is associated with the female, animals in *Kōya hijiri* are consistently linked with the male. In fact, as the reader and monk later discover, the animals are actually transformed human males, transmogrified by the woman's supernatural powers. These human animals appear again in two more important scenes in the novella. The first scene occurs after the monk and the woman return to the house and the woman is forced to strip once again to perform a magic ritual in order to soothe a horse which had taken fright upon seeing the monk. This scene encapsulates the seductive and demonic aspects of the woman and is worth quoting more extensively, particularly the actual physical meeting between woman and horse:

> She stood straight in front of the horse's long nose. It seemed as if she grew suddenly taller in one smooth movement. She fixed her eyes upon it, tightened her mouth, and drew her brows together apparently in a trance: all trace of charm or coquetry, or familiarity of manner were suddenly lost and one could have believed her god or devil. At that moment the very atmosphere of the deep mountains grew heavy . . .
>
> It seemed that the trace of a tepid wind blew, as, with her right hand, she pulled off her single garment from the left shoulder, and pulling it in front of her held it in a ball at her swelling breasts. Not even the mist veiled her body now. Drenched in rivulets of sweat, the horse relaxed the skin of his torso and back and his stiffly extended legs trembled delicately while he folded his forelegs, a droplet of white foam blowing from his downward pointed nose.
>
> Taking his muzzle in one hand, the woman used the other hand

to throw her garment over the horse's eyes. Suddenly, like a leaping rabbit, she arched her body backwards and in the hazy moonlight, heavy with strangeness, she seemed to enfold herself between his front legs. Then, tucking her robe away she abruptly passed under the horse's body and out.

(pp. 114–115; my translation)

This scene powerfully suggests the woman's shamanesslike powers. In its combination of bright moonlight (the traditional Buddhist symbol of enlightenment) with a mysterious mist, it also suggests a conflict between the powerful erotic forces at the woman's command versus the clarity of rational thought. Although the horse is in fact quietened by her actions and finally led away, the actual encounter evokes a vivid mimicry of copulation. But this is a sexual encounter in which the woman controls the male animal, just as the woman has controlled the male's metamorphosis; for, we discover later, the horse is actually the medicine peddler transformed by the woman's magic.

Animals, Buddhism, and sexuality are linked again in another important scene. This occurs after the household has gone to bed for the night and the monk is kept awake by noises outside, which he perceives as emanating from either beasts or demons. Later on, he will discover that the creatures are actually men turned into animals by the woman but, in the meantime, the monk protects himself by reciting the Buddhist sutras all night long and the creatures do not harm him. Buddhism, the rational law, is thus seen as protecting the monk against the irrationality of sexual desire.

Although highly sexually charged, these two scenes can also be read as metaphorical commentaries on the relationship between woman, the symbolic, and the imaginary order. In the imaginary world of union between infant and mother, language is not needed and, when language does develop, it marks the change into the symbolic order, symbolized by the phallic law of the father. The encounter between woman and horse, although implicitly sexual, is also in some ways still suggestive of the asexual imaginary since it occurs without any form of verbal communication. Conversely, in the scene where the monk subverts the demon/animals of lust through the words of the sutra, it can be seen as the phallic law of the father reasserting control over a pre-verbal imaginary of sexual and maternal symbiosis. The scene can also be read as prefiguring the monk's own return into the symbolic order out of the dark primordial chaos of the night.

Despite his Buddhist vows, however, the monk is still reluctant to leave on the morning following his bizarre night-time experience.

Water, in both its erotic and escapist connotations, once again becomes important at this point as the monk, in desperation over what to do, halts by a waterfall. This waterfall, known as a "husband and wife waterfall" because it has two distinct strands, is famous throughout the district for its beauty and awesome noise, another pre-verbal signifier of the imaginary. Gazing at it in despair, the monk believes he can discern the woman's form appearing and disappearing in its foam, something which she herself had predicted, asking him to remember her whenever he sees a peach blossom floating in the current. In this climactic scene the monk's longing for her can be read as initially sexual, signified by the association with the peach, a symbol of female sexuality in traditional Japanese culture, and by the description of the waterfall itself as having male and female elements.

The water also offers the possibility of a return to the imaginary, not only in its overwhelming pre-verbal roar, but in terms of the self-annihilation it invites, as the monk contemplates throwing himself into the torrent. Just before he does this, however, the old handyman appears from selling the horse at market to tell the monk he has had a lucky escape. He explains to the monk not only the woman's magical transformative powers but also something of her background. The only daughter of a doctor, the woman had early on become known throughout the countryside for her beauty and her marvellous powers of healing. While still a young girl, however, she was orphaned by a great flood that left only herself, the old handyman and the idiot alive from her household.

Retreating into the small house in the valley, with the idiot as her husband, the woman showed a new side to her nature – her ability to turn men into animals. The old man expresses surprise that the woman did not turn the monk into a beast but warns him that the time would come sooner or later.

As he explains it,

> She is by nature lustful and particularly likes young men. I suppose she said something to you sir, and indeed I'm sure she meant it truthfully but, in the long run, she would have tired of you and then a tail would grow, your ears would start to wriggle and in a twinkling you would be transformed.

> (pp. 138–139, my translation)

Kōya hijiri ends with the now aged monk telling his fellow traveller this discovery of the woman's true character and his gratitude for his lucky escape. Judging by the first narrator's description of the elderly monk as a distinguished priest, uninterested in mundane matters, it would seem that the priest's younger self has been largely put behind him. He has confronted and overcome the leeches and serpents of suppressed sexuality and he has avoided throwing himself into the reason-annihilating waterfall. Even more obviously, the sexual, "animal" side of his nature has been cast off in the form of the medicine peddler/horse. As Jackson says of the resolution to Conrad's "The Secret Sharer" when the protagonist's problematic "double" is separated from him, "This severance [is presented] as a proper resolution as 'self' renounces the libidinal other and assumes an adult life. The imaginary is relinquished with little regret."[16]

But in Kyōka's more equivocal world, still not entirely given over to "Civilization and Enlightenment," the imaginary is cast off with great regret. This is clear, not only from the tremendous struggle the young monk undergoes when he has to decide between his vows and the woman's blandishments, but also from the fact that the aged monk cannot forbear to repeat his story to a chance-met traveller. Ironically, it is through language that the monk attempts to return once more to a time of pre-verbal bliss.

The sense of regret pervading *Kōya hijiri* is not only the monk's personal nostalgia for a lost, erotically open period of youth, however. It is also an acknowledgement of the unattainability of desire on a sociocultural level, the desire to deny the workings of history by escaping into a fantasy world of "old Japan." It is this sociocultural aspect of the impossibility of desire that I would like to examine next, especially in regard to the extraordinary fantasy woman whose character dominates both the monk and the narrative in *Kōya hijiri*. Not only can she be seen as emblemizing the eternal female continuum from temptress to mother, but she can also be read as encapsulating the disappearing traditions of old Japan.

I have mentioned previously Heilbrun's point about the projection of culturally repressed values onto "outside" female characters in order to criticize the established order.[17] The irony of *Kōya hijiri* lies in the fact that these "culturally repressed" values are actually the values of old Japan, hiding at the end of the dangerous "old road" the monk is forced to travel. At the same time, the "established order" is actually the new order of Meiji Japan, toward which, as Maeda Ai says, Kyōka was "vehemently opposed."[18]

More important than Kyōka's opposition was what he offered in place of the new order, a return to a magical past. Thus, Togo equates the "old road" which the monk turns off onto as the road back, not simply to the womb, but to the premodern era. As he notes, the mountain valley cannot exist on any map, because a map signifies ordinary real space defined by modernity, and inscribed in the scientific and rational order. In other words, the snakes, leeches, and the woman have been banished by modernization and only a few remnants now lurk in the premodern darkness, nursing their hatred of modernity.[19]

Ironically, what traditionally was considered Other, i.e., the grotesque, the alien, and the female, are now seen as linked to a yearned-for old Japan which in itself has become Other.

As I pointed out previously, the woman in her magic ritual role clearly harks back to the premodern Japanese shamaness, a central figure in Japanese folklore. Her connection with animistic Shinto is further heightened by the monk's initial impression of her possessing tail and scales, metonymically linking her with the serpent on the mountain that the monk had previously encountered.[20] The snake in that earlier encounter can be seen as symbolizing the monk's unacknowledged libido, but it can also be straightforwardly interpreted, as the monk himself does at the time, as the guardian *kami* or god of the mountain. The woman's association with the snake is therefore not only sexual but also a link to the religious traditions of premodern Japan (and to its folkloric and dramatic traditions as well).

The woman's connection with water may also be read in terms of traditional Japanese religion, because water in Shinto ritual acts as an essential purifying agent. This purifying, even redemptive, aspect is evident in the scene at the spring where the water's powers have a restorative effect on the monk's wounds. Water's purifying power is also in implicit contrast to the stream which the monk refuses to drink from at the beginning of the story because he fears its contamination.

What is it contaminated by? I would suggest that the water is contaminated by modernity itself, the vulgar real world of the medicine peddler and the maid at the inn, a world from which the "old road" is both literally and psychologically a form of escape. Water here is important as well, since we know that the old road is associated with a great flood. In this regard, it is also important to note that, while in Shinto ritual water is associated with purity, in Buddhism water can be related to the mundane and the profane.

This brings me to another important critical dimension of *Kōya hijiri*, the implicit social criticism represented by the flood. Although it is difficult to be totally firm chronologically, it would seem that the "great flood" which swept away the woman's family some years before had occurred at about the time of the Meiji Restoration. The flood, therefore is evocative not only of the Restoration itself but of the sea change of modernization that occurred as a result of the Restoration, sweeping all before it except for a few remnants such as the woman and her households.[21]

Water in Kyōka's work is not always destructive of the old, it should be noted. Like women's rage, it can also be harnessed by old Japan as a form of revenge in itself, as was clear in *Yashagaike* when the supernatural heroine destroys the unbelieving villagers without a trace. *Kōya hijiri* does not allow for quite such a watery revenge, but it does contain the aforementioned vision of apocalypse that the monk sees in the leech forest which, although it does not involve water as such, does suggest a world of dissolution into a horrifying fluidity.

This apocalyptic vision is interesting for a number of reasons. Although its imagery recalls the biblical apocalypse (not unlikely since Kyōka attended a Christian mission school), the Doomsday (literally, "*daikawari*" or change of eras) to which the monk refers is at least as likely to be the changes heralded by the new order in Meiji Japan rather than a far-off Day of Judgement. Such a vision of primordial disorder may be both a commentary or even a revenge fantasy. The dissolution into blood and mud which the monk envisions suggests a world of devolution. Far from the Darwinian belief in natural selection or the nineteenth-century Western confidence in progress, human beings, along with everything else, are seen as declining into a grotesque miasmal stew.

Standing in complicated relationship to this is Kyōka's fantasy woman, a woman whom Mishima Yukio has described as "Infinitely beautiful, infinitely kind, yet infinitely terrible."[22] On the one hand, since she turns men into beasts, she seems to take part in this fantasy of regression, but this is one unlike modern transformations which, as Jackson has noted, tend to be essentially meaningless, such as Kafka's *Metamorphosis*.[23] In contrast, the woman's transformative powers in *Kōya hijiri* have a very clear point: they are the revenge of the old dark female world on the new.

This point is shown again in another less overtly fantastic work of Kyōka's 1897, "Kechō" (Chimera), a story that also illustrates the many-sided aspects of maternality in Kyōka.[24] In "Kechō" a young boy named Renya and his mother live by a river where the mother supports them by collecting tolls at the bridge. Formerly a member of an aristocratic family, the mother takes gentle revenge and entertains her son by likening each person who crosses the bridge to some kind of animal. She is especially scornful of pretentious, modern types such as a blustering government official whom she names "Professor Frogfish."

The mother is not always vituperative, however. As with the woman in *Kōya hijiri*, she is kind to those who appreciate her, such as a monkey trainer and his monkey. And she is overwhelmingly maternal to her son. Indeed, "Kechō"'s main narrative movement concerns loss and rediscovery, both of the self and of the mother. One day when the boy accidentally falls into the river he is rescued by a creature whom the mother describes as a beautiful winged woman. The boy goes in search of the woman only to become lost in the forest wherein he feels that he too is about to metamorphosize into some kind of winged beast. Just when he feels on the point of metamorphosis, he is saved, and this time very clearly by his mother, whom, he decides, with some disappointment, must all along have been the beautiful winged creature. The story ends with this realization, although the boy still hopes that he may find the other winged creature somewhere. For the present, however, he is content and the story ends on a note of acceptance, "Mother is here. Mother was here."

The use of the past tense ("*irasshatta*") for the final line is interesting, hinting that there may come a day when Mother will not be there. The prime note of "Kechō," however, is this sense of "hermetic" joy and security, as Cody Poulton puts it,[25] with boy and mother in a small safe world. This note of security linked with the mother is one found in other prewar mimetic and fantasy fiction and leads me to the second female archetype I would like to discuss, the notion of woman as oasis.

Nothing is ever lost: Tanizaki and the search for the original beloved

Clearly, the mother in "Kechō" represents an oasis of security for herself and her small son, hermetically sealed from intrusion. Many other Japanese writers, from Mori Ōgai to Shiga Naoya, have stressed this equation of women and security. But the writer who most overtly follows Kyōka's equating of woman, mother and traditional Japan is undoubtedly Tanizaki Junichirō, whose obsessive celebration of the feminine has created some of the most memorable female–male dynamics in Japanese fiction.

A writer who particularly enjoyed exploring the dark or even demonic side of sexual relationships, Tanizaki is more psychologically complex and intricate than Kyōka. Like Kyōka, however, many of his most important works such as "Shunkinshō" (1933) (trans. "Portrait of Shunkin" (1963)) and *Sasame yuki* (1943) (trans. *The Makioka Sisters* (1957)), tend to privilege the feminine as the site of a specifically Japanese past that has both personal and suprapersonal resonances. Thus, in his dreamlike 1932 fantasy *Ashikari* (trans. *The*

Reed Cutter (1993)), a woman who is explicitly linked to a lost past of refinement and traditional artistic and erotic attainments beckons the male characters to forget the modern world around them.

In *The Reed Cutter* and elsewhere, Tanizaki's use of the fantastic is far less overt than that of Kyōka. Often it is simply one subtle element in an elaborately developed artistic departure from the consensus reality of modern Japan. This is a departure which also privileges the erotic, the artificial in the form of game-playing (both within the text and with the reader), and the traditional. Within these complex literary structures, wish-fulfillment fantasies are played out in a variety of forms.

The structure of *The Reed Cutter* itself in many ways resembles a premodern Nō play: an initial character, presumably the author's persona, takes a long walk by the Minase river. As he takes pains to explain, this is an area full of historical and poetic associations, and which he ironically contrasts with the "pastoral cities" and "cultural subdivisions" of contemporary, striving Japan. As he waits for the moon to rise, he day-dreams of "past glory" and imagines the times past when courtesans used to ply the rivers, "giving their hearts over to travelers' desires" (p. 19). Lost in these reflections, in which sexuality and water are clearly linked, the narrator is surprised when, "just then there was a rustling in the reeds nearby, and when I turned to look, a man was squatting there like me among the reeds as if he were my own shadow" (pp. 19–20).

The "shadow" proves to be another fancier of moonlight, old traditions, and beautiful women, as was his father before him. It is his father's story, told in the form of the "shadow"'s childhood reminiscence, which forms the main narrative action of *The Reed Cutter*. This action is of a far slower and less immediate kind than that of *Kōya hijiri* but both narratives center around a mysterious and unusual woman who is linked to a lost past.

The second narrator explains how as a child his father would take him once a year for a moon-viewing walk, eventually pausing outside a mansion into which they would peer from a hidden vantage-point behind a hedge. Inside the mansion they could see a group of people dressed in costumes of another era playing music. The father seemed particularly drawn to the person who was probably the "young lady of the house" but whose face was always hidden. They could hear her lovely voice as she sang and played the koto, however.

The second narrator eventually discovers that the lady's name is "Miss Oyū" and that she and his father were once very intimate, although in a typically Tanizaki-esque arrangement "Miss Oyū" had been the sister of the father's wife. But it was always "Miss Oyū" who had attracted the father, especially after he heard of her unusual old-fashioned background; gently reared in a pre-Meiji style, Miss Oyū epitomized the kind of woman the father is searching for, "someone refined, like a lady of the court, one worthy to be dressed in a long formal robe, seated behind a curtain stand, and given *The tale of Genji* to read . . ." (p. 30). Although hardly fantastic in the mode of Kyōka's heroine, "Miss Oyū" is intriguing because she has something

> indistinct about her face. Her features . . . are blurred as though they were veiled by a layer of silk gauze . . . and when I gaze at her face a misty shadow seems to fall before my eyes, as if a haze floated above her and nowhere else. The word *rotaketa*, used in old texts describes such a face . . .
>
> (p. 31)

Typical of many Tanizaki heroines, Miss Oyū is an avenue back to a traditional, more elegant past, but, also typically, this past is ultimately attainable only in fleeting moments. Wanting to be close to her, the father marries Miss Oyū's sister and for a while the three live in happy fulfillment. Eventually, however, their strange *menage à trois* causes too much gossip and "Miss Oyū" is finally married off to an indifferent wealthy husband whose mansion the narrator's father now visits secretly once a year. The visit only consists of passive peeping, however, for the narrator's father is content in the knowledge that such a woman still exists. As he explains to his son, "it was most fitting for a person like her to go on forever fresh and innocent, served by a crowd of chambermaids and living in splendor" (p. 51).

The Reed Cutter ends with the primary narrator thanking the second man for a "most interesting story." He then wonders in some surprise why the man has said that he is on his way again to see "Miss Oyū" tonight:

> 'Yes' he replied, 'I'm about to set out again tonight. If I go behind the villa on the Fifteenth Night and peer through the hedge even now, Miss Oyū will be playing the koto and her chambermaids will be dancing for her.' That's odd, I thought. But Miss Oyū would be nearly eighty years old by now, wouldn't she? I asked, but there was only the rustle of the wind blowing across the grasses. I could not see the reeds that covered the shore, and the man had vanished as though he had melted into the light of the moon.
>
> (p. 53)

Unlike in Kyōka's story, there is no real confrontation between modernity and the supernatural forces which are attempting to subvert it. Instead, the text offers up a dreamlike mysterious world where all concerned are complicit in the game of escaping. Rather than the vulgar medicine peddler standing in opposition to the priest in *Kōya hijiri*, for example, there is only the shadowy second narrator, an elegant double of Tanizaki's own primary persona. There is no sense of imminent apocalypse, only a mild feeling of regret for a vanished past. As the primary narrator puts it, "for a young person, love for the past is nothing but a day-dream unrelated to the present, but an older person has no other means for living through the present" (p. 23).

Although far less overtly in its departure from consensus reality than Kyōka's story, Tanizaki's tale ends on a note of uncertainty that is almost a classic example of Todorov's theory of the fantastic as hesitation. Was the "shadow" ever really there? Did "Miss Oyū" really exist? And could she still be there now? The doubling, in fact even tripling narrative structure (the father's story told by his son to the primary narrator) also adds to the unreal aspect. This is also true of the motif of "peeping," as when father and son spy through the hedge. Although this is an obvious link to traditional Japanese literature where peeping through the fence was a highly valorized form of erotic encounter, it also complements the shadowy, dreamlike impression given by the narrative. Essentially, the reader is granted what the father and the son had, a brief, shadowy glimpse into a world that may once have existed but is now lost except in the fantasy of a moonlight night.

The Reed Cutter is typical of many of Tanizaki's efforts to create literary escapes from the reality of contemporary Japan, especially in its linking of the erotic and the traditional. Perhaps his most completely realized vision of escape is the 1959 novel *Yume no ukihashi* (trans. *The Bridge of Dreams* (1977)), a work written after the war but clearly harking back not only to a prewar but a premodern world. It is a work in which two of Tanizaki's major obsessions are most perfectly united; the search for a lost traditional Japan and the search for a lost mother who encapsulates both the maternal and the seductive. In this regard it resembles both Kyōka's *Kōya hijiri* and "Kechō," although its departure from consensus reality is far more subtly accomplished. In fact, although *The Bridge of Dreams* is included in the Japanese edition of Tanizaki's fantasies, its overtly fantastic quality is almost minimal. There is no whispering shadow in the moonlight, nor even a dream. Instead, *The Bridge of Dreams* is in its totality a wish-fulfilling departure from consensus reality. This departure centers on the creation of a perfect woman, who is, herself, a substitute for a previous ideal woman, the young narrator's dead mother. In its privileging of a clearly prewar, indeed premodern, "dream world" that is explicitly associated with the female, and with traditional Japan, the work in certain ways encapsulates more than any other the use of a fantasy woman as an oasis against change.

Like Kyōka's "Kechō," *The Bridge of Dreams* is focused through the eyes of a young boy, and is set in an "Other" world, sealed away from reality. But this Other world is far more resonant with sociocultural implications than the mother–son Utopia of "Kechō," because it is explicitly equated with traditional Japan. The work begins on a note of unreality with a quotation from the eleventh-century romance *The Tale of Genji*: "Came to Sing at Heron's Nest/I crossed the bridge of Dreams/Today when the summer thrush . . ." The narrative continues: "This poem was written by my mother. But I have had two mothers – the second was a stepmother – and although I am inclined to think my real mother wrote it, I cannot be sure" (p. 355).

The reasons for the narrator's uncertainty are elaborated upon in the course of the story. The reader discovers that the narrator, Tadasu, lost his real mother while only five years old. A few years later his father married again to a woman who not only resembled the lost mother but was instructed to act like her in every way possible. To promote the impression even further, the young woman also takes the name of Tadasu's dead mother. As Tadasu's father explains to him:

> When she comes you mustn't think of her as your second mother. Think that your mother has been away for a while and has just come home. . . . Your two mothers will become one, with no distinction between them. Your first mother's name was Chinu, and your new mother's name is Chinu too. And in everything she says and does, your new mother will behave the way the first one did.
>
> (p. 366)

The young boy, although initially surprised by this turn of events, soon acquiesces, especially after his new mother allows him to suckle at her breasts. In fact "Chinu" allows him to do this at two stages of his development. The first occurs while he is still a small boy, but the second time happens when he is a teenager. In this case his substitute mother has given birth to a child which she and Tadasu's father decide to put up for adoption. Complaining of heavy breasts caused by her still-flowing milk, "Chinu" meets with Tadasu in their garden pavilion, apparently by chance, and invites him to suckle at them. As "Tadasu" describes it,

> At first it was hard for me to get any milk, but as I kept on sucking my tongue began to recover its old skill. I was several inches taller than she was, but I leaned down and buried my face in her bosom, greedily sucking up the milk that came gushing out. "Mama" I began murmuring instinctively, in a spoiled, childish voice.
>
> (p. 375)

Far more obviously than with Kyōka, the incest taboo has been breached. Through the substitute mother, Tanizaki is able to concretize incestuous fantasies. But *The Bridge of Dreams* is not only a story of erotic longing for a maternal figure; it is also a story about death and a desire to subvert death by returning to the imaginary. This is obvious in the boy's reaction when his real mother dies. He immediately thinks, "That sweet, dimly white dream world there in her warm bosom among the mingled scents of her hair and her milk – why had it disappeared? Was this what 'death' meant?" (p. 363). Death, then, is explicitly related to what Elisabeth Bronfen calls the "lost unity" of mother and infant.[26]

This is made even clearer by the narrator's description of the first time he suckles at his substitute mother's breasts. "that warm dimly white dream world – the world I thought had disappeared forever – had unexpectedly returned" (p. 368).

But has it? In fact, Tanizaki's text is an almost classic illustration of the impossibility of desire, desire for an object (Mother) or stage (the imaginary that "dimly white dream world") that cannot return. Bronfen, in her study *Over Her Dead Body: Death, Femininity and the Aesthetic* (1992), points to the frequent use of the revenant woman (the woman who returns from the dead) in male literature. She then goes on to explain that the problem with such an attempt at identical replacement of the "original beloved" is that the replacement itself invokes the loss.

> Regaining a lost amorous unity, denying the narcissistic wound induced by death, occurs in the repetition of a beloved as an image, but an image materialized at over another's body . . . [The revenant woman] is denied her own body and is only a figure for a meaning alterior to herself, prematurely turned into a ghost. . . .[27]

In the case of the Tanizaki story, the complexities of "ghost" and "body" are given distinct and contrasting forms. Both the "original" mother and the "substitute" mother are essentially ghosts, mysterious figures whose motivation is never displayed to the reader. The "ghost" of the dead mother is invoked by the use of her name, and by the many poetic allusions which surround her and which the new mother is forced to incorporate.

The body, on the other hand, is reduced to virtually one site, the breast. At the same time this morselized body fragment is linked directly back to the dream world of the imaginary. As the story's narrative goes on to make clear, however, the Imaginary is essentially unreachable, except through death, the very instrumentality that the substitute mother is attempting to deny.

Although the story's title *The Bridge of Dreams* suggests that at some level the story is indeed enacting some form of death wish, the surface narrative in general is an attempt to deny death. This is done first through the motif of the revenant mother, of whom Bronfen says, "The double enacts that if what has been lost returns, nothing is ever lost."[28] In fact, this is a theme which is also played out in *The Tale of Genji*, as Genji restlessly seeks to replace his dead mother in a series of new lovers.

But it is not only the dead mother who has been lost in this case. Although Bronfen's book explicitly dwells only on the psychoanalytic and aesthetic aspects of the image of a dead woman, I would argue that the motif of the revenant has important sociocultural resonance as well. At least in Tanizaki's case, the "death" he is attempting to deny is also the death of a culture.

The equation of mother and a lost Japanese culture is made manifest in a variety of ways, starting with the opening poem quoted above which refers to the final chapter in the *Tale of Genji*, the greatest classic of traditional Japanese culture, and one which Tanizaki himself rendered into modern Japanese three times. Significantly, his interest in the classic began during the 1930s when what Ito calls his "dawning sense of cultural identity"[29] was beginning to crystallize in conjunction with a general *Zeitgeist* of a resurgent nativism called *Nihon e no kaiki* (a return to Japan).

Interestingly, the *The Tale of Genji* chapter itself to which "Chinu" refers is one that is a kind of elegy to an aristocratic culture that was beginning to fade, beset by outside warrior clans. The inhabitants of *The Bridge of Dreams* also explicitly see themselves in an adversarial position to the outside world. As the boy says of his father, "Father liked a quiet life. He put in an appearance at his bank now and then, but spent most of his time at home, seldom inviting guests"(p. 358). Shortly thereafter, the narrator comments, "All of my father's love was concentrated on my mother. With this house, this garden and this wife, he seemed perfectly happy" (p. 358).

The rather shadowy father can be seen as a kind of artist, perhaps even a magus figure, who creates this artificial world and then conveniently dies. His legacy, the triad of "house, garden, and wife" are resolutely, even self-consciously rendered in the most explicitly traditional fashion possible. Thus, the substitute "Chinu" is made to play the koto, a traditional musical instrument, and refers to water plants using a name from classical Japanese poetry. Needless to say, she is never shown going outside the garden into the "real world." As for the house and garden themselves, they are as lovingly described as the boy's mother, and are even more crammed with associations to Japanese literature and history, from the "bamboo mortar," a device which the narrator tells us was mentioned in a fourteenth-century Japanese poem, to the calligraphy by Rai Sanyo, the "scholar poet," which is mounted in the entrance hall.

Tanizaki's explicit use of the house and garden as a symbol for Japanese culture appears as early as his famous essay on Japanese aesthetics *In'ei raisan* (trans. *In Praise of Shadows* (1984)) written in 1933–4.[30] Already in this essay he also equated women and traditional Japanese culture as well. In *The Bridge of Dreams*, however, he also introduces a strong maternal presence into the traditional Japanese landscape. Thus, the description of the entrance to the house, down a flagstone walk to an "inner gate," is reminiscent of the entrance to the womb. Even more overtly, the scene where the now teenaged Tadasu suckles his mother's breast takes place in the pavilion at the very center of the garden.

With characteristic ambiguity, Tanizaki leaves it to the reader's imagination as to whether a sexual relationship actually occurs between Tadasu and his stepmother, but it is clear throughout the novella that some form of intense relationship has formed. Certainly, when the stepmother finally dies, Tadasu seems to lose all animation. In an interesting twist, however, he attempts a final substitution by searching for and bringing home his adopted half-brother, Takeshi, to live with him. Tadasu professes to be delighted with his half-brother. Revealingly he says, "What makes me happiest is that he looks exactly like Mother."

And yet the final part of *The Bridge of Dreams* contains a strong hint of melancholy. The narrator ends by saying,

> Because my real mother died when I was a child and my father and stepmother when I was some years older, I want to live for Takeshi until he is grown. I want to spare him the loneliness I knew.

(p. 338)

In a sense, Tadasu is following in his father's footsteps. Perpetually in mourning for a lost world, he is essentially a shrinekeeper, maintaining the faith through sacrificing first his second mother and now Takeshi.

While *The Bridge of Dreams* shares with *The Reed Cutter* the theme of evoking a lost world through an unreal female figure, its implicitly confrontational style is more reminiscent of Kyōka. Like Kyōka, Tanizaki subverts modernity both through presenting obvious alternatives to it in the form of the garden enclosing a traditional woman, and also by contrasting the keepers of tradition with ordinary human beings who belong to the mundane world outside the garden gates. While Kyōka used the vulgar medicine peddler to contrast with the monk in *Kōya hijiri*, in *The Bridge of Dreams* Tanizaki introduces the figure of the gardener's daughter who is willing to marry Tadasu because she has no other prospects. Ironically, her vulgarity is held up for contempt, in opposition to the actions of the stepmother, whose willingness to transform herself, Galatea-like, for Tadasu's father is seen as only praiseworthy.

Eventually the gardener's daughter is ejected from the garden, but not before coming under suspicion of murdering Tadasu's stepmother. Thus, reality does intrude into the garden. The story's melancholy ending suggests that it will intrude more and more with the passage of time.

Tanizaki's and Kyōka's fantasy women do differ from each other importantly in that Tanizaki's women are largely passive while the female characters in Kyōka's fantasies tend to be active. On the other hand, they both stand as sentries to a longed-for Other world of erotic and traditional richness. Their femininity, their maternality, and their eroticism are all seen as positive attributes, qualities which enhance the wish-fulfilling aspects of the fantasies in which they appear.

Femininity is seen far more problematically in Sōseki's *Ten Nights of Dream*, the last of the prewar fantasies I will deal with in this chapter. Although written in 1908 and thus much earlier than the two Tanizaki works previously discussed, *Ten Nights of Dream* displays an ambivalent and sometimes clearly negative attitude toward women which anticipates the far more overtly negative depictions of women in postwar fantasies.

Sōseki and the realm in between: "Dream of the First Night"

As mentioned earlier, *Ten Nights of Dream* consist of ten short dreams. For the purposes of this chapter I would like to focus mainly on the first one, "The Dream of the First Night." As with *The Bridge of Dreams* much of the story revolves around a dead woman and a subsequent mourning stage, what Bronfen calls "the realm in between,"[31] a place of escape from the problems of reality, one of which is, significantly, the erotic nature of womanhood.

For, unlike either Tanizaki or Kyōka, the erotic in Sōseki is seen as largely negative, a channel to a plethora of anxieties and guilt. Thus, although Sōseki's work contains many positive depictions of female characters, it is important to note that they are at their most attractive when their sexuality is most attenuated. In this regard, Sōseki's work can be seen as a bridge to our next chapter where not only sexuality but the female itself is increasingly problematized.

Sōseki was not nearly as explicit as Tanizaki in equating women with a lost Japanese Other. Even more than Tanizaki, however, Sōseki was insistently aware of Japan's problematic position *vis-à-vis* the West, and the many inadequacies involved in the country's attempt to modernize. A scholar well versed in classical and Chinese literature, Sōseki was also painfully conscious of the many traditions which Japan was giving up. Not surprisingly, women in his fiction seem to be associated with a powerful sense of loss in general and also with a means of escaping that loss, through love, art, religion, or death.

Dying women in particular seem to have strange and attractive powers in Sōseki's work. Michiyo, for example, the terminally ill heroine of his mimetic novel *Sore kara* (1909) (trans. *And Then* (1978)), perhaps encapsulates that attraction best. This is clearest in a climactic emotional scene when Daisuke, the novel's anguished young intellectual hero, buries his face in a bouquet of lilies given him by Michiyo and finds that "today for the first time, I am returning to the past, which belonged to nature. . . . In the rain, in the lilies, in the now revived past, he saw a life of pure, unadulterated peace." This life of peace is in strong contrast to the corrupt and competitive world of contemporary Japan which *And Then* delineates more sharply than any other Sōseki novel. Michiyo thus represents, in contrast, an escape into an almost Zen-like past world which can also be associated with premodern Japanese culture.

Sōseki's fantasy "Dream of the First Night" also contains a dying woman associated with flowers and, perhaps, escape. Like Tanizaki's *The Bridge of Dreams*, Sōseki's story also involves a dead woman and a form of substitution, although in this case the erotic implications of this substitution are the opposite from Tanizaki's tale. Here a woman's sexuality is metamorphosed into something non-threatening, rather than reinforced.

The story begins with the dreamer, the "I," sitting at the bedside of a dying woman. Looking down at her "large moistened eyes" he sees himself mirrored therein. He questions her, unable to believe that with her lustrous beauty she could really be dying. She tells him, however, that "it can't be helped," but also tells him that she will come again if he buries her and waits for a hundred years by her grave. The man promises he will wait and

> At that moment my image, so vividly reflected in her jet-black pupils, began to dim and crumble, to crumple as reflections in still water crumple with the wet's disturbance. The woman's eyes began to flow and the next instant closed with a snap. . . . She was already dead.
>
> (p. 25)

The man buries her according to her instructions, digging a grave with a shell of mother of pearl and putting a fragment of a fallen star at her grave. He then settles down to wait the hundred years the woman had told him it would take for her to return. He waits on and on, counting the red suns that rise and set in the sky. Just when, grown tired of waiting, the man begins to believe that "the woman must have fooled me," he sees a plant stem growing toward him. The dream ends with the following description:

> The next moment a slender bud, whose head bent lightly from the tip of that graceful swaying stalk, opened its petals soft and full. Right in front of my nose, the pure white lily poured its scent to drench my very bones. Then, as dew dropped from far high distances the flower gentled to and fro, swayed by its own white weight. I thrust my neck forward and kissed those pallid petals from which a cold dew dripped. As I drew my face back from the lily, I happened to glance up at the far off sky; where a single white star was twinkling. And only then, then for the first time, did I realize that the hundredth year had come.
>
> (p. 30)

Although brief, this evocative story weaves a complex tapestry of feminine images and associations, from the maternal to the threatening. In many ways, the quietly prone woman seems linked with the other Sōseki heroines in his realistic fiction who exist to reassure the hero that there remains a still space in the violently turning modern world to which the men can return for refuge. Indeed, most critics have seen "The First Night" as the only positive work in an otherwise extremely dark collection of dreams.[32]

From this male-oriented point of view, the metamorphosis of the woman into a plant can therefore be seen in a positive light. Not only is the man content to wait passively for the hundred years that the metamorphosis takes, but, when it actually occurs, he responds with more passion than he showed while the woman was actually alive, arching his neck, "kissing the pallid petals" and giving himself over to their heavy scent. As was the case with Daisuke in *And Then*, the union of woman, flowers, and scent seems to release something in the male, allowing him full and safe expression of his own repressed emotions.

Although the flower in "Dream of the First Night" does not stand explicitly for a return to the past as did the lilies in *And Then*, it too has a relation to time. In this case, the slow, beautiful and notably organic development of the flower stands in contrast to the red suns which streak across the sky in an artificial and mechanistic way. We know from Sōseki's fiction and essays that repetitive mechanical motion is usually associated negatively with the alienation and even madness which he saw as implicit in modernity. The slow metamorphosis of the woman, therefore, evokes another world in which time moves slowly and change is aesthetic, and perhaps even controllable.

Paired now with the slender but strong lily, the "I" finally realizes that time has stopped, that the red suns have ceased to move and only a "far away" star twinkles on the horizon. This new security given by the all-embracing "drenching" plant is almost womblike. Although motherhood is seldom explicitly depicted in Sōseki's works (in important contrast to Kyōka and Tanizaki), the nurturing, soothing plant seems to have a definitely maternal and protective aspect.

Underneath this fantasy of woman and nature protecting men from the vagaries of mechanical progress lie some disturbing implications, however. The most obvious one is the fact that the woman must be dead in order to accomplish this. As Bram Djykstra has pointed out, dying women in nineteenth-century literature and art can be seen as a form of male revenge, a desire for control over some object (a woman's body) in the face of the increasing chaos of modernity.[33] Unlike the very robust and sexually blooming women of *Kōya hijiri* or *The Bridge of Dreams*, a dead or dying woman is inherently passive and unthreatening.

In this regard, the woman's final metamorphosis into a plant is particularly interesting. As a sightless plant, the woman can no longer see the male's inadequacies, just as, without a human body, she can no longer make sexual demands. This does not mean that the plant is asexual, however.[34] Quite the contrary, the plant is still erotic but in a non-threatening way.

Not only is the man happy to kiss the plant, but the dew which drips from it has erotic connotations going back to classical Japanese literature. This dehumanized form of lovemaking is not unique to Sōseki. Fedwa Malti Douglass, for example, has mentioned a classical Arabic text describing an island where women grow like fruit on trees and have a "good, perfumed smell."[35]

Sōseki's "Dream of the First Night" can therefore be read as a fantasy of escaping or at least controlling sexuality, but it should be noted that, unlike in Tanizaki's work, the male is relatively passive. Although he is responsible for the woman's resuscitation, through his burial and his patient mourning of her, he does not direct her metamorphosis. Furthermore, this resuscitation and transformation is at the woman's behest. It is she who tells him what to do and they work together to accomplish it.

It is possible, therefore, to see this fantasy, not as a death wish, but as a form of rebirth, into a relatively sexless, beautiful, and organic world. And it is also possible to read this rebirth as not just the woman's but the man's as well, for dream images often contain various parts of the self. The man's face, we remember, is mirrored in the woman's eyes before she dies, suggesting a mutuality of identity that could well be positive.

Overall, then, I would suggest that "The First Night" is not totally misogynistic but rather simply escapist. It is an escape from both the mechanistic alienating aspects of modernity and the frightening aspects of woman's sexuality into a transcendent dream world. As Etō Jun points out, "women" and "dream" have been consistently and positively linked in Sōseki's works since his earliest poetry.[36]

Interestingly, a woman appears in the final dream of the collection, "Dream of the Tenth Night," but this time she is overtly threatening. Like the woman in "Dream of the First Night," this woman is also beautiful and mysterious and is initially associated with the organic world, in this case fruit. In the end, however, the dream turns into nightmare when the woman lures a young man to the grotesque fate of being licked by an endless series of pigs.

Where the woman in the first dream was associated with the end of mechanical repetition and the resuscitation of life, the woman in this dream is responsible for endless repetition which ultimately brings about the death of the young man. If the first dream was a dream of escape, this one, like most of the dreams, in *Ten Nights of Dreams* is a nightmare of non-escape, in which the woman exists only to traduce the man rather than to fulfill his desires.

Women and desire are associated consistently in the works discussed in this chapter. In the long run, however, all the works explored in this chapter show the impossibility of desire, whether it is the desire for escape or the desire for rebirth. Kyōka's women are part of a lost world, accessible only through the renunciation of the adult or even the human self. Tanizaki's females are also fundamentally infantalizing, either dream images or man-made constructs that can temporarily stem the tide of history but cannot ultimately reverse it. The "I" of the first dream in Sōseki's *Ten Nights of Dreams* is luckiest, but only at the price of turning the woman into a non-human entity and staying forever in a dream world.

NOTES

1   C. Mulhern, 1977, p. 34.
2   D. Shively, 1971, pp. 77–109.
3   N. Auerbach, 1982, p. 73.
4   C. Heilbrun, 1981, p. xviii.
5   Heilbrun, 1981, p. xx.
6   D. Keene, 1984, p. 150.
7   Keene, 1984, p. 217.
8   Fujimoto Tokuaki, 1980, pp. 78–80.
9   R. Jackson, 1981, p. 120.
10 Togo Katsumi, 1980, p. 145.
11 R. Girard, 1978, p. 186.
12 Slusser, G., Rabkin, E., and Scholes, R., 1983, p. xiii.
13 Togo, 1980, p. 145.
14 Auerbach, 1982, p. 55.
15 For further discussion of water imagery see C. Inouye 1991.
16 Jackson, 1981, p. 140.
17 In this regard, it is interesting to compare the woman in *Koya hijiri* with the heroine of H. Rider Haggard's *She*, a late-nineteenth-century English adventure story. Like Kyōka's woman, She Who Must Be Obeyed has supernatural powers through which she tames and thwarts any man she encounters. Also like the woman in Kyōka, she has a tender streak as well, if not precisely a maternal one. The two works also contain similar climactic scenes of suppressed sexual energy involving water and a deep womblike place. The differences between the works are even more interesting, however. For She is not only Other as a female, she is also literally a foreigner, ruler of a foreign land into which English explorers accidentally venture. And the climactic scene in *She* leads to her death rather than the male's rebirth, an event met with much relief by the Englishmen. Unlike Kyōka's woman, then, whose very Otherness represents a yearned-for Japanese past, still barely existing within modern Japan, She represents the alien

outer world of females and other races, just beginning to batter on the gates of the secure fortress of Victorian England. For a fascinating discussion of *She* in regards to both sexual and ideological politics of the Victorian period see S. Gilbert, 1993.

18 Maeda Ai, 1985, p. 16.

19 Togo, 1980, p. 84; my translation.

20 The demonic serpent woman is an archetype found not only in traditional Japanese folklore but is universal to all cultures, as Nina Auerbach explains, from the Christian iconography which makes a serpent with a female visage the agent of the fall, to the early Sumerian image of a serpent woman who was the "emblem of a prophesying female divinity" (Auerbach, p. 94). This "prophesying" element is an interesting link with the shamanesslike powers attributed to the woman in Kyōka's story.

21 Regarding the chronology of *Kōya hijiri*, and especially the notion of the "change of eras," Wakako Taneda has a fascinating suggestion. She points out that the era in which the novella is presumably set is one when the initial flood of "modernization" was being looked at more equivocally and when Japan was increasingly flexing its militarist muscles. She goes on to suggest that the woman's turning men into beasts might be related to the rise in conscription as the Meiji government drafted more and more young men in pursuit of its slogan of "Rich Country, Strong Army." W. Taneda, 1994, p. 33.

22 Mishima Y., 1981.

23 Jackson, 1981, p. 81.

24 For further discussion of the role of the "mother complex" in Kyōka see Yoshimura Hirotō, 1983, pp. 180–181.

25 C. Poulton, 1993.

26 E. Bronfen, 1992, p. 329.

27 Bronfen, 1992, p. 328.

28 Bronfen, 1992, p. 328.

29 K. Ito, 1991, p. 102.

30 Tetsuo Najita sees Tanizaki's valorizing of traditional culture in "In Praise of Shadows" as his creation of "an internalized space of resistance," a description which could be applied to the garden in "Bridge of Dreams" as well. (T. Najita, 1989, p. 12).

31 Bronfen, 1992, 327.

32 Momokawa's comment on "The First Night" is particularly interesting in this regard:

This dream is a narrative of anticipation fulfilled, in contrast to the narratives of betrayal which all the other dreams embody. The question is why did he write such a (positive) work, and I would like to suggest an answer in terms of Sōseki developing his own myth. It is certain that being able to believe in a lover and wait for a hundred years is an indication of an extremely happy time. If Sōseki had not been able to write one such blissful work, "Ten Nights of Dream" would never have been passed down to us.

(K. Momokawa, 1988, p. 67)

33 B. Dijkstra, 1986, pp. 50–63 and *passim*.

34 It is interesting to note that the "I" in the dream digs the woman's grave with a clamshell, an image in Freudian theory traditionally associated

with the female genitals. Thus, the "I" is using a fragment of female sexuality. The flower that the woman transforms into can of course be read as a non-threatening, aesthetically pleasing version of the feminine erotic.

35   F. Malti-Douglas, 1991, p. 88.
36   Etō Jun, 1974. p. 29

3 Woman lost
The dead, damaged, or absent female in postwar fantasy

[in modern fantasy] absence itself is foregrounded.
(Rosemary Jackson, *Fantasy: The Literature of Subversion*, p. 159)

Sōseki's fantasy retreat into a dream world with a metamorphosed woman was part of his own personal response to the modernity of Meiji Japan, a world which he characterized as obsessed with notions of speed, progress, and technology at the cost of humanity and tradition. In the long run, however, Sōseki believed that escape was neither a possible nor a valid alternative. Perhaps for that reason, he turned from the surreal world of *Ten Nights of Dream* and other early fantasies to the dark realistic fiction for which he is especially known. His later realistic characters still long for escape, often through the avenue of love, but are unable to accomplish this, even in their dreams.

For the characters of postwar Japanese literature, however, the urge to escape the consensus reality of contemporary Japan is still strong. At the same time, though, the unattainability of such a retreat is acknowledged even more than in Sōseki's works. Postwar writers increasingly turn to depicting the fantastic and absurd quest, not to describe a genuine escape, but instead to highlight the fundamental absurdities and impossibilities of living in the modern world.

In these postwar fantasies the world is turned upside down. The womb is now a place of terror (oozing red drops in Kawabata's phrase), and women are no longer caretakers but objects of prey, only acceptable as victims upon which to enact male rage. Water, which we saw frequently as an avenue to a lost erotic past or even to the womb has now become ominous, the raging waves around Kawabata's *Nemureru bijo* (1961) (trans. *House of the Sleeping Beauties* (1976)); dangerous, the teemingly sexual rivers of Tsutsui's "Poruno wakusei no sarumonerá ningen" (The Salmonella Beings from Planet Porno) (1982); or existing only as poisonous ooze suggestive of a diseased womb, as in the final scene of Abe's technological horror fantasy, *Mikai* (1977) (trans. *Secret Rendezvous* (1980)). Nature has become grotesque and threatening as in "Poruno wakusei", and Kawabata's "Kataude" (1963) (trans. "One Arm" 1970), or else has simply disappeared, as in *Secret Rendezvous*.

In many ways this distorted world is an amplification of the consensus reality of contemporary Japan, but it is also an attack upon it. Where Sōseki, Tanizaki, and Kyōka implicitly subverted the Meiji program of "Civilization and Enlightenment" by showing characters in desperate retreat from it, the postwar writers of fantasy explicitly confront some of the most deep-seated ideologies of modern Japan. These include the widely held notion of Japan as a homogeneous middle-class nation, supported by traditional and uniquely Japanese values founded on harmonious nuclear families. In these idealized families the roles of husbands and wives are clearly demarcated and both spouses are happy to sacrifice for each other and for the greater good of family, corporation, and society. This optimistic vision of interpersonal dynamics is in turn supported by a belief in the instrumentality of continuous technological advance leading to widespread material prosperity.

This vision of middle-class harmony and prosperity is thoroughly deconstructed in the fantasies of postwar writers. Intriguingly, some of the most savage and memorable attacks come from female writers of the fantastic whose works describe a world in which the fantasy of the harmonious nuclear family imposed by the Japanese establishment is turned into a nightmarish vision of repression and despair. Also intriguingly, but perhaps not surprisingly, it is the female in the writings of both men and women writers who is most problematically presented.

Thus, the ambivalence toward maternality and the female erotic that was implicit in Sōseki's 1908 vision becomes echoed and amplified in postwar literature. But, while Sōseki's fantasies at least allowed for the inclusion of the female, even if in transformed or desexualized guise, the postwar fantasies of male writers are notable for the absence of women characters. Women are no longer part of wish-fulfillment fantasies. Instead, they are part of the reality which the male protagonist longs to escape.

Thus, the works by male writers discussed in this chapter tend to absent or eradicate the female. In these texts women not only signify the erotic and the maternal, they also represent an affirmation of male identity within a social construct, an identity and a construct which are increasingly viewed in a negative light as part of the suffocating entanglements of both past and present.

The male characters in most of these fantasies are looking for a space of freedom that is increasingly defined by the absence of women. Women no longer offer any sort of refuge; instead they are part of the web of entrapment which modern society appears to be weaving around its citizens. Paradoxically, however, not only their presence but also their very absence can become an excuse for male rage, as is especially clear in Nakagami Kenji's passionate lament, "Fushi" (1984) (trans. "The Immortal" (1985)).

Indeed, perhaps the most striking aspect of the texts discussed in this chapter is how few of them are wish-fulfillment fantasies on the relatively simple level of Tanizaki and Kyōka. And those wish-fulfillment fantasies that do exist are largely presented by female writers such as Enchi, Ōba, and Kanai whose works often present a mirror of the male fantasy, a world without men. For these women writers it is the male who represents the suffocating constraints of hierarchy and obligation, and their fantasies attack that world by offering a solitary one in its place.

What has happened in the postwar period to render the dynamic between the sexes so problematic? Part of the explanation must lie in the problems of any contemporary industrialized society where material wealth and technological innovation have led not to increased harmony, but to increased expectations and disappointments among the sexes. Japan's case is unusual, however, in that it has only been in the 1980s that women's roles have changed appreciably. At the same time, these changes, such as delayed marriage and decreases in birth rates, have been enormous and far-reaching.

On a general level, one might also suggest the possibility that the simpler bipolarities of the prewar period, such as tradition versus modernity, Eastern ethics versus Western technology, or the West versus Japan, have become increasingly complex as Japan has become a modern country in its own right. Although remnants of traditional culture still exist, they are not necessarily identified with the female, since the traditional female of, say, a Tanizaki work has virtually vanished from the scene.

We might also look at the changing role of the Japanese male for clues to the increasing sense of despair detectable in so much postwar fantasy. Again, although the Japanese case has many universals of the modern and post-modern condition, other aspects are unique to postwar Japan. The first and most historically specific element is the loss of the Pacific War and the subsequent American Occupation, a period when the Japanese male lost power in the most dramatic and crippling way possible, as the diminished subject of a foreign occupying power.

Tadao Sato has explored the ways in which the depiction of the father changed in the cinema of postwar Japan as the tradition of patriarchal domination was virtually upended, and the father became increasingly a figure of fun or simply absent.[1] In fantastic fiction, as well, father and authority figures are also often problematized. Thus, Kanai Mieko's "Usagi" (1976) (trans. "Rabbits" (1982)) explores a bizarre sado-masochistic relationship between a young girl and her father. Often the father is simply not there and the absent father (and often an absent mother) is a staple element of many younger Japanese writers such as Yoshimoto Banana or Ōtomo Katsuhiro.

It should be noted that female characters do exist in plenty in the mimetic fiction of postwar writers, but their representation is very different from much of the fiction of the prewar period. In a world where fathers are increasingly absented one would expect that woman, in her role of caretaker, would become increasingly privileged. In fact, the opposite is true. Mothers in particular are problematized in much postwar fiction. In Mishima's *Kinkakuji* (1956) (trans. *Temple of the Golden Pavilion* (1959)), for example, the mother is seen as a betrayer of both husband and son, and stands in implicit contrast to the traditional beauty of the Golden Pavilion. In the works of Ōe Kenzaburō, such as *Kojinteki na taiken* (1964) (trans. *A Personal Matter* (1968)), or "Waganamida o nuguitamau hi" (1972) (trans. "The Day He Himself Shall Wipe My Tears Away" (1977)), mothers are seen as emasculators, criticizing the male until he appears to have no choice but to flee into madness or grotesque fantasy in order to escape the demands of marriage and social responsibility.

It is not only mothers whose existence negatively affects the male characters. Women in general are frequently seen as agents of entrapment or humiliation. Although this paradigm goes back at least as early as Sōseki's "Dream of the Tenth Night", it also may be specifically connected to the dynamics of the Occupation. Thus, Ōe's 1959 *Warera no jidai* (Our Era) introduces a sinister triangular paradigm involving a Japanese female prostitute, her Japanese pimp, and her American lover/client. This paradigm is also echoed in Nosaka Akiyuki's black-humored story "Amerika hijiki" (1967) (trans. "American hijiki" (1977)), in which his protagonist, who had actually been a pimp as a young boy in the Occupation, berates himself for his inability fully to escape that mentality even as a grown man.

Clearly, the Japanese wife/prostitute signifies the despoiled Japan, violated both by the foreign conqueror and by the weakness of her would-be protector. As such, woman becomes both victim and unpleasant reminder of male powerlessness. It is not surprising that these works, all of them written by men who were growing up during the Second World War, are both far more bitter and at least as despairing as anything in the premodern period.

This sense of despair, I would suggest, intimately affects the changing role of women in postwar literature. Whereas in the prewar period women offered an alternative to modernization, either actively in the form of Kyōka's avenging heroines, or more passively in the works of Tanizaki and Sōseki which linked women to nature and the traditional Japanese past, women in the fiction of the postwar period do not seem to offer opportunities for either vengeance against the modern or escape from the modern. Instead, women seem to have become increasingly Other, unreachable, even demonic.

Much of this, I would argue, has to do with the increasing complexities of the postwar period. As Diane Price Herndl says of late-nineteenth-century America, a period of "fundamental reorganization of culture": "male writers found themselves with the need to reassess their own roles in the culture and their relationships to women, to women's work and to their own work."[2] As is evidenced by the works set during the Occupation, postwar Japan was undergoing a much more fundamental "reorganization of culture" even than during that of the Meiji Period, and this time women could be seen as part of the problem, living reminders of male powerlessness, initially in the face of an American conqueror, and later on *vis-à-vis* an economic juggernaut which transformed society at the expense of individual fulfillment.

Deprived of the traditional masculine outlet of military adventuring, owing to the 1947 Constitution's banning of Japan's right to wage war, the Japanese male was told to compete in economic battles instead. Up till the end of the 1960s this seemed a relatively satisfactory solution, as Japan led the world in its two-digit economic growth. Even that stage of Japanese success brought its own sense of alienation, however. Moreover, the marked ups and downs of the Japanese economy, especially in the years since the 1973 oil shock, have undoubtedly contributed to an individual sense of powerlessness, especially in men, who are still the primary breadwinners in Japan.[3]

This sense of an onrush of events rendering individual action useless is echoed in all of the cultural artifacts of modern Japan, from literature and film to mass culture comic books, as will be clear in our chapter on dystopias. Lost in a world where they increasingly lack control, male characters are shown as damaged and angry. When they are not passive victims awaiting the apocalypse, as in Abe Kōbō's later works, then they are antisocial and often lunatic, as in the works of Ōe or Mishima, taking revenge on a disappointing society. In this alienating world, women become a focal point for fantasies of control and revenge.

In fact, it is possible to find any number of examples where revenge is being wreaked upon women themselves, either by virtually eliminating them from the text, or by eliminating them within the texts through a variety of forms of assault and murder. It is this new image, which I term the lost or absent woman, to which I would like to turn in this chapter.

Increasingly in the postwar period fantastic literature has been the vehicle of choice for illustrating the bitter complexities of male–female relationships. Perhaps because postmodern life contains in itself so much that would seem bizarre to traditional cultures, fantastic fiction may well be the best vehicle for its representation. The genre of realism may be simply incapable of encompassing the technological breakthroughs, social breakdowns and psychic revolutions that characterize contemporary Japan, in which people in the same generation can witness the ritual suicide of Yukio Mishima (parodied in Kurahashi Yumiko's *Popoi* (1987)) and the urban alienation of the *bōsōzoku*, the tribes of young motorcyclists whose alienated wanderings are given a dystopian spin in *Akira*.

Fantastic literature also seems to offer particularly imaginative and memorable ways of absenting women characters. This is an aspect of fantasy, incidentally, which is not confined to Japanese literature. In *Alternate Worlds: A Study of Postmodern Antirealistic American Fiction*, John Kuehl demonstrates the many nightmarish forms postwar antirealist fiction has taken in America, such as the absurd quest and the apocalypse, forms which often either exclude female characters from important roles, as in Joseph Heller's *Catch-22*, or portray them negatively as the treacherous females of Pynchon's *V* or the nurse in Kesey's *One Flew Over the Cuckoo's Nest* where the "psychiatric conspire(s) with the matriarchal."[4] In a paranoiac contemporary world where technology seems increasingly uncontrollable, the American hero has often lighted out for the "territory," in an unconscious imitation of Huckleberry Finn. Although, according to Kuehl, the twentieth-century hero's quest has been to "restore the vitality sapped by urbanized, industrialized culture,"[5] in postmodern anti-realism such a quest has become more and more unrealizable. This is certainly true of the Japanese quest stories discussed in this chapter. For example, in Tsutsui's "Poruno wakusei no sarumonera ningen," when one character seems to regain a form of vitality it is at a cost of a total metamorphosis of the self, into an asexual spider creature. As for Nakagami's and

Abe's protagonists, their quests end only in death, either of the self or a woman.

In such a world as this, the traditional comforts offered by women seem to mock the male characters by their very unavailability. As Kuehl says, "[in the postmodern American novel] paranoia and conspiracy have supplanted love and conception."[6] Or, as Patricia Waugh puts it, "[a]ttachment is viewed as regressive and as destructive of the independent self."[7] Whether the Japanese characters are attempting to create "independent selves" in these works is questionable but all of them share ambivalent attitudes toward attachment, especially love of women.

In the works examined in this chapter, by male and female writers, all forms of love, from maternal to sexual, seem to become grotesque parodies of themselves, emphasizing the lack of connection between human beings. Tsutsui's "Poruno wakusei no sarumonera ningen," (The Salmonella Beings from Planet Porno) is concerned with a quest for an abortion and privileges a male transformation into a sexless female spider. Kawabata's *House of the Sleeping Beauties* describes "relationships" between impotent old men and drugged, sleeping girls. Abe Kōbō's *Secret Rendezvous* highlights both paranoia and conspiracy in a narrative whose climax is a show of technological, dehumanized erotica. Finally, Nakagami's explicit deconstruction of *Kōya hijiri* in "The Immortal" limns a fallen demonic world where the only response of the male is to rape and rape again.

All of this is in important contrast to the roles played by women in prewar fantasy. There is certainly no postwar equivalent of *Kōya hijiri*'s magical and powerful woman who combines mother, seductress, and avenger in her attempt to protect a vanishing world. The women of Tanizaki and Sōseki are perhaps less sympathetic and more problematic in contemporary feminist eyes, but even they are delineated in highly positive terms from the male point of view, offering a refuge from a tumultuous outside reality.

Some positive portrayals of women do exist in contemporary male fantasy, of course, most notably in the works of Murakami Haruki, whose women are memorable for possessing their own independent personalities. As with Sōseki, women in Murakami's works are also clearly linked to an escape into another, better world; but, even with Murakami, this final escape will be from women, too, an aspect at which Sōseki only hints.

Thus, the narrator of Murakami's 1982 story "1963/1982-Nen no Ipanema musume" (The Girl from Ipanema 1963/1982) is musing on the 1962 hit record "The Girl from Ipanema" when he is magically transported to a beach and meets the girl from the record who shares a beer with him. This is a "realistic" fantasy, however, and the narrator realizes that the "real" girl from Ipanema would now be probably fat and forty with three children and sun-damaged skin, but he is happy to enjoy her fantasy apparition.

Although the girl's words to him are life-affirming (she tells him to "live, live, live"), the story ends with a final rejection of reality. The narrator insists that there is some sort of connection between him and the girl but, "I'm not sure just what the connection is. The link is probably in a strange place in a far off world." Revealingly, however, the narrator goes on to say that it is a link,

> joining me with myself. Someday too, I'm sure, I'll meet myself in a strange place in a far-off world. . . . In that place I am myself and myself is me. Subject is object and object is subject. All gaps gone. A perfect union.

Murakami's work essentially abandons the quest of the self for another, preferring instead the lonely happiness of autonomy. As Rubin puts it, this autonomous world is "deep within the wells of the mind, bound up with nostalgia and memory,"[8] and it is one that is not shared with anyone else. This preference for self-autonomy is apparently shared by Murakami's many young readers, and it is interesting to note that contemporary women fantasy writers also seem drawn to a vision of the solitary self, as we will explore at the end of this chapter.

Murakami's protagonist at least is happy to share a beer with his fantasy female. This is not the case in the fiction of most other postwar male writers. Although I have argued that Sōseki's "Dream of the First Night" is a relatively positive portrayal of a fantasy female, it may also be seen as giving some warning of postwar negativism, with its essential denial of the possibility of any real connection between man and woman. While Sōseki's dying woman was transformed into something beautiful and peace-giving, whose sightless eyes could no longer mirror male inadequacies, the dying or absent women in postwar works are seen as dangers to be escaped, incapable of offering any sort of peace.

SLEEPING WITH THE DEAD: KAWABATA'S *HOUSE OF THE SLEEPING BEAUTIES* AND "ONE ARM"

In two important works which may be seen as anticipating the increasingly negative depiction of women by younger postwar writers (his 1961 novel *House of the Sleeping Beauties* and his 1963 short story

"One Arm"), Kawabata Yasunari plays with Sōseki's images of an unseeing woman, death, and passivity to produce works that are both surreal yet somehow frighteningly believable. Unlike Sōseki and more similar to Tanizaki, however, Kawabata was also interested in fictional attempts to control women and to actively create worlds of escape. His fantasies problematize escape, suggesting that wish-fulfillment fantasies are no longer believable in a postwar world.

Like Tanizaki, Kawabata came to prominence in the prewar period and was especially well known for his depiction of female characters, often in traditional roles such as travelling dancers or geisha. The women in his fantastic literature share with the female characters of Tanizaki the fact that they tend to be also rather traditional, aesthetically pleasing objects to be desired. Unlike Tanizaki's female creations, however, they tend to be self-sacrificing, "good" women without even a hint of the selfish qualities that give Tanizaki's women a special edge.

Also like Tanizaki, Kawabata went on writing after the war, although with a pronounced note of pessimism. Even more than Tanizaki, Kawabata regretted the lost Japanese prewar past, but, unlike Tanizaki, he did not choose to create a fictional refuge such as *The Bridge of Dreams* where sexuality and traditional aesthetics are able to meet again. Instead, in *House of the Sleeping Beauties* he presents an artificial sterile world that becomes more a trap than a refuge, while in "One Arm"'s womblike setting he shows, quite literally, the impossibility of human connection, even in a place of apparent security.

Van Gessel says of Kawabata that after the war he "unconditionally surrendered all concrete claims to the past,"[9] and although one may quibble with the "unconditionally," since it would seem that Kawabata still at times looked back at what was lost, there is no question that he sees old Japan as dead. While Tanizaki in his mourning for a lost past made women into the main supports of a shrine to traditional Japan, Kawabata accepted death and memorialized it. As Kawabata himself said, after the war he could "produce only elegies for a lost Japan".[10]

House of the Sleeping Beauties is a work that may be said to be less an elegy than a privileging of death. Eguchi, the protagonist, is a man long past his prime but still sexually aware. A friend tells him about a certain "house" where old, presumably impotent, men are allowed to sleep next to nude young girls who themselves have been put to sleep through medicine. The most obvious aspect of the novel that makes it a departure from consensus reality is the fact that the girls never wake up, no matter how their male clients deal with them.

There are many other surreal touches as well, however, such as the "house" itself, a place of sinister, indeed gothic, privacy, located on a cliff above the ocean. The book begins with Eguchi's first visit to the house, in quest of erotic satisfaction. But this is a quest which, like the monk's in *Kōya hijiri*, will force him to confront hitherto hidden aspects of both his sexuality and his identity.

In the case of *House of the Sleeping Beauties*, however, there is a disturbing difference in the way this erotic quest is carried out, for this time the womanly Other is not an active participant in the journey. Indeed, the only woman whom Eguchi ever speaks to is the house's sinister proprietress, a shadowy but somehow repellent figure who exists basically as an enabler to help these "men who are no longer men," as the text describes them, recapture some aspect of youth at the same time as relieving them of their money.

Eguchi is led into a room whose four walls and door are covered with crimson curtains. The only other thing it contains is a girl already asleep on the bedding. The text describes his reaction: "He caught his breath. She was more beautiful than he had expected. And she was young too . . . . It was as if another heart beat its wings in old Eguchi's chest"(pp. 18–19).

Later on during the night, he gazes at the young girl wondering if she is really alive:

> Though this girl lost in sleep had not put an end to the hours of her life, had she not lost them, had them sink into bottomless depths? She was not a living doll for there could be no living doll; but so as not to shame an old man no longer a man, she had been made into a living toy. No, not a toy; for the old men she could be life itself.
>
> (p. 20)

Eguchi moves from death (the "bottomless depths") to artificial life (the "living doll", the "toy"), finally back to "life itself", but this is not the *girl*'s life but rather a life for voyeuristic old men such as himself.

Clearly, the sleeping girl is synecdotal with the dead woman whom Bronfen describes as allowing men to feel victory over the Other, be the Other death or femininity. Like vampires, the old men are able to take renewed life ("another heart") from the girl.[11] Indeed, the text contains many examples of Eguchi examining the girls' pulses and noting the flowing of blood through their veins. At one point he even has a flashback to a former lover, whose breast he had bitten till it bled.

But there is a price for this new life, and the price is that his old life returns to haunt him in the form of nightmares and evil memories, such as the aforementioned one of the girl's bloody breast. The scent and looks of each new girl he sleeps with evoke different feelings and recollections, some enjoyable but many disturbing.

Eguchi finds himself "wearying" of the house at the same time as he is increasingly drawn to visit there, even after he has heard that a friend of his had died of a heart attack in the house, giving him a presentiment of death as well. It is not Eguchi, however, but one of a pair of girls sleeping beside him, who dies mysteriously during the night. Eguchi informs the proprietress, who takes over the disposal of the body and tells him to " 'Go back to sleep. There is the other girl.' There was another girl – no remark had ever struck him so sharply" (pp. 104–105). Eguchi returns to the room and the novel ends as he gazes down on the sleeping girl while listening to the sound of a car taking the other girl's body away.

Clearly, the sealed room with its red curtains is evocative of the womb. Just before waking to discover the dead girl, Eguchi even dreams of his mother standing at the doorway saying "Welcome home" to him. But, unlike the other womblike spaces we have considered thus far, such as the spring in *Kōya hijiri*, or the garden in *The Bridge of Dreams*, this is not a place of joy and security. In the dream of his mother Eguchi sees their house surrounded by flowers from which red blood oozes.[12]

Far from being a site of rebirth or a return to a more pleasant past, this is a world where the past in the form of memories is disturbing and where only death awaits. Even sexuality, which is seen as positive, if dangerous, in Kawabata's earlier works, is viewed negatively. The girls themselves are virgins, the men impotent. Sexual activity does not even take place and the girls never see the men who sleep beside them. They are objects in the most fundamental sense, gazed at by men who cannot engage with them in any active way.

Again in this story we have the theme of the substitute, the "other girl" whom the proprietress impatiently recommends to Eguchi. But it is clear from Eguchi's reaction ("no remark had ever struck him so sharply") that this substitution is hardly adequate. After all, what can she be a substitute for? Unlike the mother in *The Bridge of Dreams*, the dead girl had no meaning to Eguchi, no personality and no associations with a beneficent past. Furthermore, unlike the flower woman in Sōseki's story, the substitute girl remains female and therefore implicitly threatening as she lies there, representing an ultimately unknowable Other.

To give Kawabata his due, much of his mimetic fiction such as *Yukiguni* (1935–1937) (trans. *Snow Country* (1956)) and *Yama no oto*

(1950)(trans. *Sound of the Mountain* (1970)) contains female characters such as Komako and Kikuko who are very much alive. Rather like
Sōseki's more positive female characters, they seem to offer the male a
chance for refuge, even redemption. But even in these mimetic works
the gulf between human beings, especially between male and female, is
usually treated as ultimately unbridgeable, and in his later fiction even
nature, initially seen as an important solace in his early writings, becomes threatening as well.

Kawabata's surreal fantasy "One Arm" exemplifies both these
themes, the gulf between self and other, and the increasingly ominous
quality of nature. (Nature is notable largely for its absence in
House of the Sleeping Beauties. Unlike many of Kawabata's other
works, the action takes place almost entirely inside the house, contributing to its claustrophobic atmosphere.) More overtly "postmodern" in
style and setting than *House of the Sleeping Beauties*, "One Arm"'s
narrative takes place in a world without rules, where anything can
happen.

Thus, the story begins with a young girl casually telling the narrator,
"I can let you have one of my arms for the night" (p. 109), whereupon,
she slips it off and hands it over. The narrator takes the arm home
with him, half pleased but half apprehensive that the arm might "cry
out or weep." Alone in his room, he caresses the arm and talks to it,
more freely than if had been talking to its owner. Outside, a heavy fog
deepens and the narrator imagines that it will soon change color to
pink or purple and wonders if he can hear wild beasts howling. Inside,
however, all is peaceful and suffused with the scent of a magnolia
blooming on the table. The narrator lies down on the bed.

> ... presently the five fingers were climbing my chest. The elbow
> bent of its own accord and the arm embraced me. There was a
> delicate pulse at the girl's wrist. It lay over my heart so that the two
> pulses sounded against each other. Hers was at first somewhat
> slower than mine, then they were together ... never before had a
> woman slept beside me as peacefully as this arm.
>
> (pp. 124–125)

Despite this blissful tranquility, the narrator cannot sleep. Muttering
"I'll have it," he abruptly takes off his own arm and replaces it with the
girl's arm. The arm trembles but tells him that it is alright. He goes to
sleep with the girl's arm attached to his shoulder. In the morning,
however, he awakens in surprise and tears the girl's arm off, hastily
reattaching his own. As he describes it "the act was like murder upon a
sudden diabolic impulse" (p. 131). He goes back to pick up the girl's

arm but it seems lifeless. The last the reader sees is of the "I" cradling the arm to his chest.

This story readdresses and highlights many of Kawabata's most important themes through its use of the overtly fantastic mode. As Gessel comments about an earlier work, "if this is a love story it is one played out with the principals at considerable distance from one another, seeking something intensely private rather than any sort of interpersonal involvement."[13]

The overt morselization of the arm rather than, say, the breast or even the foot (a favorite Tanizaki fetish) is a particularly moving aspect of the story. For the arm, although clearly erotic, also has obvious elements of the maternal to it as well, as when it embraces the narrator's neck. This maternality is then reversed most poignantly in the final scene when the "I" cradles the perhaps dying arm, embracing it "as one would a small child from whom life was going" (p. 132).

In the small room heavy with the scent of magnolia we have yet another vision of the womb. In this case it seems to be a place of security as compared to the bizarre manifestations of nature going on outside. But it is the "I" himself who brings insecurity back into the womb, tearing the arm off and insisting on the essential isolation between individuals, the fundamental inability to connect.

Both "One Arm" and *House of the Sleeping Beauties* have more sinister subtexts as well, since they also implicitly or explicitly deal with violence toward women. Eguchi dreams of "using force" on one of the young girls, thinking to himself,

> How would it be, by way of revenge for all the derided and insulted old men who came here, if he were to violate [the girl]. . . . Were not the longing of the sad old men for the unfinished dream, the regret for days lost without ever being had, concealed in the secret of this house?
>
> (p. 40)

Eguchi ultimately does not violate the girl but he fantasizes at other times about cutting the arm off one or "stab[bing] her in the chest or abdomen" (p. 83). The actual death of the girl in the final scene is also ambiguous. Eguchi's first reaction when waking beside the corpse is to think "Did I strangle her in my sleep?" (p. 104).

In "One Arm" the initial violence, the taking of the arm, is suggested and indeed performed by the girl herself, very much as if she were giving herself to the man. The "I" at first feels no guilt, but later on, going home, he sees a woman driving a car through thick fog:

I wanted to run off, fearing that the girl had come for her arm. Then I remembered that she would hardly be able to drive with only one. But had not the woman in the car seen what I was carrying? Had she not sensed it with a woman's intuition? I would have to take care not to encounter another of the sex before I reached my apartment.

(p. 113)

Despite his new-found closeness to the woman's arm, therefore, the "I" still feels threatened by the other sex. Perhaps this is what leads him finally to rip off the girl's arm the next morning, an act which he himself describes as murder. In many ways the scene where he attaches the arm in the first place is reminiscent of first intercourse, as the arm trembles in shock when the man attaches it to himself. From this point of view, the man's horror the next morning can be equated with withdrawal, the need to feel himself a separate person again, but it also suggests an essentially paranoid reaction to women. Although the "I" has initially tried to bridge the difference between self and Other, in the long run he is unable to maintain such unity for long.

House of the Sleeping Beauties, on the other hand, suggests less paranoia than a fundamental disappointment in both women and life itself. In this regard it makes an interesting comparison with a medieval tale written by Ueda Akinari. In that justly famous story, "Asaji gayado" (trans. "House Among the Thickets" (1974)), which was filmed as *Ugetsu* by Mizoguchi in 1953, the man returns from seeking his fortune and sleeps with his wife, only to wake up in the morning to discover she is dead and he has slept with a ghost. In that story the central theme was wifely devotion and man's greed, but the subtext is not so different from Kawabata's: the past is dead, one cannot re-create it except for brief moments of wish-fulfillment.

Although the two Kawabata works I have mentioned are of the postwar period, Kawabata himself is a writer whose sensibility is still formed by the prewar period. This is obvious in his treatment of female characters, whom he still believes to offer redemption; and when they do not, or cannot, the male characters are shown to be equally at fault. As in Tanizaki, women are best when they evoke positive memories such as in his short fantasy "Yuki" (1964) (trans. "Snow" (1988)) in which Sankichi, an old man, spends New Year's alone in a hotel room summoning forth images of his past, including "all the women who had loved Sankichi" (p. 227) riding toward him on silver wings. As flesh and blood, women can be more problematic, but there is still a sense of lyricism and of lost love pervading most of Kawabata's works, softening what would otherwise be extremely troubling portrayals of fantasy women. Women in Kawabata are still linked to positive elements, to a better past, to a realm which at least potentially offers some comfort, even if the realization of these desires often disappoints.

In Kawabata's works women may be silenced but they are still important concrete presences in the text. I would like now to turn to three postwar writers who do more than silence women, who actively erase women characters from the text itself. The three texts I will be discussing in detail, Tsutsui Yasutaka's "Poruno wakusei no saramonera ningen" (The Salmonella Beings from Planet Porno), Abe Kōbō's *Secret Rendezvous*, and Nakagami Kenji's "The Immortal" are all exceptionally interesting works in themselves, but two of them, Tsutsui's and Nakagami's, are also fascinating in comparison with Kyōka's previously discussed *Kōya hijiri*. Indeed, Kenji's work is an explicit deconstruction of *Kōya hijiri*. Like Kyōka's work, the texts I am about to discuss are quest fantasies with strong sexual overtones but, despite the importance of the erotic in them, women are presented largely in a negative fashion, if they are presented at all.

IN QUEST OF A DEAD CENTER: TSUTSUI YASUTAKA'S "PORUNO WAKUSEI NO SARUMONERA NINGEN" (THE SALMONELLA BEINGS FROM PLANET PORNO)

Thus, Tsutsui's remarkable 1982 short story, which translates as "The Salmonella Beings from Planet Porno," takes the reader into a world which is suffused with eroticism at the same time as it implicitly absents actual women from the text. A popular, prolific, and controversial writer, who only recently has begun to be accepted in the world of *junbungaku* (pure literature), Tsutsui first made his name as a science fiction writer. Many of his works, however, fall equally well into the category of postmodern in terms of their rapid narrative pace, grotesque imagery and lack of a moral center, and he is increasingly becoming a subject of literary criticism.

Appropriate to this sort of "postmodern" text, "Poruno wakusei" inscribes itself far from the traditional Japanese landscape, into the literary space belonging to the international territory of late-twentieth-century science fiction. Set on another planet, nicknamed "Planet Porno" for soon to be obvious reasons, and peopled by the inevitable team of scientists common to much generic science fiction, the narrative is embedded within a surprisingly sophisticated scientific discourse.

And yet, examining the work more closely, we find a number of surprising similarities in both narrative structure and content between "Poruno wakusei" and the turn-of-the-century *Kōya hijiri*. Both are quest narratives, even pilgrimages, inscribed within fantastic landscapes with only barely concealed erotic subtexts, at the end of which some measure of self-enlightenment is obtained as the result of highly charged erotic encounters. Both also deal with the issue of metamorphosis from man into beast in relation to a vision of "devolution" or "change of eras."

Perhaps the most notable difference is in language. Whereas *Kōya hijiri* kept the erotic subtext under traditional covers, the fantasy landscape of "Poruno wakusei" trumpets the sexual in all directions through the inordinate number of sexually charged place names. The ostensible reason behind this is due to the ecological make-up of the planet itself. True to Planet Porno's nickname, virtually all the species, both animal and vegetable, on the planet are engaged in ceaseless and totally undifferentiated sexual activity, regardless of gender or species.

Thus, it is not surprising that, when it comes to imposing their language on the planet, the early explorers from Earth could not help but call the swollen pink twin suns *"oppai taiyō"* (tit suns) or the swamp in which all kinds of sexually rapacious grasses and animals lurk as the *"gesen numa"* (Low, as in base or vulgar, Swamp). Most poignantly named is Yonakiyama (or Night-crying Mountain), so called because when the wind blows through it it sounds like a woman crying in ecstasy. Other creatures such as the *"yabusakawani"* (ever-ready alligator) which lurks in the "Low Swamp" suggest the kind of hypersexuality that permeates both the planet and the text.

The combination of sexually explicit names with the highly sophisticated technical chatter in which the scientists engage gives "Poruno Wakusei" an extraordinarily rich and distinctive narrative style. Although suffused with sexuality, the text manages, just barely, to distance itself from the pornographic. This is accomplished through the attitude of the scientists, a mixture of disgust and cold theoretization that accompanies their attempt to work out a theory to explain the planet's bizarre ecological system, and also through the considerable humor which permeates the story.

A further distancing mechanism is the fact that, in all this frantically sexual landscape, no women actually appear. Women are constantly evoked, as in Yonakiyama or the twin suns, and it is a woman who sets the narrative on its course and the explorers on their quest, but "Poruno wakusei" does not contain a single scene involving a female character, despite the many sexual encounters occurring on the quest.

In some ways, in fact, the quest revolves around the denial of women, at least in their maternal and sexual function.

What actually is this quest? Initially, the quest is for scientific enlightenment, as to how to prevent a birth, but the end result is closer to spiritual enlightenment and to both a spiritual and literal rebirth. Dr. Shimazaki, the only woman scientist on Poruno Wakusei's base camp, has been impregnated by a strange form of grass, appropriately known as "*gokeharami*" (or widow impregnator). The base commander calls a meeting to determine how to get rid of the "*nanika*" (whatever it is) in Dr. Shimazaki's womb, but the doctor herself, significantly, is too embarrassed to appear. At the meeting, three men are chosen to go on a journey to Mammalasia, the place where the original human inhabitants of Poruno Wakusei live, and to ask them how to abort the fetus. Although the Mammalasians are human, their attitudes toward the erotic differ significantly from the terrestrial humans, especially those of the two scientists on the team.

Indeed, the characters of the three men on the team make up an interesting sexual continuum, a continuum which goes even further than the monk/medicine peddler dichotomy of *Kōya hijiri*. The head of the group, Dr. Mogamigawa, is virtually asexual, a cliché man of learning who finds everything to do with sex (in this case almost everything on Planet Porno) to be "*iyorashii*" (disgusting). Next on the continuum is the narrator, another quintessential scientist whose special interest is in developing a theory of devolution to explain Poruno Wakusei's unique ecosystem. The narrator is also an acknowledged voyeur, in itself not an inappropriate characteristic for a scientist.

Because of their attitudes toward sex, both men would be anathema to the Mammalasians, who believe in free and participatory copulation. Consequently, the two scientists must remain outside the barrier to Mammalasia and leave it up to the third member of the party, Yahachi, a kind of handyman around the base, to actually gain the Mammalasians' confidence enough to relay information to the scientists about the means of abortion. Yahachi's sexual preferences, anything and everything, accord perfectly with the Mammalasians' own philosophy and he is delighted to be chosen for the job.

However, as is to be expected in a quest narrative, the actual journey to Mammalasia is as harrowing as that of the monk's journey down the old road. Indeed, the only really important difference between Poruno Wakusei's landscape and Kyōka's Japanese mountains is its overt sexuality, as opposed to the implicit sexuality of *Kōya hijiki*'s snakes and leeches or the swampy, muddy landscape. Like the monk, Tsutsui's explorers are also forced to confront their worst nightmares, or alternatively their most intensely erotic dreams, as they journey through a landscape which literally might rape them at any moment. Sure enough, on encountering their first obstacle, the Low Swamp, which is full of disgusting life forms such as the "*kujirimo*" (stimulating weed), the "*chimidoro*" (bloody, muddy seaweed), and the "*yabusakawani*" (ever-ready alligator), Yahachi falls victim, although he insists that the experience is a pleasurable one.

The Low Swamp is strongly reminiscent of the monk's bloody, muddy leech forest, and in its watery aspect it is in interesting contrast to the river to an erotic past of Tanizaki's *The Reed Cutter*. The Low Swamp is ultimately less important than another natural body, the forest where the explorers are forced to spend the night, the most dangerous place they encounter. There, in the forest's "dead center" (the text uses the English words *dedo senta*), they witness a particularly complex sexual orgy, which the narrator describes as a "Walpurgisnacht party", and only barely escape from being forced to participate in it themselves.

As in Kyōka's narrative, however, the journey's end, Mammalasia, turns out to be a genuinely seductive place of physical and psychological healing, at least for Yahachi, who refers to it as "Paradise." Not only does Yahachi find the secret of aborting the fetus (through copulating with Mammalasian women which will bring salmonella microbes into his sperm, rendering it poisonous to the "whatever it is" in Dr. Shimazaki's womb), but he also gains a degree of self-knowledge and self-respect through participating in the joyous and uninhibited sexuality of the Mammalasians. As he recounts to the scientists outside the fence: "I'm so happy. Here no one looks at me like I'm a dirty old man, nobody's saying 'You filthy vulgar man' to me" (p. 229, my translation). Spiritually reborn, Yahachi only wishes that Earth could learn from the Mammalasians' liberated ways.

But it is Dr. Mogamigawa, even more than Yahachi, who experiences a literal rebirth. This occurs on their return journey where once again they blunder into the "dead center" of the forest. In a scene reminiscent of an adult version of Bilbo's adventures with the spiders in *The Hobbit*, Dr. Mogamigawa is raped and bloodied by the frenzied animals, and eventually trussed up into a tree. At this point he begins to undergo a transformation into a *wasuregatami*, literally meaning "memento" but in this case referring to a kind of sexless "mother spider" whose main function within the planet's complex ecology is to save infant animals who are the products of cross-breed matings.

Fortunately for Mogamigawa, his companions save him before his head metamorphosizes, so his brains and personality are left intact, at least apparently.

To his companions' surprise, Dr. Mogamigawa is delighted with his transformation because he is "finally liberated from sex." As he himself comments,

> This must be the planet's revenge for my having thought everything on it, the humans, the plants, all its natural phenomena, to be disgusting. But what a marvelous revenge. This planet has turned a conservative obstinate old man like me, who abhorred anything erotic, into the most perfect animal possible for me, a sexless wasure-gatami, liberated me from sex and allowed me to become part of its ecology. Of course I'm no longer human. I'm a beast ... what would you call me?
>
> (p. 239; my translation)

To which Yahachi responds, "I would call you possessed" (p. 239). Possessed or not, the story ends with the transformed Mogamigawa leaping spiderlike to the base camp, laughing and shouting, "I'm so happy. I'm so happy" (p. 240).

"Poruno wakusei" thus achieves a "happy" ending. At least two of the questers have achieved their hearts' desires, while the voyeuristic narrator has found additional proof for his theory of devolution. He realizes that not only the animals but many of the plants on the planet have devolved from the Mammalasians, who themselves may have arrived from Earth centuries before. As in *Kōya*, but this time with a pseudo-scientific explanation, on Planet Porno, men are literally turned into beasts, both through devolution and through the machinations of the creatures who transformed Dr. Mogamigawa.

The importance of metamorphosis in Japanese fantasy will be discussed in further detail in the next chapter, but for now it is enlightening to compare the two forms of metamorphosis in *Kōya hijiri* and "Poruno Wakusei". In *Kōya hijiri* the men are turned into beasts precisely because of their lustful desires, the implication being that at some level the men bring it on themselves and deserve their "devolution" into lower forms. Thus "devolution" is presented as something negative, even a form of punishment. Kyōka's thinking may have been influenced both by the new discoveries of Darwin and also by Buddhism, which posits the development from animal to enlightened human to Boddhisatva.

In Tsutsui's story, on the other hand, "devolution" comes across very positively. It is either regarded with scientific excitement (the narrator) or with pleasure (Yahachi and Mogamigawa). This attitude suggests a fundamental despair at human institutions, as if modern human beings can no longer and should no longer progress. Inherently, this vision also suggests that women's maternal function is no longer useful.

In a world without maternal admonitory figures, men can regress into irresponsible boys. But without maternal affection these "boys" seem rather shallow. Yahachi glories in free sexuality while Mogamigawa is "liberated" from sexuality forever, but these apparently opposite wish-fulfillments are two sides of the same coin. By suffusing the very landscape with sexuality, Tsutsui at the same time renders sex almost meaningless.

In this regard the absent woman is crucial. The men (and animals and plants) of Poruno wakusei no longer turn to women, even sexually, except as a component of a wider sexual grouping. As for motherhood, this has devolved into either the grotesque "whatever it is" that everyone is happy to agree should be aborted, or the asexual ministrations of the *wasuregatami*. If Kyōka's sexual world is basically an innocent one where a mother's presence is still appreciated, the sexual world of "Poruno Wakusei" belongs to a pubescent boy where a mother's protection is no longer needed and where women as people are totally unimportant.

"Poruno wakusei" is a highly original work, but at its basis is a vision of an undifferentiated world of oneness common to much Utopian literature. As Mark Rose points out, "Science fiction [both] expresses the fear of the dissolution of the self and [at the same time] expresses the desire to escape the prison house of the self, the wish to merge with the other."[14]

In prewar literature this "merging with the other" meant a return to mother and to the womb. In "*Poruno wakusei*", however, the womb becomes the sinister "dead center" of the forest where even the narrator comments negatively on the sexual orgy taking place there. A "dead" center is actually the opposite of the womb. Furthermore, far from being a place inherently linked with old Japan, as are the womblike spring of *Kōya hijiri* or the womblike garden of *The Bridge of Dreams*, this "dead center" is an anonymous generic area, symbolized by the use of English words.

"*Poruno wakusei*" is the only genuine wish-fulfillment fantasy by a male writer to be discussed in this chapter. But the fulfillment achieved in it is a disturbing one, since it requires both regression into simpler forms and elimination of the more complex and unavoidable aspects of modern life. Our next work to be considered, Abe Kōbō's *Secret*

Rendezvous, acknowledges and even exploits the complexities of modernity to create a darkly fantastic vision of renunciation and abasement.

THE QUEST, SEX, AND THE TECHNOLOGICAL LABYRINTH: ABE KŌBŌ'S *SECRET RENDEZVOUS*

Although Tsutsui's satire has obvious science fiction elements, it is surprisingly free of technological elements. The explorers, for example, are forced to go by boat and on foot to Mammalasia because the base's air car has broken down, lending another traditional aspect to their quest. Moreover, the abortion they seek is to be brought about by essentially natural means, the introduction of poisonous microbes into Dr. Shimazaki's womb.

It is Abe who links women and technology in an uncompromisingly negative fashion in his grotesque dystopian satire *Secret Rendezvous*. The narrative of this surreal work is set into motion by a literally absent woman, the narrator's wife, who is kidnapped one morning by a hospital van. As he describes it (speaking of himself in the third person):

> It was an utter bolt from the blue. . . . Indeed, his wife herself, the one in question, had never complained of a single symptom. But the two men who carried in the stretcher were gruff, perhaps from lack of sleep, and paid no attention: Of course she wasn't ready, they said; this was an emergency wasn't it?
>
> (p. 8)

In a world of increasingly dizzying change, no one is ever really "ready" for whatever crisis is about to confront them. In this case the nature of the "emergency" is never made clear, but the text grows increasingly surreal as the husband goes to the hospital in quest of his wife who, he discovers, has apparently disappeared into thin air from the hospital waiting room.

Typical to both Abe and to postwar anti-realism, his quest is inherently an absurd one. Although the protagonist muses that, "if you want to find your wife, first find yourself," he ends up losing both. The loss of the self is a frequent theme in many Abe novels, but in this one, most ominously, the loss is met with resignation rather than with rage. Unlike *Kōya hijiri*, then, or even "Poruno wakusei," this quest leads not to self-knowledge but ultimately to self-defeat.

It is debatable whether the husband ever even sees his wife again. Instead, by entering the hospital, he enters an increasingly bizarre world which he characterizes as "a labyrinth." In this world the doctors and nurses behave like mental patients and criminals and seem largely preoccupied with experimenting with bizarre forms of technology, usually of a sexual sort. Thus, the husband first encounters the hospital's assistant director as he lies naked on a hospital bed listening to a recording of a woman's moans while "applying some sort of instrument to the end of his erect penis, rotating his knees and vibrating his wrists at the rate of five times per second" (p. 73).

This bizarre scene with the pedantic little detail of "five times per second" sets the tone for the rest of the novel, an increasingly anarchic vision of technology and sexuality run amok in a place which ostensibly should be a refuge for healing. The husband discovers a hospital-wide conspiracy to keep the whereabouts of his wife secret at the same time as he finds that "hundreds perhaps thousands of microphones" are hidden throughout the hospital, recording his (and everyone else's) dialogue and movements. He attempts to hear his wife's voice on the tape recordings but finds that there are too many conversations: "It's like playing hide and seek with my own shadow ... I'll never catch up" (p. 170).

Increasingly, the man begins to find the memory of his wife indistinct and even begins to question the reality of their married life. Finally, and most ironically, he actually ends up taking the job of chief of security for the hospital. As a member of the hospital staff, he is invited to its "anniversary party," one of the high points of which is a competition amid anonymous women as to who can have the most intense orgasms.

The narrator is particularly drawn to a woman whose face is painted white and who is known as the Masked Woman. Believing that she might be his wife, he buys a ticket for admission to her show and enters a reception area

> surrounded on all four sides by black cloth. When one layer was pushed aside, another appeared in its place. Pushing right and left through layer after layer of cloth ... finally, we came to a white tiled room that looked like a lecture amphitheater for a dissection. In the front of the room was a semicircular cylinder covered with curved mirrors, surrounded fanwise by rows of nearly full seats.
>
> (p. 175)

As the house lights dim, the mirrors vanish and the narrator sees the woman lying naked on a huge bed with electrodes taped to her knees, hips, and shoulders. A team of doctors measures her orgasmic intensity and announce the results to a waiting crowd. In a sense, the woman is the human embodiment of "Poruno wakusei"'s Yonakiyama or Night-Crying Mountain, but she is a human who has now become dehumanized through technology. The narrator's comment, however, is a revealing one: "Even in that state she had beauty and charm, rather like a dancer in the role of a captive Martian" (p. 175).

Neither the narrator nor the reader ever discovers if the woman is in fact his wife, and in the long run this does not seem to matter. For, if she is his wife, the woman is now utterly Other to him, "a captive Martian," reached through a technological travesty of a black curtained womb. At the scene's climax the narrator is urged to have sex with the woman to see if "his body will remember her," but he refuses and another man takes his place. As the narrator tries to get outside the room he hears,

> suddenly through the black cloth walls like a howling wind, there came the echo of a woman's deep sad moaning. . . . Swathed head to foot in black cloth, I kept pushing blindly ahead, frantically thrusting curtains aside one after another. Whether it meant that I would escape from my wife or be pulled back to her, I didn't care. . . .

> (p. 175)

This horrific journey is the emotional opposite of Tanizaki's dreamlike return to the breast in *The Bridge of Dreams*. Instead of the reassuring female symbols of milk and a mother's embracing arms, there is only black cloth that swathes him head to foot like a shroud. And far from yearning for the woman, the narrator no longer cares. Our final view of the narrator is of him with another woman, a young girl with a bizarre "dissolving disease." The narrator has taken refuge with the girl at the bottom of the hospital's sewers (another grotesque womb parody) but, even though he holds her tightly, she has almost dissolved into nothingness, another example of a female who can only be absent. Now the protagonist waits only for a rendezvous with death.

Unlike traditional myth, which started in chaos to create order, Abe's vision brings the reverse, a high-tech Walpurgisnacht, where women collaborate happily in the dissolution of all order. *Secret Rendezvous'* vision is a bleak one for both sexes: encounters between male and female are always disastrous and only lead to the final encounter, with death. But it is significant that the male characters are still actively searching for something; the narrator for his wife, the assistant director for his potency, while the women are simply passive objects, and disappearing ones at that. Women are no longer connected with a past (the narrator does not even try to find out if his body will "remember" his wife), or even a future, since their reproductive functions are not important either.

Secret Rendezvous is one of the grimmest of all Abe's works, but his other novels also often see women negatively as well. Thus, the woman in *Suna no onna* (1962) (trans. *The Woman in the Dunes* (1972)) becomes an agent of entrapment, while the mother in *Dai yon kampyo-ki* (trans. *Inter Ice Age 4* (1970)) bears partial responsibility for creating a grotesque new race of Aquans, although in *Inter Ice Age 4*'s apocalyptic view the coming flood will create a new race with no need of human mothers. Even the potentially sympathetic wife of *Tanin no kao* (1964) (trans. *The Face of Another* 1970)), is threatening to the male in that she can see through his attempt at disguise. A partial clue to the reasons behind Abe's generally negative portrayal of women may perhaps be found in his earliest novel, *Owarishi michi no shirube ni* (The Sign at the End of the Road) (1948), in which a little boy recalls being outside a wall in Manchuria with his mother's garden on the other side. Abe's characters are always in exile from both mother and garden, and this sense of exile brings both sadness and anger.

The two-way mirror at the end of *Secret Rendezvous* allows the ultimate male vengeance, for it permits the male audience to observe the woman without her seeing them. The woman's plight is also rationalized by the doctors as being the result of a form of "rape delusion" that they insist she is suffering from. They explain that the woman/wife was afraid she would be gang-raped and that her constant state of orgasmic arousal is a kind of defense mechanism for "escaping the fear of rape."

Abe's paranoid fantasy vision suggests a world where technology and human beings together collaborate to violate individuality and human integrity. As the last scene makes clear, both men and women are victims in this world, although it would appear that it is the absent woman who starts the protagonist on his course of disaster.

Abe's novel subverts the consensus ideology of modern Japan on many levels. He parodies the traditional respect for doctors and makes the hospital itself into a place of further pain rather than healing. Authority in general is questioned and confronted, but no hope is offered in its place. Technology only heightens paranoia or becomes an agent of deviant actions.

In such a society it only makes sense that a lost woman should never be found. The final auditory image of the woman who may be the protagonist's wife is a deeply disturbing one, however. The "deep sad" moan of the masked woman's lonely orgasm measured on machinery and heard through black curtains can be seen as a universal outcry of modern despair.

Our last vision of women in male fantasy, Nakagami Kenji's "The Immortal," clearly shows a woman as victim of male vengeance, raped repeatedly and left for dead. This vision is horrific in itself but it is particularly disturbing when we realize that it is part of a work that in many ways is an homage to Kyōka's *Kōya hijiri*.

THE WOMAN WHO WAS NEVER THERE: NAKAGAMI KENJI'S "THE IMMORTAL"

Like *Kōya hijiri*, "The Immortal" concerns a monk or *hijiri* who is wandering in the mountains (in this case the mountains of Kumano, an even wilder and more legendary region than the mountains in *Kōya*). Unlike Kyōka's monk, however, this is a *hijiri* who has already appropriated much worldly experience but possesses little scholarly learning. The text describes him as having learned the sutras "only as a child who had been abandoned by hill people, or valley people – or even perhaps by a monkey keeper in favor of the monkey," so that now, instead of reciting the sutras, he can only make a low growling noise, "jarajarajara", in his throat (p. 415).

It transpires that the monk lives through stealing and duping villagers in the mountains. Having killed a woman in a village he has fled to the mountains where, again like the monk of *Kōya*, he goes through a leech forest and encounters a mysterious woman beside a spring. The rest of the narrative is strikingly different, however.

Although the monk wonders if the woman might be an incarnation of Kannon, he goes ahead and rapes her anyway. Soon afterwards they are joined by strange creatures, perhaps demons or beasts, who walk with them as they approach a strange mansion by a waterfall underneath the moonlight. The woman tells him that "the noble ones" are there and in fact, these figures may be ghosts out of ancient warrior epics. Returning to the stream he has intercourse with the woman again, although this time she seems to enjoy it as well. When she gets up to bathe herself in the water, however, the monk "suddenly felt that the woman was about to disappear completely into the river and stood up to run after her"(p. 425). He asks her to stay with him, live with him, but the woman does not respond. Finally, she begs him to spare her life, which reminds him of the woman whom he had killed in the village who, too, had asked him to save her.

In the last, painful scene the monk walks away from the stream thinking that "soon it would be stained red with blood" (p. 428).

Turning back he sees only a "great flock of crows" (p. 428) apparently gathering by the woman's body. He turns back one last time to ask the woman if she will live with him. The story ends with the following vision of absence: "There was no one there. The hijiri thought he had known that from the beginning too" (p. 428).

"The Immortal" is a striking work by itself, but when read along with *Kōya hijiri* it becomes a truly shocking one. All the same elements from Kyōka's story remain – the monk, the mountains, the leech forest, the mysterious woman associated with the supernatural, a lost past, a waterfall and a stream – and yet the final impression that the reader carries away remains profoundly and disturbingly different.

Much of this difference is related to the attitude toward the woman depicted in the two works. In Kyōka's work the woman, although dangerous, is also sympathetic, capable of healing and nurturing. Furthermore, her contact with the supernatural and the old traditions have made her powerful, a force to be reckoned with.

In contrast, the woman in "The Immortal" is weak. This weakness is symbolized not only by her vulnerability to rape but by her tiny "child-sized" hands, a deformity which could also ally her to the demonic.[15] Her association with the supernatural and the traditional only serves to confuse and irritate the monk, however. As he says to himself, "He did not think that the weird monsters were phantoms. And neither did he believe they were the ghosts of the dead . . . they were here now" (p. 422).

And yet, ultimately, their presence makes no difference to him. Although Nakagami's fiction has been deeply empowered by the legends of the "dark land" of the Kumano mountains,[16] it is clear in "The Immortal" that the average human being cannot connect with legends. Unlike in works such as Kyōka's 1913 *Yashagaike* (Demon Pond), where a human writer becomes part of the supernatural world, the phantom world of "The Immortal" finally offers no connection to the monk. The phantoms cannot "save" him. Nor can the woman, any more than he can save her.

Even if supernatural creatures do exist deep in the mountains of Kumano they are capable of no action, positive or negative. The monk looks at the phantoms in the "silver moonlight" and finds that "[t]heir outlines were hazy, and they could easily have been mistaken for the grass or the branches of trees . . ." (p. 422). They are a far cry from the powerful figure of Kyōka's woman standing in front of the medicine peddler/horse. The Mansion of Noble Ones is also reminiscent of Miss Oyū's mansion in *The Reed Cutter*; but, where the phantom presence of tradition in the Tanizaki story brought a kind of solace to the peeping father and son, in Nakagami's vision the ghostliness of the mansion only emphasizes absence.

Ultimately, no one or nothing can save the *hijiri*. Although he dreams of his infancy when he makes love to the women, he cannot return to it, even though he persists in his meaningless pre-verbal chant of "jarajarajara" rather than reciting the sutras. Unlike Kyōka's monk, there is no world of the symbolic to enter either, since he has no interest in learning. As the text makes clear in its equation of the *hijiri* and the monkey, this is a man who has been abandoned by the world from the beginning.

Thus, when the woman, after he rapes her the first time, asks him "Where will you go?" he is unable to reply. But "in his heart, the hijiri replied that he had nowhere to go from the beginning, that there was nothing for him but to keep going on and on" (p. 422).

As in *Secret Rendezvous*, the *hijiri*'s quest is a meaningless one, simply haphazard, violent meandering. In the postwar world there is no womb to return to, nor even a substitute woman. At best, women are reminders of a faraway past that may never have existed. At worst they are not even there. Whereas women existed in a plethora in premodern and prewar fantasy, now "[t]here was no one there" (p. 422). In "Poruno wakusei" this absence is met with almost excessive relief and joy. "The Immortal"'s reaction seems somehow more believable and more compelling, especially the final lines, with their bitter vision of emptiness.

"The Immortal" encapsulates many of the themes we have been dealing with in this chapter in a memorably bleak and violent fashion. In place of the tall powerful enchantress of *Kōya hijiri* stands the pleading anonymous woman with her "childlike hands." The monk's actions toward her, his repeated violations of her body, seem initially shocking, but the final line explains his rage and despair: he had "always known" that there would be no one for him.

The monk's rage against abandonment is not unique in postwar fiction. As I have argued elsewhere, a sense of abandonment and betrayal is at the heart of such writers as Mishima, Ōe, and Abe, although in Mishima and Ōe's case, at least, we can see it as more of a betrayal by the father or the Emperor. What is interesting in the case of "The Immortal" is that the rage against this betrayal is taken out on a woman.[17]

To suggest that the absence of woman in "The Immortal" is equivalent to the absence of traditional Japan would be too reductive. The absence of woman implies the absence of many other things as well: love, hope, the past, and even, finally, the future. All of these absences are increasingly part of modern life anywhere and are not unique to Japan. Furthermore, Nakagami had his own personal reasons to feel abandoned by a modernity which promised egalitarianism but never gave equal treatment to the outcast class from which he came.

It is still significant, however, that Nakagami chose to wrap his bleak vision in the framework of the Kyōka story, a work that consciously celebrated the continued existence of an "old road" back to traditional Japan. In fact *Kumano-shū* (A Collection of Tales from Kumano) (1984), the work in which "The Immortal" appears in its Japanese edition, is a collection of stories which include a number of other traditional ghost stories. Just as the monk violates the woman, Nakagami is repeatedly deconstructing his own heritage, using fantasy as one of his most potent weapons. In the fantastic visions of Abe, Tsutsui, Nakagami, and the postwar Kawabata, there are no longer any old roads back to a past. And even if such a road existed there would be no woman to meet them at the end of it.

WOMEN ALONE: FANTASY FEMALES IN THE WORKS OF ENCHI FUMIKO, ŌBA MINAKO, KURAHASHI YUMIKO AND KANAI MIEKO

I would like to end this chapter with an account of some of the ways women characters have been dealt with in women's fantasy as well. Although this is a large topic, worthy of a study in itself, some interesting comparisons can be made between male and female fantasy. In other parts of this book I have interwoven fantasies by male and female writers, but in the case of the role of women, I believe a comparison of their treatment according to the writer's gender is a particularly enlightening one, both because of their differences and, indeed, their surprising similarities.

Perhaps the most important overall similarity is that both male and female fantasy in postwar Japanese fiction is strikingly pessimistic, above all about relations between the sexes. Even in wish-fulfillment fantasies (or perhaps especially in wish-fulfillment fantasies), the main desire on the part of female characters is simply to be alone and unencumbered. While male characters in the writings just discussed are still seen in search of something, often an absent woman or womb, women characters seem increasingly to turn away from the outer world and their fantasies are notably antisocial.

Fantasy has been an important part of Japanese women's fiction since the early postwar era. In fact, many of the best postwar women writers such as Enchi Fumiko (1905–1986), Kanai Mieko, Kurahashi

Yumiko and Ōba Minako have routinely used the fantastic mode in their work.[18] If anything, women writers employ fantasy even more often than have male writers. This fact is not surprising. As Patricia Waugh says of contemporary Western women writers,

> Given the acute contradictoriness of women's lives and sense of subjectivity, it is not surprising that many contemporary women writers have sought to "displace" their desires, seeking articulation not through the rational and metonymic structures of realism but through the associative and metaphorical modes of fantasy: romance, science fiction, gothic, utopia, horror.[19]

Since Japanese women have experienced at least as much of the "acute contradictoriness" of life as their Western counterparts, they, too, have leaned toward the associative and metaphorical modes, although, as will be evident in Chapter 4, the Utopian form still seems largely unexplored among contemporary women Japanese women writers. Instead, horror or the supernatural fantastic seems to have been the preferred mode. There are a number of possible reasons for this. One would be the still important influence of the greatest work of Japanese literature, *The Tale of Genji*, which contains a number of episodes involving the supernatural. Both Enchi and Kurahashi may be considered "classical writers" who have written works in explicit homage to *The Tale of Genji*. Enchi's *Onnamen* (1958) (trans. *Masks* (1983)), in fact, takes up the theme of spirit possession explored in the Lady Rokujo section of *The Tale of Genji* to weave a complex tale of female revenge against men.

The importance of revenge in modern Japanese women's fiction may also be another reason for the use of the horror or supernatural mode of fantasy, since extremely imaginative forms of revenge may be wreaked through supernatural means. Finally, horror permits a particularly memorable imagistic palette, one which makes a vivid statement, in contrast to the stereotype of Japanese women as subdued and delicate.

All of these aspects, horror (of a subtle form), revenge, and memorable images come into play in the aforementioned *Masks* by Enchi Fumiko. In *Masks* (the title suggests a woman's need to put on a false face in her interactions with society, as well as referring to specific masks in the text associated with each of the female characters) an older scholarly woman named Mieko, appears to offer her dead son's wife, Yasuko, and her own idiot daughter, Harume (the twin of Yasuko's dead husband), a kind of refuge from the disappointing outside world. But this refuge has a cost; Mieko has a hidden agenda

which is the continuation of the family blood line through the impregna-
tion of her mentally weak daughter, Harume, whose hapless partner, a
man named Ibuki, is tricked into thinking that he is having sex with
the beautiful Yasuko. Although initially somewhat resistant to this
bizarre scheme, which involves making a fool of a man who is fond of
her, Yasuko eventually gives in and is last seen playing substitute
mother to Harume.

Masks conforms to Todorov's definition of the fantastic in that the
events depicted, including a seance, can have either a supernatural or a
rational explanation, and this ambiguity intensifies the novel's eerie
atmosphere. The theme of spirit possession is invoked throughout the
novel. It appears first in an essay on Lady Rokujo written by Mieko,
and later on is explicitly discussed by two men, Ibuki and another
would-be lover of Yasuko. Neither can believe that Yasuko would will-
ingly have performed such an action and decide instead that she was
"possessed" by her mother-in-law. Or, as one of them explains it,
"Yasuko is a medium. There's no doubt about that. I'm convinced that
Mieko Togano is her motivating force."

If Mieko is a "motivating force," it is one that is clearly hostile to
men. In fact, Mieko in her essay implicitly identifies herself with both
Rokujo and the Ryo no onna Nō mask, a mask representing an older
woman "who chafes at her inability to sublimate her strong ego in
deference to any man, but who can carry out her will only be enforcing
it upon others – through the possessive capacity of her spirit" (p. 52).
Other classical allusions carry out this theme of women's rage and
vengefulness.

Thus, at one point, after her daughter's pregnancy is definite, Mieko
envisions a scene from the *Kojiki*, or *Record of Ancient Matters*, in
which the goddess Izanami takes revenge upon her husband for having
seen her putrefying corpse:

> A vision came to [Mieko] of an ancient goddess lying stretched out
> in the underworld, prey of death. Her flesh was putrid and swarm-
> ing with maggots, her decaying form covered with all manner of
> festering sores that smoldered and gave off black sparks. The lurid-
> ness of the sight sent the goddesses's lover fleeing in horror and the
> moment that he turned and ran, she arose and swept after him in
> fury, all the love she had borne him transformed utterly into blind-
> ing hatred. A woman's love is quick to turn into a passion for
> revenge. . . .
>
> (p. 127)

That such a revenge is often sexual is seen in another classical allusion, this time to the Chinese ghost story "The Peony Lantern," in which a dead woman seduces an unsuspecting young man. Thus, where dead women in the fantasies of male writers are seen as passive and unthreatening, in the fantasies of Enchi they become terrifying agents of female vengeance, walking corpses who "enchant" the men only to force them to awaken into a deeper and more horrific vision of reality.

The women's final revenge in *Masks* is to end the enchantment and to dissociate themselves from men permanently. Thus, the novel's final scene shows Mieko and Yasuko happily raising Harume's baby boy. Harume herself has died in childbirth, and there is a strong suggestion that Mieko and Yasuko welcome this. Indeed, some lesbian overtones seem to exist in their relationship. But the story's real point is less women's sexuality than women's independence and their desire to no longer subdue their "strong egos" in deference to men. In *Masks*, through a variety of arcane techniques, they seem to have achieved that.

Mieko is given a motive for her vengefulness against men: she suffered a miscarriage due to a trick played by her philandering husband's mistress. Mieko's motives are not simply those of petty vengeance, however. As Doris Bargen says, "For Mieko, mere revenge is too easily accomplished. It is not so much the destruction of male supremacy as the reconstruction of female power that is at stake."[20]

Enchi's "reconstruction of female power" requires the humiliation of the male, as a prelude to female solidarity and solitariness. In Ōba (or Ohba as in the English Edition) Minako's "Yamauba no Bishō" (1976) (trans. "The Smile of a Mountain Witch" (1982)) a woman also dreams of being left alone to fulfill her own desires, but the story clearly emphasizes the impossibility of such an achievement except through wish-fulfilling fantasy. Like *Masks*, "The Smile of a Mountain Witch" plays on the many roles women are forced to assume in society, but in this case Ōba does not go to the classics for her model but instead brilliantly recovers the age-old archetype of the mountain witch.

The work begins with a retelling of the traditional story of a young man lost in the mountains who encounters an old hag who can read his thoughts. The scene shifts abruptly, however, to the tale of a "genuine" mountain witch who lives in disguise among human beings. This woman has from girlhood onwards been able to anticipate the thoughts of others before they utter them, and has thus become capable of pandering to their every wish. Ōba's ironic point here is that every woman must become a mountain witch in order to fulfill her role as wife and mother properly. In the case of this particular mountain witch (i.e. a typical village woman), she first learns to make her mother happy and then her husband who, as the narrator comments, has been "doted upon by his mother" so that his wife too must become a kind of mother to him, learning to love him "limitlessly and blindly like an idiot." Finally, she also has to sacrifice herself for her children's happiness to the point that, after falling seriously ill, she forces herself to die more quickly so as not to be a burden to them.

The story ends with her once again reading people's minds:

> In the last smile she exchanged with her daughter she clearly read her daughter's mind. Her daughter's eyes said to her that she did not want to be tied down any longer. "Mother, I don't want you to protect me any more. You've outlived your usefulness. . . . Please don't torment me any longer. I too am preparing myself so that I won't trouble my daughter as I am being troubled by you.
>
> (p. 194)

In order to cease "troubling" her family, the mother heroically takes her own life, suffocating herself by washing the saliva she has accumulated down her windpipe.

"The Smile of a Mountain Witch" is saved from bathos by its ironic conceit of portraying an ordinary woman as a fantastic creature. It is left to the reader's discretion to be disturbed by the ideal of sacrifice that the mother calmly hands down to her daughter. But "The Smile of a Mountain Witch" does contain one clearly subversive image. This is the vision of the woman as she lies dying, looking forward to the time when she would be a real mountain witch and "would stand on a mountain ledge, her white hair swaying in the raging wind, sounding her eternal roar into the mountains" (p. 195). This vision is an echo of an earlier dream of the woman's in which she imagined escaping into the mountains, "Far off in the mountains there would be nobody to trouble her, and she would be free to think as she pleased" (p. 189)

This intense desire for solitude on the part of a character whose self had been totally defined by her familial and social relationships is surely a poignant, albeit muted protest against the culture which had created that self. In some ways "The Smile of a Mountain Witch" is a less troubling story than *Masks* since its protagonist is a less vengeful and more sympathetic character, but in its evocation of an archetypal desire "to be free to think as [one] pleased" it is a subtly powerful work.

Kurahashi Yumiko's story "Aporon no kubi" (The Head of Apollo) (1985) also privileges female solitude, but with a twist; the woman in the story lives happily ever after with the unspeaking, unthinking but undeniably beautiful head of a young man. Kurahashi's heroine is less defined by social relationships since she is still a student, but she is engaged to be married, a step that will begin to involve her in the complex web of duties of the Japanese woman.

One day after class, the young woman comes upon the head of a beautiful young man hanging in a tree. When she comes back the next day it is still there and she takes it home and plants it. Her fiancé is disturbed by her attention to the head, especially after the head ripens and flowers, and she cuts it open, planting the seeds in her sunroom to create a little garden of about a dozen heads. The story ends with her fiancé's departure for Europe, commenting that he didn't want to live with a woman who was crazy about planting heads.

Kurahashi's story is a fantasy of role reversal and brings up echoes of such Western works as Wilde's *Salome*. Indeed, the scene of the woman coolly cutting open the head might be considered somewhat disturbing in its inherent violence. Other resemblances come from closer to home, most notably two previously discussed works by Sōseki and Kawabata, although of course Kurahashi's work reverses both. One comment in particular is reminiscent of Sōseki's story "Dream of the First Night". In this scene the woman's fiancé suggests that the head is probably not human, to which she responds to herself: "Maybe it wasn't human. But if you ask me this head is much more beautiful than the head of any man.... In front of this head (my fiancé) is no more than a foul-smelling beast." (p. 76; my translation). Like the woman in Sōseki's story, the head is more perfect the more inhuman it becomes, and in this case there is an even more explicit comparison between disappointing reality and the charms of fantasy. As in "Dream of the First Night", when the head changes into a flower, its metamorphosis is welcomed with delight by the partner of the opposite sex. Indeed, in another reversal of Sōseki's tendency to put women into pictures, the woman compares the head to a picture of a youth by a European artist. The notion of scent is common to both stories as well, although in the case of Kurahashi's story it is the foul bestial smell of humans which the narrator emphasizes.

"Aporon no kubi" also strongly resemble's Kawabata's "One Arm" in which, of course, it is a woman's arm that becomes an independent appendage to be cultivated by the male. Here the differences are even more intriguing. In Kawabata's story, as we remember, the arm had clearly maternal and erotic connotations. Ironically, one might suggest that it is the very lack of any paternal or sexual connotations which draws Kurahashi's protagonist to the head. The head is "beautiful," "noble," etc. but it seems to have no sensuous qualities. Unlike the arm, it can neither move nor caress. Furthermore, since it can neither think nor speak, it is forced to remain in the pre-symbolic realm of the imaginary. This realm of course is that of mother and infant, and the young woman's care for the head could possibly be read as maternal. In any case, the head is totally unthreatening, as opposed to her fiancé, who is constantly attempting to impose his will on hers.

On the other hand, the final vision of the story is a largely asexual one. Unlike "One Arm," where the narrator himself tries to bring a form of human connection "as one would a small child from whom life was going" (p. 132; my translation) in his final (and too late) approach to the arm, Kurahashi's protagonist seems totally content to live in an essentially non-human world. Like Ōba's mountain witch or the matriarchal family of *Masks* the woman seems to feel only relief at the absence of the male.[21]

Our final example of female solitude in women's fantasy, Kanai Mieko's "Usagi" (1976) (trans. "Rabbits" (1982)) is an extraordinary and horrific version of a case of Oedipal wish-fulfillment on the part of a young girl. In many ways the story is a mirror image of Tanizaki's *The Bridge of Dreams*. In that wish-fulfillment fantasy, as we remember, a young boy and his stepmother are allowed to enact a quasi incestuous relationship with the tacit approval of the boy's father.

"Rabbits" is a more complicated text than *The Bridge of Dreams*, at least in its narrative structure, since it contains two narrators. The first, presumably a woman, goes out for a walk one day and suddenly notices a large white rabbit, which she follows, only to find that the rabbit is actually a young girl dressed in a rabbit costume. It is the girls's story which is the main part of "Rabbits'" narrative.

Although "Rabbits" explicitly echoes *Alice in Wonderland* in its beginning, it is far from a child's fantasy. Like *The Bridge of Dreams,* "Rabbits" does not explicitly admit a sexual relationship between the girl and the father, but the images of blood and the sense of intensity surrounding their relationship point to an erotic subtext. In Kanai's story the mother does not die but instead simply disappears one morning, along with the rest of the family of the young girl who narrates the story.

The father, however, remains, much to the girl's satisfaction, and the two of them embark on an independent but extremely bizarre mode of living. The girl and her father indulge in what amounts to an orgy of rabbit killing and eating, something which their conservative relatives had never allowed them to do. So absorbed is the girl in this pursuit that she ends up quitting high school in order to spend all her time at home with her father.

The text is at pains to underscore the erotic fulfillment experienced in these activities. The girl explains that while originally the job of killing and cooking the rabbits had been her father's task, when he gets too fat to move easily she happily takes over. As she describes it, "I developed the knack for this right away and set about my task with great gusto." And,

> [i]n the end, the technique [of rabbit killing] that gave me the great-est satisfaction was to strangle the rabbit while I squeezed it be-tween my thighs. . . . It did not take long for me to begin performing the mysterious rite of the bloody rabbit slaughter completely naked.
>
> (p. 11)

This description is disturbing not only for its violence and implicit sexuality but also for the delight the girl takes in it. Given that the rabbits are soft, vulnerable creatures, not unlike the girl herself, this scene hints at the girl's complicity in her own abjection.

The girl's relationship with father and rabbits grows even more bi-zarre when she puts on a rabbit costume she has made, hoping to conduct a pretend "rabbit strangling ceremony" with her father. She intends to offer herself as victim, bathing her whole body in blood "to make it look as if I were really a rabbit with its fur stripped off. It thrilled me to think of the moment when I would feel my father's hand groping around inside me" (p. 13). To her disappointment, her father is so shocked at her transformation that he dies and she is left alone.

Both "Rabbits" and *The Bridge of Dreams* operate around images of quasi-incest, parental presence/absence, and death, but the final im-pressions left by the two stories are quite different. Thus, while both deal with infantile forms of feeding, the milk-swollen breast in Tani-zaki's story suggests childish repletion while the blood-soaked rabbits point to a sado-masochistic relationship. Both works also abound in imagery suggestive of the womb, but again with very different effect. The enclosed garden in Tanizaki's story is evocative of peace, beauty, and protection. In "Rabbits" the girl and her father close off them-selves more and more from the outside world to create what the pri-mary narrator of the story calls "a rabbit hutch" (p. 4) of a house covered with rabbit blood and fur, hardly a site of peace and beauty.

There are other important differences as well. The first is the fact that, in the case of Tanizaki's protagonist, he is essentially a passive recipient throughout the story. The garden/womb has been created for him by his ancestors. In "Rabbits," on the other hand, it is the young girl who energetically sets about creating their "rabbit hutch" and it is she who feeds her father, while Tanizaki's hero is happy to suckle at his stepmother's breasts. In other words, Tanizaki's story is a story of regression while, in a perverse way, "Rabbits" is a tale of growing up.

Furthermore, Tanizaki's "regression" is a cultural one as well, back to a lost Japanese past. By contrast, Kanai's rabbit hutch is anonymous, a generic place of enclosure. In fact, the only obvious cultural reference in "Rabbits" is the one the text gives us at the beginning of the story, a quotation from Lewis Carroll's *Alice in Wonderland*: "When suddenly a White Rabbit with pink eyes ran close by her." We remember that "Bridge of Dreams" also began with a quotation from a fantasy romance, but that work was *The Tale of Genji*, the most supremely "Japanese" work of literature existing.

By quoting Lewis Carroll, Kanai brings the reader into the world of international fantasy. Furthermore, by making reference to a work full of absurd quests complicated by holes and gardens, Kanai evokes a world that is both feminine in its imagery and "modern" in its absurdity. The character of Alice herself is an outsider in the world, never quite the right size, who ends up in her yearned-for garden being greeted by shouts of "Off with her head."

Implicitly confronted by Alice's fate of never quite belonging, it is little wonder that the character in "Rabbits" rejects the confusing outside world of mature femininity and responsibility to live in happy solitude with her father. When her father dies, however, she descends into madness, dressing like a rabbit and crouching alone in her little hut. Although it is possible to speculate that the girl in the story has knowingly murdered her father by overfeeding him and causing his heart attack, thereby freeing herself from patriarchal constraints, the final vision in "Rabbits" is a very grim one.

The story's initial narrator goes in search of the "rabbit girl" again and finds her dead on the floor wearing her bloodstained rabbit suit, her house still full of living rabbits whose eyes she had gouged out. The narrator's reaction to this sight makes a disturbingly memorable ending:

> I peeled off the white rabbit's fur which had completely enveloped her body. Then I threw off what I had been wearing and got into her costume. I put on the hood and mask which were by her side, held my breath in the animal odor, and waited for a long time crouching there without moving. A group of blind rabbits gathered about

us. She and I along with the rabbits made no effort to stir and so we remained in that same spot, absolutely still.

(p. 16)

Of the works by women writers discussed in this section, at least three seem to illustrate what Auerbach says of the female demonic, that it "knows no social boundaries and no fond regrets. Instead, in its purest form it is animated by a longing not for childhood but for transcendence."[22] We may trace a kind of development of absence in the four stories considered in this section.

Masks is perhaps the most traditional fantasy, going back to the classical Japanese fantastic and showing a world which, if unusual, still seems relatively satisfying to the protagonists left alive at the end of the novel. Ōba's fantasy also recovers a traditional archetype, but this time she frees it from premodern allusions to use it as a call for women's freedom and independence, at the cost of loneliness and presumed madness. The two younger women of the last two fantasies, on the other hand, are left in a hermetic anonymous world with no past to draw on. We can assume that the narrator of "Aporon no kubi" is satisfied with her choice, but the complex relationship of the protagonist in "Rabbits" with her father suggests that she is more a victim than an active participant. In any case, her final descent into self-wounding suggests madness and loneliness, and the bleak bloody imagery surrounding her presents a very negative picture of female isolation, although even that seems preferable to "real life," since the initial narrator also chooses this condition.

Looking at the fantasies of male and female writers discussed in this chapter, we can see two general patterns. The first is the pattern of absence of the opposite sex and the isolation of the self which we have examined at length. Another important development is one linked to modern Japanese fantasy in general and that is the descent from control into chaos. This is particularly obvious in the work of male writers as we move from the enclosed gardens of Tanizaki or the hidden valleys of Kyōka to the anarchic horror of Abe's *Secret Rendezvous* or the omnipresent sexual world of Tsutsui's "Poruno wakusei". But women's fantasy too seems to be moving to an increasingly uncontrolled site. Thus, in *Masks* we had a fantasy of tight control dominated by the ominous matriarchal presence of Mieko Togano. "Aporon no kubi," as its classic name suggests, is also tightly controlled, although the fecundity of the heads hints at a possible rise of uncontrollability. Ōba Minako's "The Smile of a Mountain Witch", on the other hand, totally privileges the chaotic and the natural in its wish-fulfilling image of the witch standing naked against the wind. "Rabbits" is perhaps the opposite side of "The Smile of a Mountain Witch." It is chaotic and anarchic in its orgy of blood lust and death, but the imagery of solitude is an appallingly ugly one.

Our exploration of women in Japanese fantasy has left a grim picture of contemporary Japan. The problems of modernity are not simply political inadequacies which can be remedied. Rather, the problem seems to lie at the heart of modern Japanese society, a society in which the fantasies by both men and women can no longer envision any sort of connection or social community. The only thing left to do seems to be to revel in one's abandonment. There is only the self left; and even that self, as is clear in the next chapter, is a highly problematic one.

NOTES

1 T. Sato, 1982, p. 117 and passim.
2 D. P. Herndl, 1993, p. 79.
3 It should be emphasized, however, despite the violence in the texts discussed in this chapter, that Japan is still one of the safest countries in the industrialized world.
4 J. Kuehl, 1989, p. 242.
5 Kuehl, 1989, p. 237.
6 Kuehl, 1989, p. 247
7 P. Waugh, 1989, p. 51.
8 J. Rubin, 1993, p. 496. All quotes from "1963/1982 – Nen no Ipanema musume" translated in Rubin 1993.
9 V. Gessel, 1993, p. 194.
10 Quoted in Gessel, 1993, p. 181.
11 E. Bronfen, 1992, p. 65.
12 For further discussion on the role of motherhood in *House of the Sleeping Beauties* see C. Kimura-Steven and J. Gracewood, 1992, pp. 207–237 passim.
13 Gessel, 1993, p. 162.
14 M. Rose, 1981, p. 193.
15 As Waugh says of women in postmodern Western fiction by males, "[t]hey are in large measure projections of primitive masculine fears and desires, very often close to myth" (P. Waugh, 1989, p. 68).
16 Mark Harbison calls the historic Kumano area one of the "wellsprings" of Nakagami's "obsession" (M. Harbison, 1985, p. 427).
17 The monk's rage against women in "The Immortal" at least seems to have some basis in his own problematic history. An even more disturbing example of a rape-murder may be found in Tsutsui Yasutaka's story "Mondai gekka" (The Problem Operation) (1982). In this story two doctors are operating on a woman whom they believe to be an unconscious heart patient, only to have her wake up and reveal that, not only is she not unconscious, she is not even a patient. She is a nurse who happened to fall

asleep on the operating table. Confronted by this news, the doctors are at first panicky but they decide that there would be little point in sewing her back up and allowing her to leave, since news of the mistake would destroy their careers. Instead, they decide to kill the woman but only after they have raped her while she is lying on the table with her internal organs still exposed.

The disturbing aspects of this story should be fairly obvious, but one of the most bothersome is the doctors' total coolness towards their victim. If this is a revenge fantasy, it is one that provides no context for the revenge, unlike "The Immortal." One is left with the repellent picture of a woman who has been violated for no reason, except for the sake of a shocking story.

Tsutsui is not the only Japanese writer who depicts women in violent and negative ways, but it must be said that his visions of women are notable for their imaginative sadism. Thus, in the far cleverer, but almost equally repellent story "Nyobosatsudan" (1974) (available in English as "Such Lovely Ladies" (1982)), a group of middle-class housewives organize themselves into a gang which infiltrates the households of rich women by pretending to be from the PTA. Once inside, the "ladies" (who speak impeccably politely throughout) take only household objects that cannot be identified, such as canned goods and frozen beef. They also, however, murder whatever women they find in the house, and these murders are described in chilling, even disgusting detail. "Lovely Ladies" is in many ways a brilliant satire on consumer culture, but its portrayal of the coldly murderous yet totally feminine gang is ultimately a disturbing one, especially in light of the many other negative portrayals of women in his works.

Some Japanese critics have noted this apparently misogynistic aspect to Tsutsui. A rather tongue-in-cheek discussion of this may be found in Yahashi Ichirō (1985, pp. 162–5). Yahashi divides Tsutsui's descriptions of women into "poignant" and "sadistic," but he does not really go far in exploring the motivation behind this description.

18 In the prewar period, although important women writers do exist, their fiction tends to be mimetic and, not surprisingly, usually deals with women trapped within the confines of the domestic circle or the prostitute's world of the Yoshiwara (although there are obvious exceptions such as the unusually "liberated" writer Uno Chiyo (b. 1897)). Female characters in works of writers such as Higuchi Ichiyō (1872–1896) are usually depicted as accepting their entrapment with resignation, rather than making any attempt at escape. When women do change their lives in prewar fiction it is usually in works by Marxist writers such as Miyamoto Yuriko (1899–1951) or Sata Ineko (b. 1904), and in these works the change in life is usually an escape into the all-embracing cause of Marxist ideology.

19 Waugh, 1989, p. 171.

20 D. Bargen, 1991, p. 63. Bargen's fascinating article also deals with the theme of substitution. This substitution is of course not the substitution of the mother, as was the case of *The Bridge of Dreams*, but the substitution of lovers, and finally of children, the male child whom Mieko and Yasuko intend to raise. Substitution thus becomes a form of revenge as well, in women's fantasy at least.

21 Kurahashi has explored the notion of the severed male head in a longer work as well, the 1987 novel *Popoi*. In *Popoi*, the narrative strategy is far more complex, however. The head (whose name is Popoi) is shown to have a number of literary and historical antecedents, from Judith and the head of Holofernus to Mishima Yukio, who was beheaded at his own request. In a fascinating analysis of this work, Atsuko Sakaki suggests that Popoi is not a single self, but a "collage of others. . . . the self is not independent from others but rather subject to others." (A. Sakaki, 1992, p. 27.) I would suggest that it is this tension between independent self and the self subject to others which animates "Aporon no kubi."

22 N. Auerbach, 1982, p.104.

4   Desert of mirrors

The construction of the alien in modern Japanese fantasy

And what is identity? The cognitive system arisin' from the aggregate memory of that individual's past experiences.

(Murakami Haruki, *Hard Boiled Wonderland and the End of the World*, p. 266)

Hooray for monsters! Monsters are the great embodiments of the weak.

(Abe Kōbō, *Secret Rendezvous*, p. 172)

In the previous two chapters we have discussed the role of fantasy women in the fiction of both male and female writers. In the writings of both sexes there exists a pattern of development whereby male and female are increasingly left sundered and alone, the male characters lamenting, even raging against this fact and the women characters often celebrating it. For both male and female characters the use of the fantasy woman also became a means of exploring their own identities, often with disturbing results. If there is no *Heimat*, no womb, where is the Japanese self located? Even worse, in a postmodern world of endless change and fragmentation, is there even a fixed self to find?

This chapter continues to focus on the exploration of the self through fantasy but this time by discussing the variety of alternative beings, or, more accurately, alternative selves, that are presented in modern Japanese fantasy. Even more than the fantasy females previously discussed, these alien identities are ambivalently delineated. The presentation of the alien ranges from the threatening and grotesque to the attractive or even seductive, sometimes within the same texts, and it is this complexity which makes it so challenging a subject in both literary and extraliterary terms.

In extraliterary terms, an exploration of alien selves brings up controversial questions from socio-anthropology and linguistics as to the nature of the Japanese self. Many commentators have argued that the traditional Japanese "self" is more diffuse and other-directed than the more individualistic Western self.[1] Although this may well be true, the texts examined in this chapter suggest, at the very least, a strong concern with the notion of self in the modern period. Furthermore, there also appears to be a changing perception of the self between the generation of Meiji writers and the writers of the contemporary period.

Among such turn-of-the-century writers as Sōseki, for example, we can find a substantial sense of unease with the self. This feeling of unease undoubtedly reflected the Meiji generation's awareness of itself as profoundly different from the previous generations of premodern Japan. It is also probably linked with the fact that the whole notion of the individual was still regarded as a potentially dangerous, even frightening, import from the West. As Sōseki himself pointed out in one of his most famous speeches, "My Individualism" (1992), ". . . there lurks beneath the surface [of the philosophy of individualism] a loneliness unknown to others" (p. 309).

This unease with individual identity *vis-à-vis* society continues through the Taishō period and into the postwar period, achieving perhaps its most brilliant expression in the works of Abe Kōbō whose *Tanin no kao* (1964) (trans. *The Face of Another* 1970) is a classic meditation on the individual self in relation to others. In recent decades, however, this unease seems to be being replaced by a new sense of security and even desire for self-exploration on the part of contemporary fantasists. Thus, Murakami's protagonist in his 1985 novel *Sekai no owari to hādoboirudo wandārando* (trans. *Hard Boiled Wonderland and the End of the World* (1991)) retreats into the security of his own mind, stating that he has "responsibilities" to the thought world he created. *Akira*'s violent young protagonist, Tetsuo, takes the opposite tack, participating in a series of metamorphoses that ultimately threaten the entire world. Tsutsui's short story, "Kaomen hōkai" (Collapsing Face) (1978) goes even further than *Akira*, celebrating a postmodern collapse of identity.

In literary terms, the notion of an alien self is also exceptionally interesting. The alien in modern Japanese fantasy comes in many forms. These vary greatly from period to period, from the traditional talking beasts in Kyōka's works such as *Yashagaike* (Demon Pond) (1981), which he wrote in 1913, to the dead comrades brought back to life to help prevent nuclear war in Ōe's *Pinchirannā chōshō* (1976) (trans. *Pinchrunner Memorandum* (1994)). In other cases the alien is a sinister inner presence, an alternative self appearing in dreams as in Sōseki's *Ten Nights of Dream*, or hallucinations as in Akutagawa's "Haguruma" (1927) (trans. "Cogwheels" (1965)).

In other postwar media such as film or *manga*, the alien sometimes seems omnipresent, a staple of popular culture throughout the postwar period. One can trace a fascination with the alien back as early as 1953 to the scaly prehistoric monster in the movie *Godzilla*, which became first a domestic and then an international hit. In recent years perhaps the most striking rendition of the alien has been the aforementioned series of grotesque metamorphoses undergone by Tetsuo in the 1989 comic and animated film *Akira*.

As this chapter discloses, however, the alien is also an important presence in "pure" literature. Although it appears in many forms, two types are perhaps the most important – the ghost and the monster – both of which have their roots in premodern culture. The vengeful ghost, usually female, is the mainstay of most premodern horror stories and of the popular kabuki theater and also appears frequently in woodblock prints. But the high culture Nō plays also contain many ghosts, who are less horrific engines of retaliation than they are poignant vehicles of memory, incapable of detaching themselves from earthly passions.

In both cases these ghosts are attached to the past, an aspect which becomes increasingly important in the modern period. In modern literature both the vengeful and the pathetic ghost appear, not only as reminders of a personal past but as reminders of Japanese history as well. Ghosts also range more widely in their effect on the human characters: in the works of Sōseki and Akutagawa they are usually still terrifying, but in Kawabata's or Murakami's postwar stories they can be seen as rescuers, saving the protagonist from the miseries of modern isolation.[2]

Monsters are an even more varied category. Premodern Japanese literature contains an enormous variety of demons and ghouls ranging from the prosaic river-dwelling *kappa* or water sprite to the ominous Dream Eater of Buddhist theology. These monsters are outsiders who threaten the collectivity, but who can be avoided or appeased. In modern popular culture that tradition lingers in the image of Godzilla, whose nuclear-activated presence threatened the Japanese islands in the immediate postwar period, and whose descendants have continued into the present day in comics, animation, and live-action cinema.

Increasingly in the modern period, however, the really monstrous is located inside the self, a feared alter ego. This monster is less a menace to society (although it may be that as well) than a threat to the person it inhabits or to the people immediately around him or her. Thus, Akutagawa's short story "Jigokuhen" (1918) (trans. "The Hell Screen" (1961)) envisages the artist as monster, whose monstrousness is engendered, paradoxically, by his own prodigious artistic talent. Unlike

Godzilla, Akutagawa's artist endangers only his daughter and finally himself, but the personal quality of his attack makes him all the more terrifying.

Frequently in modern fantasy ghosts and monsters combine. Sōseki, for example, writes about a monstrous child in his "Dream of the Third Night" who, as an emblem of an unresolved past, also has a ghostlike aspect as well. Murakami's *Hitsuji o megurō boken* (1982) (trans. *A Wild Sheep Chase* (1989)) concerns a quest for a phantom sheep which is both monstrous in its bizarre powers and ghostlike in its ability to summon up certain hidden aspects of modern Japanese history.

The complexity of the alien brings forth appropriately complex and memorable literary treatments. Indeed, fantasies of the alien in modern Japanese fiction contain some of the best and most powerful works of modern Japanese literature, especially in the short story form. Many of these fantasies are of what I term the "internal alien", works where the alien presence is an interior, psychological one. They include everything from the classic horror stories of Akutagawa to Sōseki's psychoanalytically chilling *Ten Nights of Dream*, to Ōe's poignant "Agwhee the Sky Monster," or the aesthetic delights of some of Kawabata's eerier *Palm of the Hand Stories*.

Although varying greatly among themselves, one aspect that all these fantasies of the alien have in common is the importance of reader response to them. Western critics have increasingly argued that the tale of terror or horror, the genre under which the alien usually finds itself classed, is one whose effects are particularly dependent on creating certain powerful reactions in the reader. As Todorov says of the fantastic in general, "[it] produces a particular effect on the reader, fear, or horror or simply curiosity – which the other genres or literary forms simply cannot provoke."[3]

In fact, these "effects" can run a wider course than simply curiosity to horror. Reactions can range from intellectual admiration of and pleasure in the intensity of aesthetic effect, as, for example, in a work of Borges, to the enjoyable frisson of terror that the reader vicariously experiences through reading a Stephen King novel or a work by Poe. Underlying these obvious emotions,, however, are more subtle and complex ones, most importantly the sense of excitement stemming from the liberation of sublimated fears and taboos, a feeling that critics such as Terry Heller suggest is one of the major aspects of the "delights of terror."[4]

The dynamic between reader and fantastic text raises extratextual questions, since what may move or terrify a reader in the nineteenth century is not necessarily the same as what affects a twentieth-century reader. Even the most purely literary of fantasies contains a socio-cultural dimension as well: What does it mean to be "alien" in Meiji or Taishō Japan? And does the definition of "alien" change in the post-war period?

Furthermore, beyond the formal and interior fantasies, with their implicit interrelationship between text and society, there are other fant-asies of the alien that are explicitly ideological. In these works, which I have dubbed the "ideological alien," the alien is used for directly politi-cal purposes, to overtly satirize or parody the dominant political dis-course. Both these forms of the alien have played an important role throughout the development of modern Japanese fiction.[5]

Whether internal or ideological, the ultimate impact of the alien in modern Japanese fantasy is a profound one. Appearing within a soci-ety that prides itself on its homogeneity and stability, the disturbing and destabilizing function of the alien cuts across both textual and extratextual boundaries to trouble, provoke, and emancipate some hidden part of the reader's sense of self and world. Even more than the fantastic female who, as we saw, can perform a compensatory func-tion, the alien in Japanese literature is directly subversive.

Furthermore, in the literature of modern or modernizing Japan, the fantastic Other may be seen as an important means by which post-Restoration Japanese began to construct a Westernized sense of the self. While the *shishōsetsu* writers plumbed into a textualized 'real life' to find an individualized persona, writers of the fantastic took the other route, working out their explorations of the self against such textual elements as dreams, ghosts, monsters, and *doppelgängers*.[6]

Thus, to discuss the alien in Japanese fantasy is to bring up issues of identity, desire and, also, ultimately of power. The alien is the Other in its most fundamental form, the outsider who simultaneously can be the insider, and it is this polysemic potential that is so enthralling and disturbing to the reader. The alien threatens the collectivity more than any other presence.

Moreover, the alien is also a fantastic Other. Unlike the generic Other which would include such "real" outsiders as women and foreigners, it is an outsider that clearly exists outside the bounds of con-sensus reality. It is this fantastic aspect that makes the alien intriguing in two ways, literarily and socioculturally.

From a formal literary point of view, the narrative function of the alien is notably fluid; unlike a more circumscribed representation of the Other, the alien can appear in a tremendous variety of forms and formats. In general, these forms can be classified under what Todorov

calls, "the themes of the self," which include most notably the importance of metamorphosis and pan-determinism. Pan-determinism
suggests a world view in which "everything is charged with meaning"[117]
and thus all occurrences, no matter how bizarre, are seen to be
part of a master plan. As we will see, in modern fantasy the opposite
increasingly becomes true, as fantastic events seem to occur without
meaning, thus disturbing our conception of an established, knowable
order.

This leads to the alien's second intriguing function from the
psychological or social point of view: the fact that the alien's very
existence constitutes a threat to consensus reality, suggesting that reality is never entirely knowable and can, in fact, be altered. It is in this
insistent presentation of Otherness that the alien contains an insidious
and perverse appeal, becoming finally a distorting but fascinating
mirror in which is reflected the myriad faces of Japan and the
Japanese.

THREE FACES OF THE ALIEN

Mention of faces brings me to a set of examples of the alien in Japanese literature which work as a kind of continuum, both historical and
literary, through which one can examine some of the changing ways in
which the alien has been presented in modern Japanese fantasy. Although very different from each other in style and message, the works
contain two major elements in common: a horrifying face and a metamorphosis from the "normal" to the monstrous. I would like to begin
with a traditional ghost story, collected in the 1930s by the folklorist
Yanagita Kunio, in *Nihon Mukashibanashi meii* (1948):

A night school teacher was walking along a road by the edge of a
rice field late one winter night and noticed a beautiful girl standing
by the road with her face turned down at the book she was reading.
He wondered if she was a ghost and spoke to her. She did not
answer but raised her face. He took one look at the face and his hair
stood on end. He threw his coat over his head and ran home. He sat
down hurriedly at his *kotatsu* [leg warmer]. His wife seemed to
think it strange and asked him over and over what had happened.
When he told her about the frightful face of the woman his wife
wanted to know what kind of face it was. He could not explain. She
asked, "Was it this kind of face?" At that, she turned to her husband and there she was, the woman with the terrible face. He took
one look and gave a shout. Then he fainted as he tried to hide in the
kotatsu. When he awoke the next morning, the sun was shining

brightly on him as he lay down by the dam in the middle of the
field.

(p. 203, quoted in Mayer 1986)

This delightfully spine-tingling (and very popular) tale illustrates a
number of features of the classic ghost story. Looking first on the level
of narrative structure and reader response, we find that the story's
format is the archetypal pattern of a supernatural event encased in
what Grixti in describing classic horror films calls the "frame of
reassurance."[8] Unlike a genuinely "fantastic" story in Todorov's sense
of the word, the reader is initially given no opportunity to hesitate
between the supernatural explanation (the woman is a ghost) and a
realistic one (the man is mad/drunk/hallucinating). The story carries
the reader directly into the supernatural realm, and he or she vicariously participates in the man's fear of/attraction to the alien, participating even more intensely at the second revelation: that the alien does
not appear only in a dark field but also can be sitting right beside you
at your *kotatsu*.

Before the terror becomes too overwhelming, however, the frame of
reassurance starts to function. At the story's end, both the actant and
the reader are allowed to escape from the horrors of the night, or the
horrors of the tale, and awaken to a shining sun of the real world. The
response of the reader or listener thus moves from a largely pleasurable fear of the alien that lurks close around one to a sense of relief
that one can escape from it.

Another interesting and classic element of the story is its erotic
subtext. The man is clearly moved to approach the woman because she
is "beautiful" (even though he can't see her face!). Appropriately, he is
punished, first by her and then, even more appropriately, by his wife.
Of course, once could also argue that he has been traduced by the
ghostly female, a frequent theme in many premodern stories in which
animals such as foxes, badgers, cats, and even snakes take on the form
of a seductive female and either temporarily or permanently bewitch
some unfortunate male.[9] The occurrence of mysterious and dangerous
female monsters is notable not only in premodern Japanese culture,
from *setsuwa* (traditional folk tales of animals that assume human
forum) through kabuki, but it is also an important aspect of modern
fantasy, as the works of Kurahashi Yumiko, such as her short story
"Banpiru no kai" (The Vampire Club) (1985), or Uchida Hyakkens's
modern updates of traditional animal stories attest.

A number of explanations can be ventured for this frequency. The
most obvious explanation is that the very strength and fearsomeness

of the powers attributed to these monstrous women attests to the low status of women in real life. Anthropologists might suggest, however, that Japanese women historically and traditionally have been seen to possess inherently certain magic powers that men cannot encompass. Neither of these theories necessarily cancels the other out, of course, since the sphere of the sacred does not necessarily reflect the politics of the real. Or as Donald Richie puts it, "The Japanese ghost is constructed by males for males."[10]

I would like to suggest another explanation, however, that returns us to the theme of the alien. It is possible to read the erotic, seductive nature of woman as a metaphor for the intense attraction of the Other, of the outside, an Other that the collectivity seeks to shield its members from. Although she is formally a ghost, the woman in this story functions more as the monstrous outsider. Thus, the man is shocked to find something horrible and frightening in what he expected to be beautiful and appealing.

Even more frightening, of course, is the fact that, after having returned to the bosom of the collectivity, his own home, he finds the alien lurking within it. In a sense, he has been punished twice for his transgression, and the second punishment, the revelation that the alien can exist within the collectivity, is by far the most frightening.

The text, almost of necessity, ends on a falsely optimistic note of closure. As Grixti says of the stock monster characters of the horror genre, they can become a means by which society both confronts its fears and also "evade[s] the implications of unpleasant social and existential realities."[11] Thus, the tale can ultimately be read as a warning that is both frightening and cathartic, whose threat is finally softened by the reassurance provided by the morning sunlight. Although not formally "fantastic" in the Todorovian sense of sustaining hesitation throughout, the tale does conform to Todorov's framework of the themes of the self in the fantastic by including both metamorphosis and pan-determinism. The metamorphosis in this tale is "charged with meaning", suggesting a world in which supernatural beings punish those who attempt to go outside the law.

Although Yanagita collected this tale in the 1930s and his intention was to show the survival of Japanese folk roots, the ideological framework of the tale is obviously that of a world before the Meiji Restoration. This is a world "charged with meaning" that can be understood and analyzed, even if it is full of supernatural complexities. In fact, the supernatural as a presence that can taken for granted and is ultimately understandable, is one fundamental aspect of premodern cultures.

Moving chronologically to our next example, Abe Kōbō's *The*

Face of Another, we come to a very different world, the world of Japan in the 1960s. This is a world in which paranoia reigns and where there is no comforting *kotatsu* to return to, and no way to awaken from a nightmare vision. It is a world in which technology takes over the instruments of the supernatural to create a nightmare vision even more terrifying than the one in the Yanagita tale.

Among modern Japanese writers, Abe is perhaps the master of conveying the alien, and his approach is, appropriately, far more psychologically complex than in the traditional tale. Like the story from the Yanagita collection, *The Face of Another* revolves around a horrifying face and a frightening metamorphosis of an intimate. In this case, however, it is not the wife who turns into an alien but the husband, and the psychology of the husband as monster and wife as unwilling participant in his monstrousness are intimately explored.

The narrator/protagonist of the novel is a scientist whose face has been turned into a mass of keloid scars owing to an explosion in his laboratory. Unlike the ghost woman, who appears to enjoy the frightening power of her face, the scientist fears and loathes his monstrousness and eventually devises a means to conceal it, a mask that perfectly reproduces human features. Not content with the passive perfection of the mask, however, the scientist begins to play with its possibilities, finally deciding to pretend to be a stranger and seduce his unsuspecting wife while wearing the mask.

The experiment is apparently a success, as the scientist records in the series of notebooks which constitute the actual text of the novel. The notebooks go on, however, to record a bitter letter from his wife. In this letter she states that she knew all along that it was her husband behind the mask but only went along with the game for his sake. The novel ends with the scientist, once again wearing his mask (which seems increasingly to be taking on a personality of its own), crouching in a ditch in the darkness, waiting to take revenge upon his wife.

Abe's novel turns the classic horror elements embedded in Yanagita's story into a complex meditation on male–female relations, identity, Otherness and, finally, society's conception of what is "normal." Although it uses the generic horror tropes of science gone amok and a monstrous face, it is much less dependent on any visceral reader response than on reader appreciation. The goal is not so much to horrify the readers as to make them think. To this end, the scientist's terrifying visage is given two important functions within the narrative.

The first is as a confrontational device. By pointing out the similarity of the scientist's scars with those of Hiroshima victims and by implicitly comparing the scientist's fate with Japan's Korean citizens who are habitually discriminated against, despite being physically indistinguishable from their Japanese co-residents, Abe forces the reader to re-examine his or her conception of what is alien. In a scene toward the end of the novel that is eerily reminiscent of Yanagita's tale, the scientist recalls a poignant film he had recently seen about a female Hiroshima survivor whose face is half horrifically scarred and half transcendently beautiful. Like the woman in Yanagita's story, she first attracts men, although in this case unwittingly, and then terrifies them. Finally, in desperation to achieve some sort of human connection, she seduces her brother and then commits suicide.

This story within a story points up some of the important ways in which the modern Japanese conception of the monstrous has evolved from the traditional. In Abe's reading, the woman is a victim and the lines that are being transgressed are arbitrary ones, imposed by an uncaring society. The alien is used not simply to shock readers but to shame them out of the smug comfort of the collectivity. A committed Marxist, Abe here seems to be suggesting the opposite message of Yanagita's tale; that it is not the alien but society's conception of the alien (perhaps especially industrial capitalist society's conception) that is truly the frightening element at work here. This is what can be called "message" fiction, forcing the alien to work as an ideological pointer.

As in the best of Abe's stories, however, the work can also be read on the psychological level, beyond the political dialectic. In the case of *The Face of Another*, it is the tortured character of the scientist that generates this welcome complexity. This brings us to the second function of the alien in *The Face of Another*, as a device for psychological introspection, the internal alien, in other words.

It is the scientist's rational desire to control his fate, mixed with his own spontaneous squeamishness toward his monstrous face, that ultimately brings out the truly monstrous in his own personality. This monstrousness is paradoxically signified by the blandly handsome mask of normality that he creates and which goes on to take over the scientist's personality or, perhaps, to release it.

Like the traditional tale in Yanagita's collection, *The Face of Another* is a story of metamorphosis from normal to monstrous, but with a twist. In contrast to the Manichean Jekyll-and-Hyde view of an evil that is in direct opposition to the normal, Abe suggests that it is in the seemingly attractive and normal that the really alien lurks. Even more ominously, this alien is within oneself.

Abe's novel is not totally unsympathetic toward the scientist, however. The text delineates in a surprisingly moving way the protagonist's rage and humiliation when he finds that his wife has seen through him.

The scientist's final cry of despair reverberates more profoundly than most of his abstract theorizing: "My mask, which I had expected to be a shield of steel, was broken more easily than glass" (p. 227).

In the end the scientist is also a victim, not simply of society but of his own egotistical nature. As his wife says:

> You don't need me. What you really need is a mirror. Because any stranger is for you simply a mirror in which to reflect yourself. I don't ever again want to return to such a desert of mirrors.
>
> (p. 212)

The wife in *The Face of Another* has put her finger on an essential point of modern identity, its isolation from others and finally from itself. Or, as Christopher Nash puts it,

> [t]he dilemma, now, lies not in the mere possibility that in actuality no one is "out there", that one is *only* in a world of mirrors ... the possibility that – alone or in company – one's very self is something other.[12]

Even worse, in modern industrial society there may be no self at all, only a "desert of mirrors." Nash says of a Calvino hero, that "self now has nothing to do with any inward sense of identity. To be 'identical' only with what is outside is to submit to the instruments of ... appearances."[13] This is also true of the mask, and indeed is an increasingly universal aspect of modern capitalist society where one cannot escape the emphasis on appearance reflected in the critical mirrors of consumer culture.

Abe's novels are unusual for seeing both the world of mirrors that the solitary individual creates and the world of mirrors erected by society. This attitude often verges into paranoia as the scientist reflects on society in the following manner:

> No matter how much television dramas go on singing the cloying praises of the family, it is the outside world full of enemies and lechers, that passes on a man's worth, pays his wages and guarantees him the right to live. The smell of poison and death clings to any stranger, and people have become allergic to outsiders without realizing it. Loneliness is terrible of course but being betrayed by the mask of one's fellow man is much worse.
>
> (p. 214)

Abe looks beyond the mirrors that society builds for itself to distort the real and finds the "strangers" all around us and within us. In Abe's fiction the stranger/alien is both terrifying and pitiable, a despairing comment on human nature. On a personal level this despair may be traceable to Abe's own deracinated background. Given his birth and subsequent life in Manchuria it is not surprising that he is a brilliant conveyor of outsiders.

It is important to note, however, that Abe's outsiders have struck a common note among the Japanese reading public. Although never bestsellers, Abe's works have always been highly regarded in Japan. Part of this may be due to the fact that his works challenge on both an intellectual and a political level. In this regard it is also worth noting that *The Face of Another* is also a meditation on the power of fiction and the danger of believing that mimesis, be it fiction or a mask, is really possible. In Abe's classic left-wing vision, one must finally go beyond the writing. As he puts it in the novel's last lines, "So nothing will ever be written down again. Perhaps the act of writing is necessary only when nothing happens" (p. 237).

Abe's politically involved sense may be viewed as linked inextricably with the political movements of the 1960s, a period when Japanese radicalism did go beyond "the act of writing." It was a time when young Japanese people in particular were trying on new identities for themselves in direct confrontation with their elders. The hypocrisy that many young Japanese saw as characterizing those in authority may help place the work's obsession with masks and strangers in a more universal light. Despite the decade's extraordinary economic growth, an increasing sense of nihilism was capturing many students and intellectuals, as is evidenced not only in Abe's works but throughout the writings of other young authors of the period such as those of Ōe Kenzaburō and Nosaka Akiyuki.

In contrast, our last paradigmatic text to be examined, Tsutsui Yasutaka's "Kaomen hōkai" (Collapsing Face) (1978), comes from the late 1970s, a period when Japanese politics had moved back to "business as usual" and young people were beginning to be more interested in conspicuous consumption than in radical politics. One element which they consumed with particular voraciousness was the image, whether it was in clothes, videos, or advertising. This "image culture" is also linked to the international movement of postmodernism, although it is entirely possible to find a fascination with the image in traditional Japanese culture as well.

Thus, "Kaomen hōkai" moves away from the explicit ideological comment of Abe's novel and in certain ways is closer to Yanagita's traditional tale in its emphasis on sheer effect. I have mentioned that Tsutsui, a noted science fiction and fantasy writer, has recently been moving toward acceptance by the literary establishment, although initially his works were considered too popular. One reason for their popularity has been the stunning verbal pyrotechnics in his fantasies which tend to overwhelm any particular "message."

This does not mean that Tsutsui's satire is without sociocultural relevance. Any ideological point is usually a subtle one, however, more often generated through his clever and imaginative satire than through any overt ideologizing. Unlike Abe, whose ideology springs from more doctrinaire sources, Tsutsui seems to be content to be a general iconoclast, skewering hypocrisy wherever he finds it.

Although it was written in 1978, less than 20 years after Abe's *The Face of Another*, Tsutsui's story clearly belongs to another generation of literature. The title "Collapsing Face" more or less sums up the narrative action, but a few quotations from it will help to give the story's idiosyncratic and memorable flavor.

"Kaomen hōkai" begins, "I hear you're going to the Sharaku Star system. You'd better be careful. Sometimes really strange things happen on that planet" (p. 60; my translation here and subsequently).

The narrator goes on to explain what the "really strange things" are, and it is this extremely detailed explanation of them which constitutes the greater part of the text. It turns out that on the Sharaku planet grows a kind of bean that explodes in one's face under pressure. Not only does this leave the face pockmarked with huge pits and scars, which the narrator describes with great relish, but the larvae and worms that grow inside the holes create bigger holes which lead to the blood vessels. Or, as he explains:

> When the deroren worm finds a vein large enough in the face or eyeball that looks as if they can dig into it, they quickly open a hole in the blood vessel and penetrate into it. As a result, the blood starts spurting all over the face. Now, this blood is actually not a big deal. . . .
>
> (p. 70)

For, as the narrator further explains, the real problem is when the larvae worm their way further and further into the blood vessels of the head and into the vein of the tongue, although the narrator adds that you'd be surprised how even that is really not all that painful. It does play havoc with the sense of taste, however, causing one to have taste hallucinations. Worst of all, though, eventually several dozen insects will congregate on your tongue and harden. The only way to get rid of them is to cut the tongue off. The story ends as follows:

> Well, of course your tongue gets shorter. It's a little harder to talk,

but if you just discipline yourself, then you can get like me, to the point where other people can understand just fine. What's that you say? Oh yes. You're saying that my face doesn't look like its's been in such a disaster. That's because I'm wearing an artificial face. Shall I take it off for you? See? Recently the artificial ones have gotten so good they can even mimic facial changes. Your color doesn't look so great. Are you feeling sick? Wait a minute. What's wrong? Hey! Get a grip on yourself. For heaven sakes, get a grip on yourself!

(p. 72)

Tsutsui's tale steps over the complexities, both political and psychological, of Abe's alien *The Face of Another* to return us to the nightmare supernatural world of Yanagita's terrible face. Both of these texts' primary aim is to arouse horror and fear in the reader and both works succeed most effectively. There are some important differences, however. One striking dissimilarity is the importance of description in Tsutsui. While the folk tale depended for its final effect on the indescribability of the face, leaving it to the reader's/listener's imagination, and Abe's story too only hinted at the ugliness of the scientist's keloid scars,[14] Tsutsui's story revels in the disgusting and unforgettable details. This richness of description is unusual in Japanese literature, especially when the subject is the face, revealing some of the international, postmodern flavor of Tsutsui's work.

This abundance of grotesque detail has an almost overwhelming effect on the reader, making him or her feel as if they were virtually present at the metamorphosis. In this emphasis on the process of transformation, rather than the psychological effect, Tsutsui's work shows commonalities with contemporary Japanese *manga*, both comic book and film, and with the avant garde and science fiction in general. Indeed, the discomfiture one feels on reading "Kaomen hōkai" is very similar to what many viewers feel watching Tsukamoto Shinya's 1990 avant-garde film *Tetsuo*, in which a man mutates into a machine. The Yanagita story is also uncomfortable in a pleasurably spine-tingling sort of way, but its disturbing aspect is also related to the fact that it, like Abe's story, contains a message: Do not stray from the collectivity!

While the threat of alien metamorphosis was ultimately contained in the Yanagita story by the work's fictional frame of reassurance, Tsutsui's story breaks through any fictional frame through its provocative final lines. This development is foreshadowed in Abe's novel, in which the scientist is writing his notes to "you," his wife. The reader of *The Face of Another*, however, is still able to maintain some comforting fictional distance through the novel's emphasis on writing. "You," the reader or the wife, are only reading words. As Abe's last line says, writing will not change things. Tsutsui's work crosses over the boundary of insistent fictionality, first by overwhelming the reader with horrifying sensations and then by directly warning the reader that the same fate of monstrous metamorphosis may befall them as well.

Where the two previous works contain messages founded on the fear of alien metamorphosis, and appeal to our desire for stability, there would appear to be no such didactic element in Tsutsui's work. This is not a metamorphosis "charged with meaning" as were the two previous ones. At the same time, this metamorphosis takes to the extreme another of Todorov's themes of the self, "the effacement of the limit between subject and object."[15]

Indeed, the very Grand Guignol aspect of Tsutsui's text, with its emphasis on collapse in front of one's eyes, is virtually a celebration of metamorphosis and perhaps of monstrousness as well. Unlike the previous tales, where at least one of the actants kept a fixed identity (the man in Yanagita's tale, the scientist's wife in the Abe novel), in Tsutsui's story the only certainty is fluidity. Difference is dissolved, and not just between genders but between writer and reader. For "you," too, the implied listener/reader, will be going to the Sharaku Star system and the same grotesque fate may befall you. In "Kaomen hōkai" the alien confronts us, mocks us and glories in its fluidity and power.

I have suggested that these three stories form a paradigmatic continuum of the alien in Japanese literature from the traditional through the modern to the postmodern. Although there are obviously going to be exceptions in every period, I believe one can find a definite pattern of development in these works that relates to some of the cultural and social changes undergone in Japan since the Meiji period. In the traditional tale, collected by Yanagita in the 1930s but presented as an ancient story, the collectivity is threatened but still fundamentally secure, and the threat of the alien represented by the ghostly woman is ultimately contained. In *The Face of Another*, it is the collectivity itself, in terms of postwar capitalist society, which produces the alien.

If the Yanagita tale is traditional horror, *The Face of Another*, and much of Abe's work in general, can be seen as belonging to the genre of paranoid horror. This genre, significantly coming to the fore in the socially conscious and politically activist 1960s, delineates a world in which the supposedly normal is actually threatening and sinister. As Andrew Tudor puts it, "Gone is the sense of an established social and moral order."[16] It is a world where paranoia makes sense because the collectivity is the threat, not the protection.

Finally, Tsutsui's work dismisses all notion of the collectivity, presenting a world in which identities collapse into each other and there is no secure point either to protect or to attack. "Kaomen hōkai"'s subtextual celebration of a boundaryless world is in some ways even more threatening than the overt message of Abe's work. It seems to embody some of the most disturbing aspects of the postmodern subject, a subject which, as Douglas Kellner sums it up, "Has disintegrated into a flux of euphoric intensities, fragmented and disconnected [which] no longer possesses the depth, substantiality and coherence that was the ideal and occasional achievement of the modern self."[17] Even the narrative format of "Kaomen hōkai," with its pretense of being an oral tale, helps to undermine the power of the symbolic, while the story's refusal of closure (except for the satirical invocation to "get a grip on yourself") is also insidiously threatening.

Where Abe's work ultimately cries out for action, Tsutsui's text constitutes an attack on modern assumptions of stability and security in and of itself. In both cases the works break through any traditional frame of reassurance. The alien is no longer a nightmare from which one can awaken.[18]

METAMORPHOSIS AND IDENTITY

Despite their significant differences, the three texts discussed above do contain one important constant, and that is their reliance on the notion of metamorphosis. Metamorphosis is so indispensable to much of fantasy literature in general and to the imagination of the alien in particular, that it is sometimes taken for granted as a narrative tool. In fact, the theme of metamorphosis has both literary and sociological aspects as well, all of which interrelate with modern Japanese history and with modern history in general.

Thus, although the West has had a fascination with metamorphosis from at least the time of Ovid, Rosemary Jackson in her book on fantasy has found a resurgent obsession with metamorphosis in nineteenth- and early-twentieth-century Western literature. Jackson links this with Darwin's discoveries and the public's subsequent fascination with both evolution and, more threateningly, devolution.[19]

It is also possible to link this interest in metamorphosis to a new concern with identity. W. R. Irwin suggests in *The Game of the Impossible: A Rhetoric of Fantasy* (1976) that the action of metamorphosis is so highly charged because of the "widespread assumption that form is a determinant of identity, even of being."[20] If form is taken as a determinant of identity, then it is hardly surprising that a cultural preoccupation with metamorphosis should surface at times of deep social transition.

Certainly this is true, although in somewhat different ways, for the nineteenth- and twentieth-century West. It is in this period, after all, that Western nations at the forefront of the Industrial Revolution were attempting to define themselves in new forms, while the old traditions, religious, philosophical, and social, were collapsing around them. And, as the twentieth century continues, it is perhaps no coincidence that Jackson finds an increase in what might be called "transformations without meaning"[21] as the old ideological certainties of Christianity and general morality begin to collapse.

This sense of established identity under attack, and a concomitant fascination with new forms of self-definition is even truer for the citizens of nineteenth- and twentieth-century Japan. But it is also true that the theme of metamorphosis has as deep roots in Japanese culture as it does in Western civilization. From the traditional *setsuwa* describing animals turning into humans, to the many depictions of the so-called transformer robots in contemporary science fiction comics and films, Japanese culture also shows a consistent fascination with transformation, in particular the crossing of boundaries between human and inhuman.

At first glance, this fascination with boundary crossing might appear surprising. The stratified nature of both traditional and contemporary Japanese society would seem to leave little room for fluidity. But, conversely, it is possible to argue that the very existence of consciously constructed social barriers may actually have stimulated an interest in transformation across them.

Traditional Japanese culture, while on the one hand hierarchical, is also marked by an extreme sense of the fluid relationships between human and natural. The Shinto religion posits the *kami* nature in humans, animals, and inanimate things such as rocks and waterfalls. Buddhism takes the idea of metamorphosis even further, with its notion of a karmic cycle suggesting potential bestiality in humans and potential humanity in animals. From this point of view, the notion of metamorphosis is a largely positive one, suggesting a philosophical acceptance of a universe where boundaries between the human and the natural are constantly fluctuating.

If metamorphosis is philosophically acceptable, it may be more problematic socially. Emiko Ohnuki-Tierney, whose book *The Monkey as Mirror: Symbolic Transformations in Japanese History and Ritual* (1987) chronicles the reflexive function of the monkey in Japanese culture, has suggested that, although the dualistic order on which

Japanese culture is based lacks the Manichean dichotomies of Western culture, it still retains its own classificatory boundaries. She asserts that transgressions of these boundaries are encouraged so as to elicit meaningful interactions between categories, and to define the category even further. Ultimately the boundaries become well marked precisely because they are transgressed.[22]

The most obvious example of this is the notion of *gekokujō* (the inferior overpowering the superior) in traditional Japanese culture, especially in *kyōgen* comedies, in which those conventionally considered inferiors (women or servants) outwit and overturn their masters. The humour, of course, results in the basic unlikelihood of such events occurring. But it is possible to argue that the actual notion of metamorphosis itself also exemplifies a similar boundary-marking function. In a society where social mobility was largely circumscribed, the "mobility" implied in metamorphosis must have seemed both tantalizing and subversive.

Boundary crossing and collapse can also be frightening, both in art and in reality. It is interesting to note that the proliferation of demonic and grotesque images in woodblock prints and on the kabuki stage really began at the end of the Bakumatsu period in Hokusai's superb ghosts, and carried on into the beginnings of the Meiji period in the depictions of ghosts and monsters in the works of such masters as Yoshitoshi. Commenting on this, one Japanese writer has called the Bakumatsu period a time "when dreams appeared in the upper levels of consciousness,"[23] another form of boundary transgression appropriate to a time when boundaries were broken as never before in Japanese history. Not only did samurai lose their swords and merchants and farmers become (supposedly) empowered, but the entire nation attempted to don a new identity as a modernizing state under an enlightened emperor. This process of metamorphosis led inevitably to tremendous psychological and social dislocations.

MONSTERS FROM THE ID: THE INTERNAL ALIEN FROM SŌSEKI TO MURAKAMI

Natsume Sōseki, perhaps the most important writer to arise out of this period, described Meiji Japan's condition as a national nervous breakdown. It is appropriate that the next part of this chapter, an examination of the internal alien from Meiji to the contemporary period, should begin with a discussion of Sōseki's version of the alien, since he was perhaps the most acute observer of modern Japan's metamorphosis. Yet, despite his almost hypersensitivity to cultural dislocation, the alien in Sōseki remains largely an interior one. Although he was acutely aware of Japan versus the Western Other, and in *Wagahai wa neku de aru* (1905) (trans. *I Am a Cat* (1986)) gives a brilliant example of an early form of the ideological alien, Sōseki's best works describe human beings oppressed, not by some alien outside force but through some frightening power inside themselves – what I have termed the internal alien.

Among the three works previously discussed, the internal alien was represented in Abe's *The Face of Another* in which the scientist's mask took on a life of its own corresponding to a hitherto unsuspected side of the scientist's personality. I have drawn a link between Abe's work and the paranoia of the 1960s, but the notion of an internal alternative self is one that appears in both premodern and modern literature. For the purposes of this chapter it is interesting to see how this self is presented and how this presentation changes over the course of the century of Japan's modernization.

The four writers principally dealt with, Sōseki, Akutagawa, Endō and Murakami, form a chronological continuum from the Meiji period (Sōseki) through the Taishō period (Akutagawa), through postwar Japan (Endō), to the Japan of the 1990s (Murakami), and they show some intriguing changes in their representation of the alien. These changes range from seeing the internal alien as a threatening, oppressive presence in Sōseki, and to some extent in Akutagawa and Endō, to the notion of the internal alien as a comforting, even empowering version of the self in Murakami's works.

Important similarities of presentation also exist. All the works considered in this section are notably concerned with the same sets of dualities: escape versus entrapment, art versus the real, and, most importantly, the self (or selves) in confrontation with others. It is this notion of various forms of insider and outsider which is perhaps the most subversive aspect of the alien, inherently questioning the framework upon which society rests by allowing for an outside observer.

Thus, what might be called Sōseki's first and most famous fantasy *I Am a Cat* creates one of the most famous outside aliens in modern Japanese literature. By focussing his narrative through the gaze of an intelligent and critical cat, Sōseki was able to bring humorous and accurate observations of contemporary Japanese society. While the cat is of course powerless to change society, its acute and often savage commentary makes for a brilliantly subversive satirical vision.

I Am a Cat emphasizes what I have called the ideological or "message" alien over the internal alien, but at the same time it also provides a vision of another self as an outside observer, a kind of alien superego. This outside observer self is one that is an important part of the fantasy of Sōseki and the other writers as well. This strong sense of self as outsider is of course typical to many writers, but in the case of these four it may also be related to their exposure to foreign influences.

Sōseki, Endō, and Murakami actually lived abroad, while Akutagawa studied English literature at university and remained a voracious reader of the Western classics throughout his life. Of course, not all their experiences abroad were positive ones. Sōseki's two years in London, for example, apparently provoked extreme paranoia, if not an actual nervous breakdown. This experience too may have contributed to his sense of alienation.

It is also possible that the internal alien itself is a construction deeply rooted in modernity. Indeed, Sōseki and the other writers who use this are usually writers at the forefront of literary modernism. Modern psychology with its new awareness of the self obviously stimulated a consciousness of the psyche's complexities. Stories revolving around the internal alien tend to be profoundly psychological. Often using the motif of the double, they delve into the protagonist's inner states which are usually characterized by a sense of vulnerability and paralysis against another unknown power, be it guilt, heredity, sin, or simply one's alter ego.[24]

At times the inner alien can wear a more positive aspect, particularly in the myth of the artist and his genius, a turn-of-the-century phenomenon found in the West in writers such as Oscar Wilde and in Japan in the fiction of such writers as Akutagawa and Tanizaki. This internal alien can be both frightening and empowering. As such, it might be likened to the "muse" of classical Western literature.

Western influences undoubtedly had a powerful effect on the development of the Japanese internal alien, but it is also the case that the Meiji and Taishō periods were times of a distinctive Japanese exploration of the self.[25] With the entrance of the philosophies and religions of the West the notion of the self and identity in general became widely discussed.[26]

On the other hand, it should also be mentioned that the inner alien is not exclusively a product of modern self-consciousness. The psychological linking of self and internalized alien Other is brilliantly encapsulated in the tenth-century *Tale of Genji* in the tormented figure of Genji's lover, Lady Rokujo. Lady Rokujo's jealousy is so powerful that her "spirit" possesses and murders another of Genji's lovers and then his wife. Although the text plays up the more conventionally supernatural elements of the possession, it also includes some ambiguous passages where Lady Rokujo's tormented and guilt-ridden state and her horror at this alien side of herself are movingly delineated.

Guilt and jealousy and a sense of intense vulnerability are emotions with which modern fantasy writers are also very familiar. This is certainly the case in the works of Sōseki who has long been known for his anguished explorations of the self in relation to both the outside world and to its own ego. He explored this problem in a series of brilliant mimetic novels, the most famous of which is *Kokoro* (1914) (trans. *Kokoro* (1992)).

But it is Sōseki's hauntingly beautiful collection of dreams, *Ten Nights of Dream* (of which "Dream of the Sixth Night" was mentioned in the my Introduction and "Dream of the First Night" was discussed in Chapter 2), which remains one of his most memorable meditations on such issues as guilt, insecurity, and crises of faith. They also present a fascinating and varied range of creatures who can be characterized as "internal aliens."

Although the motif of dreams in literature is a traditional one, Sōseki's use of dream is archetypally "modern." He presents the reader with dreams that are full of darkly evocative imagery, and leaves it to the reader to interpret them. As is appropriate to dreams, virtually all of the short fantasies assembled in *Ten Nights of Dream* are full of mysterious creatures, from the woman who turns into a flower in "Dream of the First Night" to a ship full of foreigners.

But what is most interesting in the dreams is the interaction between the strange dream creatures and the usually passive, dreaming "I." This dreamer is ghostlike in many ways, a shadowy figure forced to take part in situations which he does not understand and wishes only to escape from. Indeed, in these dreams the "real" alien is the "I," an "I" whose anguished self-consciousness and isolation reminds us of a famous line from *Kokoro* in which the protagonist sums up his condition in the following agonized manner: "loneliness is the price we have to pay for being born in the modern era, so full of freedom, independence and our own egotistical selves" (p. 29).

Given this problematic interaction between the "egotistical self" and others, it is not surprising that much of the narrative action in the dreams involves questions of identity. "Dream of the First Night," as we remember, explored the relationship between the dreaming "I" and the object of his gaze, a dying woman. Although the dream can be interpreted straightforwardly as an example of male sexual unease *vis-à-vis* a fully sexual female, it is also possible to read the female figure as another part of the self. Thus, the natural world that the woman-as-flower represents can be seen as a kind of escape from the

consciousness of the self, an idea explored more concretely in
Sōseki's mimetic *Sore kara* (1909) (trans. *And Then* (1978)). This notion
of oblivion through transformation may relate as much to the "I"'s
own insecurities of identity as to any deep-seated fear of women.[27]

While the female self in "The First Night" is able to transform
herself into something more positive, at least from the "I"'s point of
view, many of the protagonists in *Ten Nights of Dream* feel a need to
change or escape that they cannot fulfill. In one of the most strongly
sociocultural of the dreams, "Dream of the Seventh Night," the "I"
finds himself incapable of entering a new world, that of the West.
Trapped on a giant ship that sails forever westward and surrounded by
foreigners who ask him meaningless questions about God's existence,
the "I" grows increasingly "forlorn" and desperate. Like a lonely
ghost, he moves endlessly around the ship finally determining to
escape by jumping overboard. Even after jumping, however, he remains suspended in mid-air, in a liminal state between the Western ship
and the death-promising sea until he finally goes down, "infinitely
regretful, infinitely afraid . . ." (p. 52).

"Dream of the Seventh Night" shows two kinds of aliens, the incomprehensible (monstrous?) foreigner and the ghostlike "forlorn"
Japanese, who does not belong on the ship but knows no way of getting
off without self-annihilation. It is perhaps one of Sōseki's most powerful fictional statements about his ambivalence toward Westernization
and his own Japanese identity.[28]

Interestingly, the emotions portrayed in "Dream of the Seventh
Night" echo another one of Sōseki's writings which, although supposedly autobiographical, is close to being a fantastic text as well. This is
the famous story from Sōseki's time in England when he saw what
appeared to be a hideous yellow dwarf coming down a London street
toward him. The dwarf turned out to be his own reflection in a shop
window. Sōseki's own "desert of mirrors" can thus be seen as beginning with his initial experience abroad, an experience which affected
his self-conception in an entirely negative way, forcing him to see himself as something monstrous *vis-à-vis* the West.

The mirror in Sōseki occurs frequently, from his autobiographical
fiction through his early fantasies, to his final unfinished novel *Meian*
(1916) (trans. *Light and Darkness* (1971)). In this mimetic work the
protagonist goes on what is essentially a journey of self-discovery to a
country inn where, at one point, he is startled to find see his reflection
in a mirror. In the scene that ensues it is clear that the protagonist is
beginning to build a new, more positive identity. In this regard it is
important to remember that the so-called mirror stage, as Lacan tells

us, is the one in which the infant constructs his own identity for the first time.

In Sōseki's fantastic fiction the mirror plays many roles. Thus, in "Dream of the Eighth Night" the "I" goes to a barber shop and watches a parade of passing humanity reflected in the shop mirror. When he looks through the shop's window, however, he sees nothing. The mirror is merely a literally self-reflexive fantasy, one that ultimately rejects the outside world, leaving the "I," as usual, passive and alone. Even his attempt to change his appearance through barbering seems to make no real difference.

The inability to transform either oneself or the world around one comes to the fore in the famous "Dream of the Sixth Night," discussed in the Introduction to this book. Although there are no mirrors in this tale there is a kind of *doppelgänger* for the "I," the famous Kamakura period sculptor, Unkei. We remember that the "I" tries to follow in Unkei's steps, attempting to carve guardian gods out of logs in his garden, only to give up in frustration, concluding that "guardian gods were not, after all, buried in the trees of the present age" (p. 48).

As in "Dream of the Seventh Night," which is set on the ship, there are again two aliens in this tale. Unlike that dream, however, although one of the aliens is familiar to us, in the person of the forlorn, passive "I," the other alien is perhaps a surprise. This alien is the Japanese past, signified both in the ghost of Unkei and the magical guardian gods who can no longer exist in the "present age." Unlike the strange Westerners, this is a longed-for alien but, as in "Dream of the Seventh Night," it is just as unattainable.

"Dream of the Seventh Night" contains elements of both the ideological and the internal alien. The ideological alien is clearly the unattainable guardian gods, while the deracinated, helpless "I" is the alienated self. In the dream, the "I" tries to transform the contemporary trees, but is unable to do so. His attempt at metamorphosis blocked, the "I" is left back in his familiar liminal state, unable to return to the past but ill at ease in the present.

A past that is both alien and frightening at the same time as being appallingly intimate is the background to the extraordinary "Dream of the Third Night," the most fascinating and enigmatic of all the dreams. In this dream a man (the "I") is walking through a dark wood carrying a child on his back. He knows that the child is his and that the child is blind, but he does not know where he is going or why. The child jeers at him, telling his father that he will be "heavy soon." As they go further into the forest depths, it grows darker and darker. But the child shines like a mirror, "like a mirror that revealed my past, my present, and my future" (p. 37). Eventually they reach a place beneath a cedar tree where the child tells him, "It was exactly one hundred years ago that you murdered me" (p. 38). The story concludes:

> As soon as I heard these words, the realization burst upon me that I had killed a blind man at the root of this cedar tree on just so dark a night in the fifth year of Bunka one hundred years ago. And at that moment when I knew that I had murdered, the child on my back became as heavy as a god of stone.
>
> (p. 38; stone reads *Jizo* in the original)

The third dream is such a brilliant and disturbing *mélange* of archetypal horror that it seems almost reductive to dismember it. From the point of view of this chapter, however, it is worth examining for its powerful depiction of an identity in serious conflict with itself. Indeed, with its combination of blindness, murder, and a search for origins, the story can easily be interpreted as a slightly displaced Oedipal fantasy, as Japanese critics have suggested.

The story contains many other layers as well, however. Like all good nightmares, it starts with the alien in both setting and character. The dark wood is a classic fantasy site, at the same time as the journey suggests a quest into a psychological "heart of darkness," a journey toward recognition, not simply of the Oedipal conflict but of the self as well.

In fact, there are three selves in the dream: father, son, and murdered blind man. These three selves or, perhaps more correctly, alter egos, create a fascinating and disturbing triumvirate of identity, incorporating transgression, guilt, and vulnerability. Each reflects, distorts, and controls the other in a perfect realization of paranoid fantasy.

First let us examine the "I." Like the "I" in most of the other dreams, this dreamer initially seems to have no control over his destiny. Driven by an alien compulsion upon his back, he tries to present himself as passive. Unlike the other "I"'s, however, we find that he has once acted, i.e., committed murder. Now his memory, itself an alien force beyond control, has come back to him in the form of the child.

But the blind child is not simply alienated memory but incorporates many other elements as well. The monstrous child that both is and is not of the self has become such a staple of horror fiction that at times the reader tends to take for granted the very elements that make it so monstrous: as the "I"'s child it is both an insider and an outsider, both threatening and vulnerable, and the child's prescient blindness emphasizes both its outsiderhood and its vulnerability all the more.

Perhaps even more significant than its blindness is the child's function as a mirror, echoing the Lacanian mirror stage even more obviously than in "Dream of the Eighth Night." In Lacan's thesis, the child looks in the mirror and sees a construction of itself, thus leading it for the first time to become aware of itself as an identity separate from its mother. In "Dream of the Third Night"'s far more fearsome version, however, the child is blind, it cannot see itself and cannot therefore create an identity. "Dream of the Third Night" thus plays on the theme of vision, one of the themes that Todorov identifies as a "theme of the self." But in the "Third Night"'s case, vision is not part of the "road to the marvelous," but rather reveals that the road is blocked.

Thus, the shining child supposedly acts as a mirror to its father, but this is a mirror that rejects the father. For, rather than showing the father his reflection, it shows him "his past, his present and his future." The father now has neither identity nor control, since his history is being played out in front of him continuously, without any will on his part.

The murdered blind man is in some ways a more simple construction of the self. Apparently vulnerable, like the child, the blind man is also threatening, like a vengeful ghost, since he does not rest but comes back to haunt the "I"'s memories. The blind man, then, is another disappointing self that cannot be willed away.

Finally, there is a fourth self[29] that appears at the end of the story: the stone *Jizo* that the child metaphorically turns into. Not only does the buried self/selves return from the dead but other negative selves are always there. Jizo is known in a positive fashion as the god of children but, in this case, the sacredness of the deity only emphasizes the awesome burden of guilt and responsibility which the "I" must carry around with him.

The feeling of being overpowered, be it by outside events, other selves, or a past and a future over which one has no control, is an important aspect of Sōseki's other writings, both fictional and autobiographical. But in no other work is this sense of psychic claustrophobia so effectively conveyed. It is interesting that *Ten Nights of Dream* was one of Sōseki's earliest works and was also written soon after his return from England, a journey of self-discovery more fearsome and more frustrating than any dream.

The sense of the self as alienated from its past, present and future, forced into various manifestations, but all largely negative, runs through *Ten Nights of Dream*. More than dreams these are nightmares, nightmares of paranoid horror where the world is either frighteningly meaningless or, even worse, threateningly meaningful.[30] Terror fiction,

Heller suggests, can offer the delight of the "unchosen self," but this is a delight only offered the reader, and a reader who consciously chooses to participate in the "delights of terror." It is perhaps not surprising that, compared to the funny and satiric *I Am a Cat* of 1905, Sōseki's early works were not as well received.

This was not the case, however, for the next writer of the inner alien this chapter deals with, Akutagawa Ryūnosuke (1892–1927). Akutagawa's entire oeuvre is far 'weirder' than any one story of Sōseki's but, on the whole, his bizarre and grotesque fantasies were well received by critics and reading public alike. Perhaps this is because, with the exception of the posthumously published dark *doppelgänger* fantasy "Haguruma" (1927) (trans. "Cogwheels" (1965)), Akutagawa maintained, at least in his early works, a brilliantly controlled aesthetic and ironic distance from his fantastic creations. At the same time, Akutagawa's fantasies of the alien explore very similar issues to those of Sōseki, particularly the problem of defining the self in relation to others. The way he treats these problems, however, shows some important generational changes.

Although Akutagawa revered Sōseki as a mentor, he was fifteen years younger than Sōseki and his sensibility is very much representative of the Taishō period (1912–1926). This was a time of intense urbanization and industrialization, when the initial unity of the Meiji period had been replaced by an increasing tendency toward conflict on the part of political and other pressure groups, and by a fascination with self-discovery and self-transformation on the part of the newly urbanized, newly consuming population. Thomas Rimer describes the *Zeitgeist* of this period as "a move inward," when, the younger generation, troubled and moved by the power of

> the writings of their precursors, now felt a need to seek out a sense of interiority, which seemed a mandatory first step toward an understanding of the relationship between the individual and the surrounding culture.[31]

Thus, the problems of identity with which Akutagawa deals are different from those of Sōseki's generation, which still had one foot in premodern Japan. The inner self may still be alien but it is in some ways a more attractive alien, hinting both at a new, more interesting self, and at new ways to understand the society around it.

Akutagawa does share with Sōseki a strong preoccupation with individuals entrapped by powerful forces beyond their control, be it their own genius or their egos. Also like Sōseki, his fantasy works show a consistent preoccupation with outsiderhood, either willed or enforced. But Akutagawa's outsiders are usually more monstrous than ghostly, more determined to try and change themselves, often through the medium of art or artifice.

This fascination with both outsiderhood and change leads to a pre-occupation with metamorphosis and boundary transgression as well, such as in "Hōkyōjin no shi" (1918) (trans. "The Martyr" (1952)), where a young Christian accused of fathering a child is revealed upon his death to be a woman. This story, with its transgression of gender boundaries and its exotic Christian framework, recalls the work of another writer contemporary to Akutagawa, Yumeno Kyūsaku, who wrote a number of stories depicting androgynous characters often in an international setting. Although Kyūsaku's work has only recently begun to become well known again, the popularity of his writings at the time is such as to suggest that the Taishō fascination with identity ambivalence was a widespread one. As Donald Roden says, "[t]he sexual ambiguities in Taishō Japan reflect the transition from a civiliza-tion of character to a culture of personality."[32] While Sōseki's dream-ers are constantly trying and failing to find their identities against a larger background of history or philosophy (such as the protagonist's attempt in "Dream of the Sixth Night" to unearth guardian gods in the trees of the Meiji period), Akutagawa's characters explore the alien on a more personal and direct level. Although his works, especially the dystopian satire *Kappa* (1927) (trans. *Kappa* (1974)), can indeed be highly critical of Japanese society, Akutagawa's approach is usually more intimate than Sōseki's carefully structured works.

A short-story writer rather than a novelist, Akutagawa's genius was in creating memorable characters trapped in bizarre situations and trying to escape them. Often his works end with might be called the Akutagawan twist, a kind of epiphany experienced by either character or reader. This epiphany can be a positive one but often it is simply an awareness of the absurdity and uncertainty of life.

All the above features are on view in Akutagawa's first important short story, "Hana" (1916) (trans. "The Nose" (1952)), a story which is both a brilliant dissection of how identity is formed and also an explora-tion of how the alien and the grotesque can be part of the self. In this case the alien takes the form of the monstrously large nose belonging to the protagonist, a prominent monk in medieval Japan.

In this narrative of what might be called counter-metamorphosis, the priest succeeds in neutralizing his alien member by shrinking it back to normal size. Only temporarily, however; embarrassed by the taunts and innuendo of his fellow acolytes, the priest wishes miserably for his grotesque appendage to return, and one morning, magically, it does. "Now, no one will laugh at me any more," the priest whispers softly, his nose wafting in the breeze.

The notion of the alien in "The Nose" is a teasingly ironic one, suggesting that the monstrous is very much a product of one's own perceptions. For, like Abe's far darker *The Face of Another*, Akutagawa's story is really a commentary on the desire to be "normal." Unlike the protagonist of *The Face of Another*, however, the priest is finally willing to accept his deformity rather than withstand the ridicule of pretending to be something he is not.

If the nose is the sign of the self (traditionally Japanese people point to the nose in referring to themselves), then the priest's acceptance of his nose can be seen as either healthy or resigned. By accepting his nose he acknowledges his essential estrangement from the main run of humanity, an acceptance which makes him, paradoxically, more human, and more accepted, than before.

The sense of unease with one's own identity does not have to be read purely in personal terms, of course. It is even possible to read "The Nose" as Akutagawa's ironic judgement on Japan's attempt to Westernize itself, although the comparison is never explicitly stated. The priest's torturous attempts to transform his nose, including boiling it and wrapping it, can be read as a subtle satire on the Taishō generation's fascination with donning the trappings of the West.

A far more overt political statement that involves the notion of the alien and estrangement in relation to modern Japanese identity can be found in Akutagawa's bleakly dystopian fantasy *Kappa*. I will discuss *Kappa* more fully in the chapter on dystopias, but certain aspects of it in relation to the treatment of the alien are pertinent here.

Kappa extends the implicit equation of the Japanese with their traditional gods and spirits that we saw in Sōseki's "Dream of the Seventh Night" dream about "guardian gods" to a rather problematic fantastic creature, the Kappa or Japanese water sprite. A clever fantasy, it is also a troubling one. Its disturbing quality may lie in the fact that it amalgamates the notion of an internal alien with that of an ideological one through the use of a grotesque monster as a double, both for the protagonist and for the entire Japanese race.

The fact that the narrative begins in a mental asylum, where the first narrator goes to visit his friend who tells him his story of his adventures in Kappaland, suggests that Akutagawa is still playing with the problem of perception as to what is "normal." This is even clearer in the second narrator's description of his initial encounter with a Kappa: looking at his watch to find out the time, he sees reflected in it the face of a Kappa.

The monstrous Kappa is thus immediately equated with the protagonist himself, a distorted "mirror" image. Not only does the protagonist see a hideous double, but, since he can see neither the time nor his own face, he is about to be lost in a timeless "Other" world, which is potentially dangerous. The Kappa thus subverts both the protagonist's sense of self and the reality of modern Japan.

The protagonist's adventures in Kappaland will be described in greater detail in Chapter 6, but for now I would like to examine the role of the Kappa as grotesque double. Ohnuki-Tierney has pointed out that the Kappa has traditionally been considered evil, the trickster version of the reflexive monkey figure previously mentioned. Actually, Akutagawa's Kappa are no more evil than the average human, but they do perform the trickster function of giving a distorted reflection of contemporary Japanese society.

Akutagawa uses the Kappa's pretensions, their avid capitalism, their artistic affectations, and their imperialist assertiveness against the Otters, to satirize many of the major movements of the Taishō period. This is dark satire, however. Perhaps the most shocking scene in the book is that of the birth of a baby Kappan who declares its unwillingness to be born. In explaining its intentions, the fetus says simply, "It makes me shudder to think of all the things I shall inherit from my father – the insanity alone is bad enough. And an additional factor is that I maintain that a Kappa's existence is evil" (p. 62).

It is interesting to compare this scene with Sōseki's "Dream of the Third Night." As in Sōseki's third dream, a monstrous child speaks of an inescapable past, in this case hereditary insanity, and a bleak future, although the child in Akutagawa's story intends to repudiate it. In some ways this scene is highly personal, related to Akutagawa's fear of inheriting his mother's madness. It is important to remember, however, that a fascination with genetic inheritance is common to the literature of the Taishō period. Yumeno Kyūsaku's 1935 novel *Dogura magura*, for example, interweaves notions of heredity with the story of a magic curse in an extraordinary fantasy narrated, it turns out, by the diseased fetus itself.

But, as Akutagawa's work and the Sōseki story also suggest, the notion of a deformed coming generation is related to more than an interest in heredity. If existence is "evil," and populated by alien creatures, then the future too must be "evil." If there is no hope even in the future, then it appears that the only way out is through total alienation from the self through madness.

The alien in *Kappa* comes in many forms, from the most obvious representation of the Kappas themselves to the more subtle horror of madness which leaves the protagonist happily outside society. The novella's "happy" ending, with the protagonist comfortably ensconced in an insane asylum, interweaves madness, art, and language; the protagonist inscribes himself into his own version of reality with help from props such as the telephone book and the flowers. With these he is able to make the alien intimate and the familiar alien. Through art, the telling of his tale, and the verbal transformation of homely objects into the exotic, the narrator is finally able to achieve his own escape.

This notion of the liberating and seductive power of art ties in with another, generally more positive aspect of the internal alien, the idea of the artistic force itself as an alien, potentially overwhelming power. This valorization of art is extremely important in Akutagawa's work. His contention seems to be that if one cannot achieve metamorphosis in reality, as the priest discovers in "The Nose," perhaps one can change the world through art.

This theme of the power of art and the imagination is given a lighthearted treatment in Akutagawa's short story "Ryū" (1919) (trans. "The Dragon" (1952)), in which a monk invents a prophecy that a dragon will arise from a nearby pond at a certain date. On the date in question a crowd gathers excitedly waiting for the dragon to appear. Meanwhile a thunderstorm begins to brew. As the storm breaks, the crowd gasps in awe as what appears to be a huge black creature erupts out of the pond's waters and rises to heaven. Even the monk is finally uncertain as to what he has seen, but everyone has enjoyed themselves greatly. The monk's imagination has summoned forth an alien creature but this version of the monstrous is shown as something comfortably outside the collectivity and fundamentally unthreatening.

Akutagawa gives a similarly lighthearted treatment to the power of art in his lovely story "Shūzanzu" (1921) (trans. "Autumn Mountain" (1972)), in which the role of the phantom dragon is played by a landscape painting, which may or may not exist but whose presumed presence makes reality more easy to bear.[33] In both stories artifice and the alien are seen as basically pleasurable, even humorous.

This fascination with the transformative powers of art and the artist may also be related to several of the Taishō period's fascinations. Of these, the most important are the period's obsession with the self and its potential, which the artist seemed to most perfectly embody, and a related obsession with artifice and ambiguity in popular culture. This latter was expressed in the popular fascination with the Takarazuka review or the emerging culture of the cinema.

The potent combination of art and personality had its negative aspect as well. Akutagawa's most memorable look at the dark side of art and the artist is his famous story "Jigokuhen" (1918) (trans. "The Hell Screen" (1961)). In this story a court painter, Yoshihide, rumoured to practice the black arts, is so consumed by his art that he paints a picture of a subject burning in hell, even though the dying model is in fact his only daughter. Yoshihide himself is clearly represented as a demonic figure, metonymically and metaphorically associated with owls and monkeys, but it is also emphasized that his art is of the highest. The price he pays for giving in to the internal alien is high, too, however. One week after finishing the painting, Yoshihide hangs himself.

In "The Hell Screen" Akutagawa portrays an artist who transgresses moral boundaries to become essentially a demon. The artistic presence in him has overpowered the human to the detriment of all around him. The fact that the painting is his greatest masterpiece only adds to the irony.

The darkest vision of the artist and his internal demons appears in Akutagawa's posthumous story the surreal "Haguruma" (1927) (trans. "Cogwheels" (1965)). Less a coherent fantasy than a surreal *tour de force*, "Cogwheels" explores the mind of its narrator, a writer, as he wanders through the Tokyo night, attempting, essentially, to escape himself. He externalizes this alien self into a variety of visions, especially a vision of cogwheels turning in front of his eyes and, even more sinisterly, a ghost in a raincoat. Returning home, the narrator discovers that his brother-in-law has committed suicide wearing a raincoat. The discovery fills him with further foreboding.

Eventually, everything he sees, from crows on a swing to a passing cyclist, serves to remind him of death. Even language, especially certain foreign words, seems to take on an alien power. The protagonist finally returns home to hide. Even at home, however, he cannot escape as, in the last scene, his wife comes running upstairs telling him "I felt that you were dying."

"Cogwheels" deserves to be ranked with Sōseki's "Dream of the Third Night" in its claustrophobic vision of a self lost in a nightmare world, and what it loses in formal structure in comparison to the Sōseki work it gains in its frightening intensity. The ghost in the raincoat is obviously not merely the past in the form of the narrator's suicidal dead brother-in-law but a double of the narrator himself, a potential future that came true for Akutagawa – he committed suicide soon after he wrote "Cogwheels." As Donald Keene says of the story, "After reading 'Cogwheels' we can only marvel that Akutagawa did not kill himself sooner." [34]

We can trace a kind of trajectory of the self and the alien in

Akutagawa's work from "The Nose" to "Cogwheels." This is a move-ment from a distanced ironic perspective on the grotesqueness of the self in his early years through an attempt to escape the self or create a new self, the self as artist/superman in works such as "The Hell Screen" or "The Dragon," or even "Autumn Mountain," whose dual-ities between "the real" and "art" inherently privilege art. In his last years Akutagawa is known for turning away from his earlier fascina-tion with the fantastic and the grotesque toward a more overtly autobio-graphical mode, as is evident in the personal elements in "Cogwheels." It is important to note, however, that *Kappa*, in its own way as an-guished an inquiry into the soul as "Cogwheels," was written in 1926, the year he committed suicide. But while the ghost in "Cogwheels" haunts the protagonist like both a reminder of the personal past and a grim harbinger of the future, the *Kappa*'s monstrousness mocks humanity on a more general level.

Although of different generations, Sōseki and Akutagawa do share certain important aspects in their general conception of the internal alien. With only a few exceptions (the phantom picture in Akutagawa's "Autumn Mountain," the flower-woman in Sōseki's "Dream of the First Night"), the internal alien is inherently frightening. It is a part of the self which the protagonist usually does not wish to accept. Whether it is the blind child of "The Dream of the Third Night" growing heavier and heavier upon the dreamer's back, the Kappan double reflected in a wristwatch, or the raincoated ghost haunting the narrator of "Cogwheels," the alien invades the soul of the protagonist and refuses to leave. In the case of *Kappa*'s protagonist this refusal is finally welcomed with relief, since he clearly does not wish to live in the "real" world of the sane. Sōseki's protagonists usually struggle for a while but eventually resign themselves to their fate, even though "infinitely regretful" and "infinitely afraid."

Sōseki's and Akutagawa's aliens are subversive in that they bring to the surface many of the unconscious conflicts of identity occurring in the prewar Japanese soul. The notion of the self as mutable or mon-strous suggests an enormous degree of insecurity lurking just below the surface of Japan's military and economic successes. Even the impor-tance of the androgynous self at this time can be read as either a celebration of uncertainty, as may be the case in Yumeno Kyūsaku's works, or an expression of the dangers inherent in the lack of a fixed sexual identity, as was the story in Akutagawa's "The Martyr."

The association of the self with ghosts is also important. Many of Sōseki's dreamers are essentially ghostly, passively watching others in action. These ghosts are forlorn rather than sinister, suggesting a tragic inability to fit into a new, Other world. The ghost that appears to the writer in "Cogwheels" is more sinister, bringing both a dismal personal past and a tragic personal future with it.

The only major prewar writer that I know of who depicts the alien positively is Kawabata Yasunari, and two of his short stories are worth mentioning as a bridge to the postwar aliens of Murakami. These stories "Yuki" (1964) (trans. "Snow" (1988)) and "Fushi" (1963) (trans. "Immortality" (1988)) privilege what are essentially ghosts of the past as liberating forces, rescuing the protagonists from living in the real.

Unlike Akutagawa's protagonists, who are still creating their identities, Kawabata's male characters are usually fixed in a lonely outsiderhood where art and fantasy help them mediate between their inner and outer worlds. There are few doubles in Kawabata. Rather, as we saw in Chapter 3, his male protagonists tend to see themselves in relation to women.

Thus, in his exquisite short story "Snow," a man retreats to a hotel room each New Year where he lies in bed and watches the walls dissolve into his private fantasies, a childhood walk with his father in the snow, or a group of winged women who turn out to be all the women he ever loved, flying toward him in a cloud of silver wings. Unlike almost all the writers mentioned so far, these ghosts of past erotic involvements or generational differences are positively presented, metamorphosed through the transforming and distancing power of fantasy into dreams. Here the alien is presented as wish-fulfillment of the most appealing kind.

The alien in the form of a ghost is directly liberating in one of Kawabata's most explicitly fantastic works, "Immortality." This work, whose structure resembles a Nō play, begins in the quotidian surroundings of a golf course through which an old man and a young girl are walking. Gradually, we learn that the girl is a ghost, having thrown herself into the sea for love of a youth who is now an old man walking by her side. As they walk, the old man relives the torments and humiliations of his youth, reaching a Nō-like climax when he acts out his memories of being pelted with golf balls while performing his job. It is only at the end of the story, through the girl's surprised recognition that the man, too, is dead, that we learn that he is now a ghost as well. On this note of recognition of their mutual alienness, the couple walks into a tree and disappears.

The strangling, overwhelming power of the past that is evident in Sōseki's *Ten Nights of Dream* is obvious here as well as the old man relives his humiliations. Unlike in Sōseki's works, however, death allows the protagonist to escape by affording him the metamorphosis into a ghost. Unlike Sōseki's ghostly protagonists, this is a ghost who can walk away from his old, humiliated self, forever. Typically for Kawabata, it is a combination of woman and nature in the form of the tree that welcomes the duo at the story's end that allows him finally to escape.

The notion of the alien within continues in the postwar period, in works such as Abe Kōbō's many stories of bizarre metamorphoses. These works, however, also tend to have a strong ideological component, as was obvious in *The Face of Another*, so I will discuss them under that section. Perhaps the most negative portrayal of the alien within in the postwar period is in Endō Shūsaku's 1986 novel, *Sukyandaru* (trans. *Scandal* (1988)).

This work revolves around a respected Christian writer's discovery that he has a double who roams the Tokyo red-light district participating in what, to the novelist, appear to be depraved sexual activities. He is also persistently bothered by phone calls from a source who remains silent when he answers the phone. The writer, Suguro, decides to search for his double and through the search begins to realize that the black and white verities of truth and evil no longer seem applicable. He is particularly drawn to a beautiful widow, Madame Naruse who, despite her many good works in a children's hospital, has a darker side based on sado-masochism. Eventually, in a classic example of Todorovian hesitation, Suguro confronts his double only to find that the double is probably himself, although the text remains suitably ambiguous on this point. Returning home after the confrontation, hoping that at least the nightmare is over, he awakens in the middle of the night to the sinister sound of the telephone jangling.

Scandal ends with the ring of the phone suggesting that there is finally no escape from the other self within us. Unlike Sōseki's other selves, which are often ghosts of the past, Suguro's *doppelgänger* is clearly a monstrous other, a more obvious manifestation of the mask in *The Face of Another*. The combination of Endō's own Christian faith with a Todorovian acknowledgement of uncertainty, however, makes it a memorable work in its own right.

Both Abe and Endō, although writing into the 1980s, were born in 1926, long before the war, and their negative sense of the inner alien may well be a generational one. Murakami Haruki, the last writer of the inner alien to be discussed, was born in 1949. Probably due to the fact that he grew up in a culture more comfortable with ideas of the Western self, Murakami depicts his other selves in a largely positive fashion, as gateways to a deeper understanding of the self as a whole.

Murakami uses the fantastic perhaps more than any other writer discussed in this chapter, but he uses it with remarkable effectiveness, exploring the problem of self *vis-à-vis* others in a number of imaginative ways.

His novel *Sekai no owari to hādoboirudo wandārando* (1985) (trans. *Hard Boiled Wonderland and the End of the World* (1991)) can be read as both an apolitical dystopia and a brilliant satire on technology, at the same time as it can be analyzed as a meditation on the self in contemporary culture. Since I discuss *Hard Boiled Wonderland* at greater length in the chapter on dystopias, I will simply mention here the fascination with the *doppelgänger* that is the thematic basis of the book. For the final and most important duality in *Hard Boiled Wonderland* is the existence of two protagonists, "Boku" and "Watashi," who are actually two parts of the same person. "Watashi" lives in the future "real world" of technological dystopia, while "Boku," who is further divided between himself and his shadow, exists inside a fantasy world inside "Watashi"'s head. This fantasy world is called appropriately "the End of the World," for "Watashi" eventually loses consciousness in the "real world" and escapes or is reborn into the fantasy of the End of the World, where everything is "perfect" and nothing changes.

Murakami's fantasy has been harshly criticized by the more political members of the Japanese literary establishment for being "escapist," and indeed it is hard to avoid being somewhat troubled by the novel's ending.[35] The self in Murakami seems finally to be rejecting "others" in toto. Furthermore, like Akutagawa and Kawabata, Murakami seems to be privileging art at the expense of life by creating not only a fantastic Other self in the form of "Boku," but also a fantastic other world to put him into.

There are some important differences, however. While Akutagawa's valorization of the fantastic Other clearly came out of despair, and even Kawabata's retreat into fantasy can be seen as stemming at least from profound disappointment, *Hard Boiled Wonderland*'s depiction of the construction of a fantasy double seems strangely positive. As mentioned in the Introduction, the last scene of the "End of the World" section of the novel shows "Boku" consciously choosing to stay inside his mental fantasy world because it is his "responsibility." Far from the madness and despair of *Kappa*, *Hard Boiled Wonderland* seems to exult in the mind's ability to create a haven for itself.

Murakami's works are also redolent of both ghosts and monsters, but these aliens are usually positive, even humorous creations. In his short story "The Little Green Monster," for example, a housewife who clearly has no identity problems whatsoever, calmly confronts a little green monster who climbs out of her garden one day and declares itself in love with her. Like the monstrous child in Sōseki's "Dream of the Third Night," the monster can read all her thoughts, but even this does not faze her. Instead, she turns this ability against him and destroys him by "thinking at the creature increasingly terrible thoughts" until the monster shrivels away, leaving only his mournful eyes:

> That won't do any good, I thought to it. You can look all you want but you can't say a thing. You can't do a thing. Your existence is over, finished, done. Soon the eyes dissolved into emptiness, and the room filled with the darkness of night.
>
> (p. 156)

Unlike the "Dream of the Third Night," the housewife has no trouble getting rid of the monstrous presence. Far from being burdened by guilt or other painful emotions, she is able to turn her thoughts outward into weapons. In this interaction between self and alien the self is barely affected.

Murakami's ghosts can be more disturbing than his monsters, but they are usually well intentioned. Thus, the ghost of the protagonist's friend Rat in *Hitsuji o meguru bōken* (1982) (trans. *A Wild Sheep Chase* (1989)) helps destroy the real monster, the all too human henchman of a sinister right-wing politician. In *Dansu dansu dansu* (1988) (trans. *Dance, Dance, Dance* (1988)) the protagonist's murdered girlfriend Kiki returns as a sobbing presence, crying for the protagonist who is too frozen in cool emotionlessness to be able to shed tears for himself.

Murakami's ghosts are internal ones in that they have a strong personal relationship to the protagonists in his works. Thus, in *Dance, Dance, Dance*, the narrator asks the ghost of Kiki, "But you did call me, didn't you? It was you who guided me along, wasn't it?" She answers, "It was you who called yourself, guided yourself, through me. I'm your phantom dance partner. I'm your shadow. I'm not anything more" (p. 371).

These ghosts are thus related to Murakami's conception of the *doppelgänger* developed in the "End of the World" side of *Hard Boiled Wonderland and the End of the World*, a shadow self who takes care of the other self. But the protagonist responds to Kiki's answer by putting himself in the mind of Kiki's murderer (another potential *doppelgänger* of the protagonist). "But I wasn't strangling her, I was strangling my shadow. If only I could choke off my shadow, I'd get some health" (p. 371).

Paradoxically, it is the shadows/ghosts who are the "healthiest" entities in *Dance, Dance, Dance*. It is they who mourn and sob for the protagonist's emptiness. And it is they who are willing to try and help him.

Murakami's ghosts are hardly subversive. Indeed, a case might be made that they act as palliatives for the difficulties of reality. At the same time, however, their existence suggests alternatives or at least emendations to that reality.

"HOORAY FOR MONSTERS!": THE IDEOLOGICAL ALIEN

In this next section we turn to a group of works in which the alien is blatantly subversive. In these works the alien is there to disrupt consensus reality as much as possible, to forcibly place alternatives to it in the reader's vision. Unlike the works previously discussed, which were intensely personal, inner-directed, and sometimes escapist, the direction of these works is outward, toward the "real" world. Where the alien in the works of the previous section was usually seen as something to be concealed if at all possible, these aliens are highly public, glorying in their exposure.

Power is also an explicit issue in works dealing with the ideological alien, in quite different ways than works treating the internal alien. While the strategies of texts dealing with the internal alien also often revolved around issues of power and control, these were of a personal kind. Sōseki's dreamers are almost all passive, unable to do more than observe or at best engage in futile struggle with the complexities of modern life. Akutagawa's artists long for power but are ultimately unable to control it when it is granted to them.

In contrast, while the ideological alien often seems powerless *vis-à-vis* society this alien is usually intent on changing the equation. Thus, Kyōka's demons bring floods down on disbelieving villagers and cut off the heads of ignorant men trespassing in their castle. Ōe's dispossessed marginals in *Dōjidai gēmu* (The Game of Contemporaneity) (1979) engage in an elaborate series of games with the central government in an attempt to deceive the authorities.

Aggressive and extreme, the ideological alien is usually a monster rather than a ghost. It forces readers to confront not so much their own inadequacies and fears as those of society around them. At its most extreme, this type of alien is used to construct a wide variety of revenge fantasies, often within an overtly political framework that ranges from the reactionary to the liberal. Rather than escape reality, the ideological alien directly subverts reality through a celebration of the monstrous, the marginal, and the outsider.

This subversive function of the alien initially seems quite modern but, if anything, the ideological alien has as long a tradition in Japan as the internal one. The twelfth-century animal scrolls caricaturing priests as frogs and monkeys are a pictorial forerunner of this sort of imaginative subversion. The entire Zen tradition, both pictorial and literary, may be seen as an attempt to look at the world from the outside. But the most obvious use of the alien as satire occurs in the literature of the Edo period, especially in the works of Hiraga Gennai, whose fantastic worlds included a good share of bizarre and grotesque creatures. The Edo period is also the time when the first Japanese robots, the mechanical dolls known as *karakirijin* were invented, and they too were used for comic satire on society.

It is perhaps not surprising therefore, that Izumi Kyōka (1873–1939), the first modern writer of the ideological alien I will be discussing, was a thoroughgoing conservative who was far better versed in traditional literature, particularly that of the Edo period, than in contemporary Western fiction. As was discussed in Chapter 2, Kyōka's personal or perhaps professional misfortune was to be a traditional writer doomed to forge his career at the height of the Meiji fascination with the West. In literary terms this fascination was particularly allied to the Naturalist movement, a movement which Kyōka regarded as anathema. Paradoxically, however, this professional misfortune may have had good effects on Kyōka's writing. Although his traditional romantic style led to his vilification by the Naturalists and to a certain amount of critical disregard for many years following his death, the tension between modernity and tradition may actually have empowered Kyōka's literature. The exquisite yet passionate intensity with which Kyōka evokes his monstrous ghosts makes him perhaps the greatest fantasist of the writers to be considered here.

Kyōka's fantastic landscape and characters (ghosts, demons, talking animals, and enchantresses figure prominently in his fiction) are both alien in the eyes of modern Japan at the same time as they are as intimately familiar, rising from the woodblock prints, kabuki drama, and legends of the late Edo period. They are thus what might be called the "familiar alien," similar to the guardian gods which Sōseki's dreamer tried so fervently to discover in the trees of the Meiji period. The difference is, however, that Kyōka's protagonists can and do discover the alien in the present age, often through the motif of a physical journey that is also a journey in time and psyche as well. Furthermore, although Kyōka presents these demons and ghosts at times as simply a refuge from modernity, more often he shows them attacking and triumphing against the modern, symbolized often in the figure of disbelieving materialistic males.[36] In these revenge fantasies it is finally the modern characters who become, often literally, dehumanized, turned into beasts or else destroyed by the powers of old Japan.

Like his longtime friend Yanagita Kunio, Kyōka found and presented a traditional Japan which, although filled with the grotesque and the bizarre, ultimately offered a more attractive alterity, one that was warm and familiar in comparison to the new and alien collectivity symbolized by the ideals of "Civilization and Enlightenment." At first glance this alternative collectivity is a frightening one, alien in its own way. It is a world of literally bloodthirsty ghosts, gigantic talking crabs and enchantresses who turn men into beasts.

But this grotesque world is actually attractive in many ways. Like a late Edo print, it is both highly colored and exciting. Also like a woodblock print, it is a known quantity. Audiences and readers could relax in a literary world that they remembered from childhood, full of striking transformations and bizarre manifestations that were, withal, more understandable than the real transformations going on around them.

Thus, Kyōka's metamorphoses are seldom "meaningless" in a Kafka-esque sense. Like the frightening woman who teaches the man a lesson in the Yanagita tale quoted at the beginning of this chapter, these are metamorphoses with a message. An interesting example of the two different kinds of metamorphoses, modern versus traditional, occurs in Kyōka's masterpiece *Kōya hijiri*, where a Darwinian/apocalyptic vision of devolution into leeches is contrasted to a very traditional form of what might be called "revenge metamorphosis," the transformation of evil/lustful men into animals.

Another revenge fantasy which also includes metamorphosis is Kyōka's extraordinary play *Yashagaike* (Demon Pond) written in 1913. In this work a young writer from the city finds happiness in the depths of the mountains with a beautiful wife and a strange duty, that of tolling the village bell every night at midnight. If he fails, legend goes, the village will be destroyed by a flood unleashed by the demon princess who lives at the bottom of the pond. Kyōka's work effectively counterposes the normal life of the young writer and the villagers with the highly colored dramatics of the monstrous denizens of Demon Pond.

Ultimately, however, the two worlds meet in tragedy. The writer, visited by a long-lost friend from the city, is unable to return to toll the bell and his wife is prevented from doing so by the oafish, disbelieving villagers. The demon princess finally escapes and the villagers receive their appropriate punishment of death by drowning. As for the young writer and his wife, there is at least a suggestion that they are granted a transformation into the new king and queen of Demon Pond, a meta-morphosis for the better, apparently.

Kyōka's demons are fascinating in their many manifestations. Some, especially his female ghosts, are genuinely frightening, but even at their most bloodthirsty they remain far less threatening and three-dimensional than the internal aliens conjured by Sōseki or Akuta-gawa. Even a story with some psychological suspense, such as "Sannin no mekura no hanashi" (1912) (trans. "A Tale of Three Who Were Blind" (1956)), suggests a strong division between the spirit world and the world of the real in Kyōka's work.

This is also true in the architectural and landscape features of Kyōka's tales. His demons tend to be in hidden valleys or enclosed in black towers, or pent up in ponds. They are a hidden menace that might leap out at one in the dark, but they do not come from inside the psyche.

Ultimately, of course, Kyōka's demons cannot venture much further beyond the haunted inner valley, and they remain powerful but safely removed from modern life. Other writers besides Kyōka, however, have seen traditional Japan as a fantasy world that offers an alternative to the modern world. Of these, Kawabata is the most famous, but most of his "worlds," although imbued with a fairytale quality, are not strictly fantasy. Furthermore, his magical Japan is offered more as a refuge than as a gauntlet to the modern world.

Surprisingly, one writer who followed in Kyōka's footsteps to use the myth of an alien old Japan was Akutagawa, whom we dealt with in the section on the internal alien. The story that most effectively exemplifies his use of the ideological alien is his surprisingly poignant "Kamigami no bishō" (The Faint Smiles of the Gods) (1921). In this short, provocative tale the alien is initially seen in the form of a Western-er, one Padre Organtino, a Christian missionary in Nagasaki during the Edo period.

In contrast to Sōseki's dream of the Western ship where the West-erners are viewed as outsiders, however, Akutagawa focuses the story sympathetically through the Westerner's eyes. He thus forces his reader to "identify" with the missionary *vis-à-vis* the foreign land of Japan. In this story it is Japan which is the alien rather than the Westerners.

Japan becomes even more alien when the priest is treated to a vision straight out of the *Kojiki*. In this vision a group of ancient Japanese gods appear in front of him in a re-enactment of the scene in which Ameterasu, the sun goddess, is lured out of hiding by the lewd tricks and noisy dancing of the other gods.

Akutagawa presents this scene as a frighteningly pagan vision of almost orgiastic intensity, thus heightening the priest/reader's sense of difference. Stunned and discouraged, the priest goes on to encounter another Japanese god, in the guise of an old man who delivers the story's final warning:

> Perhaps even the Christian God will become a native of this country. China and Japan changed. The West must also change. We are among the trees, in the current of shallow water, in the evening light that falls on the temple walls, in the wind that blows through the rose bushes. Everywhere and at all times. Watch out for us!

(my translation)

Akutagawa's text offers an overtly ideological message but one that is hardly surprising. What is surprising is the way "Kamigami no bishō" uses difference to inscribe the message. Rather than encoding the Westerner as alien, the text clearly shows the Japanese as exotic, frightening deities, and finally celebrates this very exoticism, even monstrousness, suggesting that it is the West rather than Japan which must transform itself.

This celebration of monstrousness becomes an increasingly important trend in postwar fiction, although in this case the ideological framework is radical rather than conservative. The most obvious and fervent exponent of this form of linking the political with the alien is Abe Kōbō, whose *The Face of Another* we have previously discussed. *The Face of Another* demonstrates Abe's ability to blend the inner with the ideological alien, but other texts are far more explicitly political. Thus, in "Shinda musume no uta" (1954) (trans. "Song of a Dead Girl" (1986)) Abe shows the variety of downward transformations of a young farm girl, from factory worker, to prostitute, to corpse, to finally a ghost. Unlike the vengeful female ghosts of Tokugawa fiction, this girl's power is of a quieter, more passive kind: her dead self functions as an eternal comment on an oppressive and exploitative system.

As should be clear from the examples already given, Abe's fiction often turns on metamorphosis. Sometimes it can be a subtle one as in his 1967 play *Tomodachi* (trans. *Friends* (1977)), when the smiling normal family "turns into" a demonic form of thought police. In other works Abe pulls out all the fantastic stops to depict a society in which metamorphosis is pushed from outside by some evil, or at least overwhelming, force which the victim is powerless to counter.

Abe's famous early story "Bō" (1955) (trans. "Stick" (1966)) is one such example of a metamorphosis that is both internal and ideological in that the character, a typical salaryman father who just happens to turn into a stick one day, clearly represents the passive everyman of the modern condition. Less sinister than the pathetic scientist in *The Face of Another*, he is still no hero. The story ends with the stick being examined and tossed away, found wanting for having led a boring useless life.

The combination of inner alienation and outer conspiracy leading to metamorphosis occurs in innumerable other Abe stories from his 1949 story "Dendorokakaria" (trans. "Dendracacalia" (1991)) to "S. Karumashi no hanzai" (1951) (trans. "The Crime of S. Karma" (1991)) to *Mikai* (1991) (trans. *Secret Rendezvous* (1980)) in which virtually all the characters have turned into the demonic. As was evident in the works discussed in Chapter 3, Abe's later work seems increasingly nihilistic. Where "Song of a Dead Girl" gave some dignity and meaning to her transformation, much of Abe's late work seems more and more to revel in transformation for the sake of itself. But this is not transformation for narrative excitement as in the postmodern terms of Tsutsui's "Kaomen hōkai" (Collapsing Face) (1978). Instead it may be seen as a nihilistic comment on the absurdity and horror of modern life.

Perhaps his most complete comment upon the alien is in his early novel *Dai yonkampyō-ki* (1958) (trans. *Inter Ice Age 4* (1970)). In this work a man is first alienated from himself by having his personality "doubled" by being fed into a computer. He is then alienated from his son and indeed from the next generation of human beings by having his embryonic child transformed into an Aquan, a creature with gills developed to survive an anticipated ice age.

Inter Ice Age 4 is another brilliant meditation on the *doppelgänger* motif and it contains certain features reminiscent of Sōseki's "Dream of the Third Night" and of Endō's *Sukyandaru* (1986) (trans. *Scandal* (1988)). As in Sōseki's story, there is an all-knowing other self, this time the computer, and a monstrous baby. Also like the Sōseki story, and like the child in Akutagawa's *Kappa*, this baby is related to past, present and future. In the case of the Sōseki work, the tale ends with man and child welded together forever in mutual guilt and self-loathing. The Kappan child, we remember, rejects the future because of the past (heredity), and refuses to be born. In the case of Abe's Aquans, they already are the future, and their very existence is a rejection of their parent's past. Not only are people alien from each other but the future itself is alien.

The theme of father and grotesque child is given another twist in the fiction of Abe's near contemporary Ōe Kenzaburō. In this case the son is a brain-damaged child who, with his father, appears in various guises throughout Ōe's oeuvre. In "Sora no kaibutsu Aguii" (1964) (trans. "Aghwee the Sky Monster" (1977)), for example, the handicapped infant is explicitly identified with the liberating power of the imagination: a young musician, who allowed his brain-damaged infant son to die, finds himself followed constantly by a gigantic baby in the sky. His father hires a young student to look after the musician, and the two men plus the phantom baby go on a number of amusing expeditions. In the end, however, the composer dies, walking in front of a truck in an apparent attempt to save his baby.

The young student is not so sure. He confronts the dying composer suggesting that "Aghwee" was just an excuse for the composer to commit suicide. The composer says nothing as the student shouts, "I was about to believe in Aghwee!" (p. 433). In the long run, however, Aghwee's existence or absence proves immaterial, for the student himself finds that he can now see a group of aliens, lost parts of himself, in the sky.

The delightful "Aghwee" harks back to some of Akutagawa's early fantasies about the transforming power of art and the imagination. In other of Ōe's works, however, the brain-damaged child becomes a heavily charged symbol of the marginalized and disenfranchised Others of modern society. Furthermore, these marginals are often aggressively aligned against society.

In *Pinchirannā chōshō* (1976) (trans. *The Pinchrunner Memorandum* (1994)) a fascinating variation on the father and monstrous child theme occurs. A thirty-eight-year-old father and his brain-damaged son literally change places, the father becoming a teenager, the son becoming his thirty-eight-year-old protector. Here the bond between the two is as intense as in "Aghwee," but it is also liberating, with both generations encompassing the future and the past. Their mutual identification with the monstrous now complete, the two join a drear group of bizarre comrades, including ghosts. The dead and the transmogrified go on a long march that hopes to rescue the world from the prospects of nuclear annihilation.

In a world of grotesques, Ōe's angry satire forces the reader to choose among the varieties of monstrousness. Language also becomes part of Ōe's weaponry, since the idiot child, unlike the preternaturally articulate babes of Sōseki and Akutagawa, speaks only nonsense, lost in a prelinguistic world of the imaginary where the loneliness of the self has not been recognized.

Ōe also brings up to date the notion of an alternative collectivity of the alien introduced in Kyōka. His most complete version of this is in his 1979 *tour de force*, *Dōjidai gēmu* (The Game of Contemporaneity).

Like Kyōka's *Kōya hijiri*, *Dōjidai gēmu* revolves around a hidden valley full of aliens, in this case a group of villagers who are equated both with rebels against the shogunate and with Ōe's notion of the rebel deities who were forced out of heaven by the gods of the Japanese imperial family.

Not content with being exiled, however, the outcasts are actually willing to wage war against the central power symbolized by the Japanese imperial army. Even though they inevitably lose the war, the marginals win in another fashion, through staging two disappearing tricks, once through a maze constructed by the village children, and once from the records of Japanese history and from the census book through the non-registration of twins. These are aliens, then, whose powers lie in the "normal" person's inadequate perceptions of all that reality can encompass, as "Aghwee" also suggested.

The aliens are led by The Destroyer, a figure who, like the idiot child in Ōe's other works, mixes both past and future, and infantile and adult. At the novel's end The Destroyer is reported to have been reborn and is perhaps ready to lead his people into confrontation once more.

Ōe's marginals use different, more sophisticated weapons than the demons of Kyōka, yet, surprisingly, the two writers ultimately share a common perception; that the best of Japan lies hidden in the dark spaces of Japanese culture. Ōe, Abe and Kyōka also share an anger against society and an unwillingness to subdue that anger. In their privileging of the marginal they recall the section from *Secret Rendezvous* quoted at the beginning of this chapter, "Hooray for Monsters! Monsters are the embodiment of the weak" (p. 172).

It is interesting to pose the question as to whether the ideological alien is entirely ascendant in modern Japanese fiction. We remember that our continuum of alien faces ended with Tsutsui's postmodern celebration of change for the sake of change. In a still hierarchical Japan, such a highlighting of change may perhaps be read as anti-authoritarian.[37]

The emphasis in "Kaomen hōkai" (Collapsing Face) on agonized metamorphosis is echoed in other contemporary media as well. Perhaps the best-known example is Ōtomo Katsuhiro's bestselling comic and animated movie *Akira*. Although *Akira* will be discussed in more detail in Chapter 6, it should be mentioned that both film and comic book contain some extraordinary scenes of mutation on the part of the work's teenaged anti-hero Tetsuo. As with Tsutsui's "Kaomen hōkai," the effect of these transformations on reader/viewer is less ideological than visceral. The dissolution of boundaries expressed in Tetsuo's mutations is both shocking and exhilarating, even disgusting.

Tetsuo's metamorphoses, with their privileging of a fluid subject, seem a long way from the variety of fixed and lonely selves described in Sōseki's *Ten Nights of Dream*. In that respect they are perhaps fundamentally more subversive than Sōseki's characters, who accepted the fact of a fixed identity. Tetsuo's awesome transformative powers as well as those of the other mutants in *Akira* suggest a subverting of all boundaries, especially the hierarchical ones that still characterize contemporary Japanese society.

Ōtōmo's monstrous characters confront and even directly attack the Japanese establishment. In some ways they may be seen as the comic book versions of the monstrous new generation that Sōseki, Akutagawa and Abe depict so fearsomely. In Tetsuo's case, his new powers come very close to destroying the world, although, in *Akira*'s dystopian view, this is a world which will not lose much by its own destruction.

If *Akira*'s new generation seem bent on asserting their alienness in order to destroy, the characters of his bestselling contemporary Murakami initially seem bent on using their alien associations only to escape. This difference may be due to the fact that Murakami's protagonists are almost always of the "everyman" type. It is usually not they who suffer metamorphoses but those around them, most frequently turning into ghosts. Yet, Murakami's use of ghosts hints that, even for an everyman, it is, finally, impossible to escape either oneself or the past (unless, like Boku in *Hard Boiled Wonderland and the End of the World*, we build our own fantasy world inside our heads).

Thus, in *Dance, Dance, Dance*, the protagonist tries to find the hotel where he and his girlfriend Kiki had previously stayed on their journey to Hokkaido depicted in *A Wild Sheep Chase*. He finally finds the hotel, but it has been transformed, knocked down and rebuilt into a glittering symbol of what the protagonist sourly calls "the elephant's graveyard of advanced capitalism" (p. 123); it seems that only the name remains the same. The protagonist discovers, however, that there is a phantom sixteenth floor, onto which he steps one night. There he finds a familiar ghost, The Sheep Man, who talks to him about "thethingsyoulost" and "thethingsyou'regoingtolose [sic]" (p. 83).

Loss and memories pervade *Dance, Dance, Dance*, from the obliterated hotel sacrificed to rapacious real estate developers, to the many obliterated relationships in the protagonist's life. In some ways the protagonist prefers this. For example, he says of a potential new relationship, that it would be just "another thing to lose."

At the same time, however, the protagonist longs for connection. The Sheep Man knows this and tells him, "We'lldowhatwecanto-connectyouwithwhatyouwant," but he adds, "... evenifwesucceed,no-promisesyou'llbehappy" (p. 85).

Ultimately, the protagonist realizes that identity is indeed the aggregation of experiences mentioned in *Hard Boiled Wonderland and the End of the World*, a collection from the past which he cannot escape. Thus, toward the novel's end, still searching for Kiki, he finds himself once again in a place of phantoms, a living room with six skeletons on the sofa, five of whom he identifies as dead friends or lovers. As for the sixth skeleton, could it be the protagonist himself?

In Murakami's world the self rather than society is the final adjudicator. But he acknowledges a multiplicity of selves, of projections, some of which are more positive than others. Murakami's protagonists may also end up in a desert of mirrors, but at least in those mirrors they see different potentials of the self. While Ōtomo's transformations go outward to the monstrous, Murakami's go inward to help his protagonist find unexplored parts of the self.

It is still arguable that Murakami's vision is less subversive than compensatory, but his insistent use of ghosts can also be read as having ideological implications. As Lois Zamora says, "ghosts are liminal, metamorphic, intermediary, existing in/between/on modernity's boundaries of physical and spiritual, magical and real, and challenge the lines of demarcation."[38]

Murakami's ghosts are not only personal ones. The phantom Dolphin Hotel carries "the burden of traditional and collective memory,"[39] as Zamora puts it, existing in stark contrast to the anonymous new hotel which replaces it. By insisting on the Dolphin's absence, the Dolphin remains present. And in a Japan where the self is increasingly seen as images, the protagonist's final acknowledgement of the importance of memory and experience can be seen as a gauntlet thrown down against an impersonal desert of mirrors.

NOTES

1 The literature on the Japanese self is enormous and varied. Two works that usefully compare the Japanese sense of self with that of the West are G. DeVos, 1985, and N. Rosenberger, 1992.

2 Ghosts are an extremely popular subject in Japanese folkloric and literary critical studies. One particularly interesting discussion between Matsuda and Yura asserts that the Japanese word for turning into a ghost (*bakeru*) actually means to turn into one's real self (Matsuda, 1974, p. 17). This would suggest that even premodern Japanese understood that the ghost

was not necessarily something outside the self but rather a manifestation of a hidden aspect of the soul.

3   T. Todorov, 1975, p. 92.

4   T. Heller, 1987, pp. 46–8.

5   The ideological alien also plays an important part in Japanese film and popular culture as well, as the anti-nuclear message of *Godzilla* attests.

6   The importance of the alien is not confined only to Japanese fantasy, of course. Christopher Nash discusses the increased fascination with "Otherness" and metamorphosis in twentieth-century anti-realist fiction, noting the existence of many characters who are "perpetually in flight from the unstable external identities of which they're composed and cry for escape into the artificial act of private creation or into death itself" (C. Nash, 1987, p. 181).

7   Todorov, 1975, p. 112.

8   J. Grixti, 1989, p. 17.

9   Animal possessions can sometimes be male as well but the overwhelming preponderance is by the female. Interestingly, even in contemporary Japan one can find instances of fox possession among the so-called "new religions". Winston Davis records some cases, "undeniably sexual in nature" (Davis, 1980, p. 178; see also p. 90).

10 D. Richie, 1983, p. 9.

11 Grixti, 1989, p. 172.

12 Nash, 1987, p. 181.

13 Nash, 1987, p. 185.

14 This subtlety is in interesting contradistinction to Japanese graphic art, which throughout the nineteenth century depicted the monstrous in extraordinary and grotesque detail. From that point of view, Tsutsui's vivid descriptions, although arguably postmodern, do contain an aspect of the traditional as well.

15 Todorov, 1975, p. 116.

16 A. Tudor, 1989, p. 222.

17 D. Kellner, 1992, p. 144.

18 Tatsumi Takayuki has suggested that Tsutsui's story actually revolves around the threatening power of language and the act of reading itself. Just as the hypothetical face is penetrated to the point of experiencing hallucinatory sensations, so is the reader invaded and forced into experiencing the unreal (Tatsumi, 1988, pp. 79–80; my translation).

19 R. Jackson, 1981, pp. 116–18 passim.

20 W. R. Irwin, 1976, p. 101.

21 The most paradigmatic of these "meaningless transformations" can be found in Kafka. See Jackson, 1981, p. 160.

22 E. Ohnuki-Tierney, 1987, pp. 158–59.

23 Oka Yasuo, Kasahara Nobuo and Soya Shinpei, 1979, p. 2.

24 What Nash says of the *doppelgänger* in Western anti-realism is even more pertinent to modern Japanese fantasy:

In the single image of the doppelganger a double anguish may now be invoked. The Realistic struggle for objectivity, even about oneself – and the struggle to get out of, to be free of oneself ... meets the thwarted yearning for oneness which for some is the very motive impulse behind traditional fantasy. Nash, 1987, p. 183.

25 See, for example, the essays collected in J. T. Rimer, 1990b.

26 For what is perhaps the classic discussion of the Meiji-Taisho period's interest in the new individual see Sōseki's famous essay "My Individualism" in Sōseki, 1992, pp. 285–315.

27 Regarding "Dream of the First Night," Atsumi Koko suggests that the woman in that dream represents transcendent lyricism in contrast to the "reality" of the woman with pigs in "Dream of the Tenth Night." K. Atsumi, 1989, p. 135.

28 It is also possible to interpret this dream as symptomatic of sexual unease. In this case the ship which thrusts endlessly forward to the sinking red sun can easily be read as a phallic symbol. The "I"'s decision to leave the ship can therefore be interpreted as a desire to escape the sexual through death, a theme already played out in "Dream of the First Night." I am indebted to my student Jane Britting for pointing out this interpretation to me.

29 Actually there is still *another* buried self in the forest, and that is the female one. Formally and significantly absent from a story that has clear Oedipal implications, the female presence can still be found in the brooding womblike presence of the forest itself.

30 It is interesting to compare this *doppelgänger* drama with Henry James's famous double story "The Jolly Corner." Although very different in style and content, both works may be seen to have been written by men of letters attempting to work through their mixed feelings about their native country and their own past. In the case of James's story, it is an alternative past that "might have been" and he is able to excoriate the double, "haunt the ghost," as he puts it. In Sōseki's story it is a past event which cannot be escaped, because the burden of self-consciousness is too heavy to be ever fully lifted. Commenting on James's story, Karl Miller points out how often what he calls "dualistic writers" have "suffered the excitements and uncertainties of dual nationality" (K. Miller, 1987 p. 239). Sōseki also wrote mimetic fiction involving the double as well, the most famous example being *Kokoro*.

31 Rimer, 1990, p. 4.

32 D. Roden, 1990, p. 55.

33 Another vision of the fantastic power of art, this time a gently ironic one, is Nakajima Ton's "Sangetsuki" (1942) (trans. "Tiger Poet") (1962). In this funny but poignant story a would-be poet is so consumed by his artistic arrogance that he turns into a tiger, but a tiger who, pitifully, still insists on repeating his less than inspired verses.

34 D. Keene, 1984, p. 584.

35 The critical literature on what Murakami "represents" in terms of the new generation of writers is already so vast as to constitute a scholarly cottage industry in itself! One of the most interesting of the many books on him, however, is Kuroko Kazuo's *Murakami Haruki to dōjidai no bungaku* (Murakami Haruki and Contemporary Literature) (1990). In this work Kuroko discusses the notion of "reality" in contemporary literature. He also sets Murakami and Ōe Kenzaburō at opposite ideological poles in the current Japanese literary world and extensively quotes Ōe's thoughtful assessment of Murakami. Oe sees Murakami's protagonists not so much as "escapist" but rather as passive consumers of a materially abundant but spiritually empty society (p. 33).

36 See Fujimoto Tokuaki, 1980, p. 80.
37 For a discussion of Tsutsui's anti-authoritarianism in relation to Ōe's ideological positioning see Teruhiko Tsuge, 1984, pp. 120–123.
38 L. Zamora, 1995, p. 7.
39 Zamora, 1995, p. 1.

5 Logic of inversion
Twentieth-century Japanese Utopias

In our discussions of the alien and women in modern Japanese fantasy we have seen a variety of different and sometimes contradictory impulses at work. On the one hand, we have seen the fantastic used as a wish-fulfillment strategy. In the prewar period, for example, fantasy women were often seen as saviors, rescuing the male from the complexities of modernity. More rarely, the alien has also fulfilled that function, particularly in the form of Kawabata's ghosts, who transport his protagonists into a better world or compensate them for the disappointments of the real world.

We have also seen the fantastic used as a form of revenge or attack. Izumi Kyōka's supernatural women and demons are examples of prewar resistance, maintaining premodern beliefs and traditions in the face of modernity's onslaught. In the postwar period the grotesques of Ōe Kenzaburō and Abe Kōbō confront and horrify established society.

Both of these impulses are implicitly or explicitly involved in another strategy of the fantastic, its use as a form of 'message," highlighting the problems of modernity through defamiliarizing them in the most extreme fashion possible. Thus, Ōba Minako's "Yamauba no bisho" (1976) (trans. "The Smile of the Mountain Witch" (1982)), in which an ordinary woman sees herself as a mountain witch, alone in the wilderness, is both a wish-fulfillment fantasy and a message concerning the inadequacies and frustrations of women's lives.

All the above impulses, wish-fulfillment, confrontation, and expressing a message are important subtexts to the subjects of the next two chapters, the fantastic worlds of Utopia and dystopia. More than any of the fiction thus far explored, the fantasies examined in these two chapters are "message fiction." Using the fundamental Utopian/dystopian tropes of a journey to an alternative world, the writers in these two chapters consciously confront the disappointing consensus reality of twentieth-century Japan.

These worlds are clearly meant to subvert the *status quo*. Far from being isolated wish-fulfillment fantasies (although they can function in that way as well), the Utopias described here are presented as urgent possible alternatives, blueprints for a better Japan. The dystopias described here, on the other hand, are warnings, fantastic extrapolations of alarming trends that are meant to disturb, shock, and ultimately move the reader to action.

This chapter will concentrate on Utopias, examining the Utopian novels of Miyazawa Kenji, Inoue Hisashi, Ishikawa Jun and Ōe Kenzaburō. It will also include a discussion of Kurahashi Yumiko's fascinating but problematic deconstruction of Utopia, *Amanonkoku ōkanki* (Record of a Voyage to the Country of Amanon) (1987) to serve as a bridge to our next chapter on the dystopian imagination. All these novels differ significantly from each other in terms of style and content but they also contain enough important similarities to develop a general paradigm of the twentieth-century Japanese Utopia: In fascinating contrast to the general stereotype of the monolithic Japan Incorporated, these are worlds that are fluid, heterogeneous, and united only in their opposition to hierarchy and the central establishment. Even at their most moderate, as in Miyazawa Kenji's work, they are notably progressive, even radical Utopias, highlighting movement over stasis, anarchy over control.

Where do these radical Utopias come from? Are they part of an indigenous Japanese tradition or do they stem largely from Western influences? In fact, these Utopias are a largely modern phenomenon, although they do maintain some important connections with the past, notably the privileging of the pastoral over the urban on the part of Miyazawa, Inoue and Ōe. It is useful, therefore, to examine the Utopian impulse in relation to Japanese culture as a whole.

UTOPIAS IN JAPANESE CULTURE

Utopias, one of the most central images in all fantastic literature, have an interesting relationship to modern Japanese history. Based on the definition of a Utopia as a "place of ideal perfection, especially in law, government, and social conditions,"[1] it might be said that modern Japanese culture has been founded upon consciously Utopian longings. More than any other non-communist country, Japan in the late nineteenth and twentieth centuries has been animated and directed by a clear-cut ideology that looked forward to a Utopian form of progress.

Obviously, other non-communist nations, most notably the United States, have been guided by ideological principles as well. What makes Japan unique is the remarkable involvement at every level, on the part of the government, private citizenry, business, and educational institutions, in a highly conscious ideology of progress. The fact that this ideology was clearly promoted in relation to the ideal of catching up with and surpassing the West does not make it any less Utopian, but it may be one of the major reasons why it was so successful.

Thus, Carol Gluck notes that "the late 1880's marked an upsurge of ideological activity ... prompted in part by a surfeit of change."[2] Attempts were made to stop change by turning back the clock but this proved impossible. As Gluck sums it up,

> In any case, by 1890 too much had changed; there was no possibility of going home again. It was partly because so many recognized this – some with fear, others with anticipation – that the ideological momentum gathered as it did in the late 1880's.[3]

What Gluck calls "the ideological momentum" ebbed and flowed throughout the prewar years and changed from a politically based pattern to one based more on economic attainments in the postwar period. Even so, an arguably Utopian belief in progress seems a fundamental part of both periods. In the prewar period, until the rise of the militarists in the late 1920s and early 1930s, this notion of progress consisted of modernization and Westernization, advanced through slogans such as the idealistic "Civilization and Enlightenment" and the more pragmatic "Rich Country, Strong Army".

In the postwar years, after the Occupation, the program shifted to economic advancement and democratization. The postwar ideal was a more personal one, based on a vision of a materially comfortable and homogeneous middle-class culture supported by double-digit economic growth. Appropriately, its slogans were expressed in the material imagery of the "three c's" (car, cooler, color) in the 1960s or the "three v's" (villa, vacance, video) of the 1980s.

While modern Japanese society seems to be built on genuinely Utopian aspirations, the premodern period is more problematic. Certainly, a number of Western scholars of Utopianism such as Frank and Fritzi Manuel (1979) or Krishan Kumar (1987) flatly state that true Utopias are impossible to find outside the Western tradition.[4] Kumar and the Manuels base their assertion on a rather narrow definition of Utopia, derived from their analysis of the influences behind Thomas More's original *Utopia*.

In their version, there are two traditional Utopian paradigms: the first is the city-state based on the writings of the ancient Greeks, above all of Plato's *Republic*, combined with the post-apocalypse heavenly city of the Judeo-Christian tradition. It is this combination which produced the carefully planned, even static, ideal city-states of More's *Utopia* and Campanella's *City of the Sun*. The second paradigm is that of the pastoral Utopia, the Arcadia of the Greeks combined with the pre-Lapsarian Eden of the Bible, modernized in the nineteenth century into the agrarian-socialist visions of such writers as William Morris.

Even if we agree that these two paradigms are the fundamental models of Utopia, and they do appear to be the most universal,[5] there seems little difficulty in finding their functional equivalents in premodern East Asian culture, although perhaps not the detailed blueprints for a perfect society that the Manuels assert are essential to Utopia. For the static worlds of *Utopia* and *The City of the Sun*, one could easily substitute the whole Confucian tradition, with its emphasis on using order and hierarchy to create the perfect man, and, more specifically, we could mention the Confucian doctrine of a golden age under the Duke of Chou. For the Arcadian paradise, the obvious candidate would be found in the Taoist ideal of simplicity, in particular T'ao Ch'ien's essay-poem, "Tōgenkyō" (The Peach Blossom Spring), a tale of a lost village which has inspired countless generations of East Asian writers and philosophers up to the present, where the Chinese Communists have paid it the ultimate compliment of finding the roots of a primitive socialist society inscribed in the poem.

The Japanese enthusiastically took up both of these Chinese Utopian paradigms. As mentioned above, Confucianism became the basis of the Tokugawa state, while *Tōkengyō* has passed into common parlance in Japanese to mean the equivalent of the Western Shangri La. Like Shangri La, the term *"Tōgenkyō"* not only connotes an ideal world but also one that can be reached only through fantasy.

Perhaps the Chinese archetypes were particularly popular, because the early, indigenous, Japanese tradition does not seem to contain a Utopian ideal that approaches anywhere near the complexities of the Utopian archetypes found in either the West or China. The heavens where the gods dwell in the *Kojiki*, the earliest Shinto writings, is neither morally nor politically superior to life on earth. Although such premodern fantasies as the legend of Urashima Taro posit a world of material abundance, in this case the palace of the Dragon King beneath the sea, this refuge has no pretensions to any spiritual or moral higher ground. Nor is there much evidence of a deliberately constructed society with superior institutions that the philosophies of both China and the West contain.

Yura Kimyoshi, a scholar of English literature, and the writer Nakamura Shinichiro put forth a number of possible reasons for the absence of Utopian vision in Japanese culture. One cause is simply the
overwhelming dominance of China as an intellectual and cultural
model in premodern Japan. Not only were such stories as "Urashima
Taro" or the popular fantasy "Taketori Monogatari" (Tale of the
Bamboo Cutter) probably Chinese in origin but, generally, all visions
of ideal societies were based on Chinese models, thus making a specifically Japanese Utopia almost impossible. Yura and Nakamura also put
forth more culturally based reasons. Perhaps the most interesting one
is that the Japanese people did not see themselves as taking government and politics into their own hands, and thus were less likely to be
either politically discontented or to envision political change as a
remedy for problems around them.[6]

Nakamura and Yura find in the tradition of *shukke* (the forsaking
of the world on the part of a Buddhist priest) a possible Utopian
model. But this form of ideal life, as they admit, is in many ways the
opposite of the Utopian ideal, which has at its base the belief that
society, rather than the individual, should change. *Shukke* can consequently be seen as the recognition that Utopia is fundamentally impossible to realize on a society-wide level. Intriguingly, Nakamura suggests
that the *shukke* tradition lives on in Japanese fiction in the form of the
resolutely apolitical *shishōsetsu* (autobiographical novel), where the
writer consciously turns his back on society.[7] This "world-rejecting
tradition" can also be found in postwar women's fantasy, as was seen
in Chapter 3.

To return to the premodern tradition, however, we can discover a
specifically Japanese yearning for a kind of aesthetic Utopia, as in *The
Tale of Genji*, which speaks nostalgically of a vanished world of an
elite in possession of aesthetically, if not morally, superior accomplishments. It is this ideal that Hino finds in his book *Edojin to yūtopia*
(1977), where he suggests that upper-class interest in ancient poetic
form proceeded from an aesthetic escapism that sought a better, i.e.,
artistically superior, world in which people were valued for their artistic accomplishments rather than their power or learning.[8] Hino also
mentions the development of *Kokugaku* (National Learning), in particular Motōri Norinaga's conception of the Way of the Gods, as evidence of an interest in a native, Utopian tradition. But it must be said
that the *Kokugaku* scholar's ideal of *mono no aware* (the sadness of
things) is a long way from the complex and rigorous moral thought
posited by Western or Chinese Utopianists or even by the Japanese
Confucianists of the Edo period.

A more politically confrontational philosophy which also upholds a better world can be found in the writings of Andō Shōeki, a "forgotten thinker" of the Tokugawa period, who has been rediscovered by Japanese and Western scholars. Andō created a dystopian critique of contemporary Japan through the use of satirical animal legends. He also posited a Taoist style "Natural World," which he placed in Hokkaido, the then remote northernmost part of Japan. In Andō's fictional world, class and hierarchy, the cornerstones of Tokugawa institutions, were abolished. This "Natural World" has clearly Utopian elements, quite radical for the time, but Andō's works were never widely read; in fact, he was not even published during his lifetime. Furthermore, although Andō professed to despise Chinese culture, his Utopian ideals can still be seen as having clearly Chinese influences.

If we cannot find an indigenous political Utopia in the Edo period, we can find the beginnings of the literary format that Utopian writing would eventually take: the travel narrative. In it a person from the real world voyages to various fantastic countries. Saikaku's amorous hero's setting sail for the Isle of Women at the end of *Kōshoku ichidai otoko* (1682) (trans. *The Life of an Amorous Man* (1963)) is one example, but the most carefully worked of these fantastic voyages is Hiraga Gennai's mid-eighteenth-century *gesaku* (light or playful literature) work *Fūryū shidōkenden* (The Tale of the Free and Easy Asanoshin). This imaginative narrative follows its hero Asanoshin's adventures on a magic fan to such places as the Land of Giants and the Land of Pygmies, the Land of Play and the Land of Blockheads (this last being a satire on Confucian scholars).

Fūryū shidōkenden's fantastic countries do not approach the Utopian ideal, but their existence allows the narrative to perform one other important Utopian function – that of a highly conscious form of estrangement. The contrast of Utopian idealism with a defective reality is always implicitly in the background of any Utopian or fantastic work. Thus, as Adriana Delprat points out, *Fūryū shidōkenden*'s elaborate celebration of magical eroticism is in many ways an imaginative satire on the hypocrisies and repressions of the Tokugawa period.[9]

Utopias, then, are more than the dictionary definition of "an ideal state," they are alternative states. As such, they perform an important extra-literary role: to hold up an ideal as a challenge to their audience, thereby attacking either implicitly or explicitly the consensus reality. Or, as Yura Kimiyoshi in a discussion of Inoue Hisashi's *Kirikirijin* (The People of Kirikiri) (1980) puts it,

I call it the logic of inversion: the contrivances of reality, what we see with our own eyes, if you turn them around, they become some-thing completely strange . . . the great Utopian novels all have this kind of logic. They usually overturn reality.[10]

It is this inversion of reality that I would like to focus on for the rest of this chapter. To do so, we must be aware of the reality that is being inverted in order to understand the marked difference between the Utopias of the twentieth century and those of the Meiji period, for it is in the Meiji period that the first overtly Utopian novels were written. These novels were the well-known political novels (*seiji shōsetsu*) of the period and are little read today because of their didactic nature and simplistically allegorical narrative structure. Yet the Meiji political novel performed a vital function: it inverted the reality of post-shogu-nate, "backward," agricultural Japan and presented its readers with an alternative vision of a different world that was clearly better on many fronts, at least according to the Meiji government.

Just as premodern thought had privileged China or the remote past as ideal places, Meiji Utopias were set either in the West, or (typical of the so-called "euchronic" or "ideal-time" form of Utopia) in a future, better Japan. One of the most overtly Utopian of these works is the 1886 novel *Setchūbai* (1966) (Plum Blossoms in the Snow) by Suehiro Tetchō, whose prologue posits a Japan of 2040 stocked with modern technology, including warships and factories, where political rule is evenly administered between the emperor and a freely elected Diet. This combination, or perhaps conflation, of modern weaponry and technology with democracy is one that the Japan of the post-war era has learned to be wary of. Indeed, the evils of technology have become a key element in most twentieth-century anti-Utopian fiction, but it is very much a positive element of Meiji ideology and therefore of the Meiji political novel as well.

Given the importance of clearly Western elements as a basis for Utopia, it is not surprising that the West looms large in the political novels of this period. The Utopias depicted in these novels naturally belong to the city-state paradigm since, in a world where Confucian values had shattered, the relatively urbanized and rationalized West offered the only other paradigm of this sort. As is clear from a cursory look at Japanese history, the West itself has been a kind of Utopia for many of the enthusiastic young writers, intellectuals, and politicians of the Meiji period. Or, if not the West *per se*, then the vocabulary of Westernization, its technology, its ideologies, and its literature all suggested Utopian possibilities.

Turning now to our major examples of twentieth-century Utopian novels, we find the notion of the Western Other to be an important element in virtually all of them, although the attitude toward the West changes markedly by the late twentieth century. The early Meiji faith in the West becomes ever more attenuated as we move from the prewar Miyazawa and even Inoue's works of the 1960s, where the West is still seen as the site of exploration and Utopian possibilities, to the late 1970s and 1980s where Inoue, Ōe and Kurahashi regard Western hegemony with an increasingly jaundiced eye.

This change in attitude to the West is no doubt due at least partly to Japan's new prosperity and concomitant changing role in world politics. Given Japan's increased independence from Western aid and Western role models, it is not surprising that we find fewer and fewer cases of the West as an ideal. In fact, Kurahashi's *Amanonkoku ōkanki* (Record of a Voyage to the Country of Amanon) (1986) savagely satirizes Western theological, philosophical, and intellectual imperialism in the form of her main character, the aggressive missionary P from the aptly named Monokamikuni (One God Country). Ōe and Inoue are somewhat more tolerant. Although they also give short shrift to the Western establishment, their Utopian visions do allow for the possibility of a union of marginals from all countries.

As we examine twentieth-century Utopian novels more closely, we will see other important changes in the Japanese Utopian imagination that are clearly related to alterations in Japan's historical and global position. In general, the works discussed in this chapter move from an open-ended belief in progress and scientific enlightenment in the 1920s, i.e. Miyazawa's short children's novel *Ginga tetsudō no yoru* (Night Train to the Stars (1986)), to an increasingly narrow and less optimistic belief in change and subversion simply for their own sake, with less and less hope of a saving ideological framework. Finally, in Kurahashi's 1986 work, the whole notion of Utopianism is called into question. Utopian visions are an important part of Japanese fantasy, as we shall see, but by the end of the twentieth century they seem increasingly difficult to implement.

MIYAZAWA KENJI'S TICKET TO PROGRESS: *GINGA TETSUDŌ NO YORU* (NIGHT TRAIN TO THE STARS)

We begin our explorations of Utopias with a largely positive vision, however, *Ginga tetsudō no yoru* (Night Train to the Stars) by Miyazawa Kenji (1896–1933). Miyazawa, a poet, essayist, and writer of children's stories, is the most consistently optimistic of the five writers

I will be discussing. This is surprising, considering that Miyazawa spent most of his short life in poverty as an agronomist in northern Japan. What sustained him was his devout belief in the Hokke sect of Buddhism, combined with a perhaps naive faith in Western-style progress. This ardent optimism marks him as an obvious descendant of the Meiji ideology of "Civilization and Enlightenment," although the Taishō period during which he lived was, as we have seen in Chapter 5, a more complex and ambivalent time.

Miyazawa's writings themselves are a sometimes surreal but effective blend of his rather disparate beliefs. His works casually mix vocabulary from Buddhist doctrine with Marxist or revolutionary rhetoric, and often juxtapose this mixture against theoretical science. Thus, in one of his final poems, he challenges his readers to "try to form a new nature" and goes on to call for a "Marx of the new age" to:

reform this world that moves on blind
impulse
and give it a splendid, beautiful
system
Darwin of the new age:
board the Challenger of Oriental
meditation
and reach the space beyond the galaxy.
New poets:
Obtain new, transparent energy
from the clouds, from the light, from the storms
and suggest to man and the universe the
        shapes they are to take.[11]

Although strikingly unusual and almost verging on pastiche, these surreal combinations are held together by Miyazawa's basic philosophy, his delight in the beauty and mystery of the cosmos and his belief in the need to understand the world through a continuing process of education. For the universe, as he says, is "ceaselessly changed by us." Miyazawa's "beautiful new system" is an open-ended one, a philosophy that significantly contrasts with the static Utopia traditional to both the West and to East Asia.

Nowhere is that philosophy more evident than in his famous children's fantasy *Ginga tetsudō no yoru* (Night Train to the Stars). Written, and continuously revised throughout the 1920s, it was finally published posthumously in 1934 to immediate popular and critical acclaim. One of Miyazawa's American translators even proclaims that "[n]ever before had a Japanese writer attempted a fantasy of such sustained intensity."[12] While we may suggest Sōseki's *Ten Nights of Dream* or Akutagawa's *Kappa* as other possible candidates for such a description, it is certainly true that Miyazawa's story is remarkable for its originality and sheer imaginative scope.

Ginga tetsudō no yoru is not a description of Utopia *per se*, but rather a narrative dealing with ways to achieve Utopia on earth. It also differs from the other Utopian works to be discussed in that its geography is overtly fantastic. But, in the long run it remains true to the Utopian ideal of inverting and ultimately improving upon the real.

Miyazawa's tale begins with its young protagonist, Giovanni, being asked the question: "This vague white thing that some call a river, some call the Milky Way, do you know what it really is?" (p. 172) Giovanni is unable to give the technically correct reply of "stars," but the rest of the story is really an open-ended narrative answer to that question. In Miyazawa's vision, fantasy and science work together, so that when Giovanni finds himself aboard a train to the stars he finds that the stars are not merely balls of gas, but rather a variety of other worlds. These worlds range from the so-called "Pliocene Beach," where a scholarly man digs up dinosaur bones, to the "Southern Cross," a way station saturated with such Christian symbols as crowds singing "Ave Maria."

These worlds are stops on the Galactic Railroad, which Giovanni unwittingly finds himself riding along with his best friend Campanella. Although this device of placing a representative from the "real world" on a journey to the fantastic one is typical of Utopian fiction and of fantasy in general, Giovanni's "real world" hometown in *Ginga tetsudō no yoru* is a little more exotic than most. Apparently a small rural village, the hamlet contains almost no specifically Japanese elements: Giovanni searches for milk for his sick mother rather than Japanese-style gruel; he works in a small factory, rather than traditional rice planting; and his name and that of his best friend are of course Italian. Campanella, the name of Giovanni's friend, is the same as that of one of the earliest of European Utopianists, the author of *City of the Sun*! Whether this exoticism is meant to deepen the fantastic quality of the story or to make it more universal (or both) there is no question that the disappointments, humiliations, and poverty that afflict Giovanni are typical of the real world and of the early stages of a children's fantasy novel.

The train itself, the central symbol of the narrative, is also appropriate to both Utopian and children's fantasy. As a Western import, something new and exotic, it is a more appropriate vehicle for a modern journey to new worlds than was Asanoshin's magic fan. It is also a potentially dangerous piece of machinery, something implicitly high-lighted by Giovanni's discovery that all the people on the train except for him are dead. His friend Campanella has drowned in the village river, and the two children across from them are victims of a ship-wreck. This is, indeed, as Kurihara points out, a "journey of the dead," casting Miyazawa's fantasy in a somewhat grimmer light.[13]

The train also has an important narrative function. It is a continu-ously moving vehicle for which Giovanni is given a ticket that will "take him anywhere," as one character explains. The train's journey is an endless one, cutting across both space and time, in contrast to the closed, cyclical world of Giovanni's life in the village.

Makoto Ueda has pointed to the Buddhist influences underlying *Ginga tetsudō no yoru*, in particular the doctrine of *samsara*,[14] re-peated birth and death, as is seen when the train is delivering its load of passengers to their respective forms of heavenly rebirth. But, al-though the passengers on the train seem happily resigned to their fate, Giovanni's "go anywhere" ticket suggests that he, at least, is expected to break out of the cycle, as he does, by being returned to his village and told to continue his education.

In keeping with the technological and Western implications of the train, the ticket itself suggests a Western-style valorization of progress. At the end of the journey, Giovanni is told to "hold on to your ticket . . . you've got to stride through the fire and the fierce waves of the real world. You must never lose that ticket. It's the only real one in the Milky Way" (p. 240).

Despite its otherworldly setting, *Ginga tetsudō no yoru* is a Utopian fantasy that inverts reality only to insist ultimately that Utopias can and should be constructed on earth. Although the stops on the railway have a fairytale appeal, and the idea of a heavenly life after death may have initially assuaged Miyazawa's anguish over the death of a much loved younger sister, there is no suggestion that seeking life after death is a genuine solution to problems on earth. Thus, when Giovanni meets the two victims of the shipwreck who are about to get off at the Southern Cross and go to the Christian heaven, he asks them indignant-ly, "Why do you have to go to Heaven? My teacher said we should build a better place than Heaven, right here" (p. 232).

Ginga tetsudō no yoru hints at the actual parameters of this "better place," giving certain outlines of Miyazawa's ideal of Utopia. Educa-tion is clearly important; at the end of the story a mysterious man, holding a big book, exhorts him to "study for all you're worth" (p. 238). Miyazawa also valorized work as an art in itself, in a way reminiscent of William Morris, to whom he has been compared by

Japanese scholars, and there is a short scene at the beginning of the story describing Giovanni cheerfully at work in a small factory.

But *Ginga tetsudō no yoru* is more than simplistic exhortations to work and study hard. Through its own narrative structure it conveys a sense of intellectual excitement and discovery. At its best, the story is a self-reflexive example of the joy of knowledge itself, leaping from the Pliocene epoch to the Christian heaven and evoking the mystery and grandeur of the universe along the way.

From the point of view of its sociohistorical context, however, Miyazawa's apparently boundless optimism may seem a trifle disturbing, leading to a potentially one-note encomium to modernization and progress at all costs. In the world of the train, science is positively presented and authority figures are never questioned. The characters passively accept their fates.

The final message of *Ginga tetsudō no yoru* is more complex than a simple exhortation to acceptance, however. The subtext of the novel is based on both open-endedness and fluidity that were not a part of the rigidly authoritarian framework of the Meiji state. Not only is the train in constant movement, but the text is replete with images of fluidity, including the watery deaths of several protagonists, the seafaring work of Giovanni's father, the Milky Way itself, and the milk that Giovanni goes in search of. All these images emphasize a world in constant flux.

Furthermore, although not overtly confrontational, Giovanni and his mother are clearly marginals, outsiders who are humiliated by the other villagers. For Giovanni to avoid the fate of his father, a seasonal worker on a fishing fleet who has possibly been imprisoned, his only way out is through education. Giovanni's ticket is a ticket of change. Although hardly revolutionary, the story suggests that the established order must be altered. Either one escapes through death, hence the underlying grimness of the train's basic function, or through "building a better world," as Giovanni is advised.

Miyazawa's fantasy is not a sophisticated vision of Utopia but it is worth examining because it provides a stepping stone between the Meiji political novel and the postwar radical Utopias to be dealt with later in this chapter. On the one hand, Miyazawa retains a conservative belief in authority and a naive faith in the potential for an earthly Utopia brought about through progress. At the same time, however, he undermines this message through various subtextual and intertextual hints.

In the works of the three writers I am about to discuss, belief in "progress" has completely disappeared, to be replaced by an anarchistic belief in "movement" or change as a value in itself. Technology and the urban world are evil, while authority figures are dangerous. There are no central beliefs to which one can adhere.

Much of this change has to do with the realities of the postwar era. The Japan of the 1950s and early 1960s was a country bereft of any overarching ideology, thanks to the wholesale discrediting of emperor-centered militarism brought about by the country's crushing defeat in 1945. As we have seen in our previous chapters, the loss of belief in traditions was replaced by a national faith in an all-out economic drive. This faith, while it brought about an excellent educational system, an impressive corporate culture, great technological progress, and an extraordinary economic record, did little for the individual on a personal level. Male and female lives became increasingly separated as women ruled the household in their small nuclear families while men worked long days in industry and management. Children too, once they were of school age, were channelled into a demanding and hierarchical educational system that left little room for creativity or freedom.

It is not surprising that a variety of new religions appeared promising wealth and success. Perhaps most importantly, these religions offered in their very structure a sense of community which was fast disappearing in the increasingly fragmented urban landscape which makes up most of Japanese society. For those who did not embrace these new religions there seemed little else of psychic or emotional sustenance. It is also not surprising, therefore, that the postwar fantasies discussed in the previous chapters should chronicle a world in which men and women are alien beings to each other and wish-fulfillment becomes solipsistic.

What is perhaps unexpected is that during this increasingly alienating period a number of genuinely Utopian works were written, offering richly drawn alternatives to the unfulfilling material prosperity of postwar Japan. These Utopias are far more radical than the gradualist exhortations of Miyazawa's authority figures in *Ginga tetsudō no yoru* (Night Train to the Stars), however. In these works Utopia is now deemed no longer possible without violent change in society as a whole. Indeed, lurking at the heart of these postwar Utopian novelists is the insistent fear that Utopia is both desperately necessary and increasingly impossible.

THE ENERGY OF THE SPIRIT: ISHIKAWA JUN

The allure, and the impossibility, of Utopia is fascinatingly explored in the works of Ishikawa Jun (1899–1987). Ishikawa follows Miyazawa chronologically, but his visions are far more radical and all-encompassing, including both modern Japanese society and Japanese history in their range. He is also a far more sophisticated writer than Miyazawa, with a unique and powerful vision.

Ishikawa is perhaps the least well known in the West of the writers discussed here, regrettably, because he is one of the most exciting and unusual of modern Japanese authors. Writing in a consciously anti-Naturalist style, he began creating in the 1930s what he called the "*jikken shōsetsu*" (experimental novel). This metafiction blended surrealism and self-reflexivity with something rare in that period, an intense and overt concern for the political problems of the time. Although never a purely Marxist writer, Ishikawa consistently wrote what has been called "resistance literature," even during the politically repressive decade of the 1930s. Until his death he possessed a sharp eye for the problems of contemporary Japan, which he satirized savagely, while presenting fictional visions of a very different world, what his American translator has called his "lifelong dream of an unfettered existence in an anarchial millennium."[15]

To this end, Ishikawa produced a number of works highlighting what he termed "*seishin no undō*" (the energy of the spirit). In these works, often fantastic in nature, the characters, narrative structure, and language exist in a rapidly changing continuum where anything can happen and frequently does. Ishikawa's writings are particularly concerned with groups and individuals who turn their energy toward revolutions.

A number of his works involve schemes to achieve Utopia on earth. These include the tawdry plot by a sinister business consortium to build a paradise in his 1961 play *Omae no teki wa omae da* (Your Enemy Is You), his dystopian vision of underground revolutionaries in his novella *Taka* (The Hawk) (1953), and his 1965 *tour de force Shifuku sennen* (The Millennium) (1980). In *The Shifuku sennen* he offers a fresh vision of the *bakumatsu* (end of the shogunate) years through his depiction of an alternative Edo period in which hidden Christian groups attempt to take over Edo as the shogunate crumbles.

Shifuku sennen is a dense and fascinating work, but for the purposes of this chapter I will only mention a few of the most relevant features of the novel. As in Miyazawa's story, the protagonists who are given hope of a better world are outcasts, in this case the truly wretched of the earth, beggars, street entertainers, and those belonging to the so-called "inhuman" caste. The outcast groups are inflamed by a vision of "paradise on earth" presented to them by Kaga Naiki, the unscrupulous leader of one of the Christian factions. The beggars come close to rioting after magically Naiki heals their wounds and poverty during a sermon, only to release them back into misery when he finishes preaching.

Unlike Miyazawa, Ishikawa explicitly undermines the promise of a better world, not only by the transitoriness of the magic but also by the extreme unsavoriness of the supposed authority figures in the novel. Naiki, although mesmerizing, is also heartless and dangerous, even Satanic, as his mastery of magic suggests. Another leader is a bourgeois merchant using Christianity to further his own interests in trade with the West. The only truly Christian figure in the novel, a master dyer who follows in the steps of Saint Francis, perishes pathetically alone, pursuing an hallucinatory figure. Even the most disinterested observer, a haikai poet and perhaps the author's representative, ends up seeking a passage aboard ship to the West.

The West is not only a refuge in Ishikawa's novel, however; it can also inspire flights of fantasy. Thus, one of the novel's most poignant lines occurs at the end, when one of the protagonists dreams of escaping on the Black Ships of the American commander, Admiral Perry. As he explains excitedly:

> In the harbor there are great Western ships at berth, and among them is one of the new three-masted ones that breaks the high waves. It is so beautiful, like a fallen star, it makes me tremble. I fell for it the moment I saw it. I must board that ship.
>
> (p. 394; my translation)

Ishikawa's privileging of the West as both escape and inspiration may recall Miyazawa's use of Western imagery and vocabulary to inspire his readers, but a key difference between them lies in Ishikawa's more tempered view of the West as an Other that cannot be re-created in Japan. Miyazawa's heroes are expected to return and make use of their acquired knowledge, while Ishikawa's become self-determined exiles. In both writers' works, however, Western symbols suggest a dizzying world of freedom and excitement.

Miyazawa's *Ginga tetsudō no yoru* (Night Train to the Stars) begins and ends with the fluid image of voyaging the Milky Way. *Shifuku sennen* (The Millennium) also has a subtext of fluidity. The novel's first words are "*mazu mizu*" (first of all, water), and several important scenes take place on the rivers of Edo. But the novel's end hearkens far beyond Edo to a vision of the greater waters of the Pacific as the crowds of Edo, no longer controlled by either the shogunate or the hidden Christians, burst forth, shouting "the ships, the Black Ships."

Shifuku sennen thus ends with a glimpse of the tidal wave of the West that is about to engulf old Japan.

Miyazawa and Ishikawa concentrate more on the potential for Utopia than on its actual realization, but one short story of Ishikawa's, "Tora no kuni" (The Country of the Tiger) (1980), should be mentioned here as an example of one of his few visions of a successful Utopia. Although set in his favorite Edo period, "The Country of the Tiger" is a long way from the urban excitements of the capital. Instead it belongs to the pastoral paradigm, being a hidden mountain community tucked away on the borders of the far provinces of Echizen and Kaga.

A young samurai, Muriemon, lost on a hunting expedition, discovers the community, and acts as the reader's "this-world representative" to the Utopian settlement. He discovers that the Country of the Tiger is a refuge for the outcasts of the rigidly hierarchical Edo system. Criminals, actors, masterless samurai, and prostitutes have all escaped there, but not to re-create the rigid Tokugawa polity. Rather, as one of them explains to Muriemon, "Outside they were called samurai, townsmen, tradesmen, or farmers, but here there is no such foolish name division. No one asks you your name or history. Here everyone is the same" (p. 319; my translation here and subsequently).

Even women, it seems, are treated more equitably, so that many of the prostitutes from surrounding areas come to settle there freely. There are no marriage laws. People mate with whom they please and, according to the same spokesman, "The men are happy and the women also enjoy. This is the basis of human harmony" (p. 320).

Other aspects of the community are less obviously Utopian by present-day standards. The inhabitants are much concerned with martial arts and comparing the fighting styles of different fiefs. Perhaps because of this martial emphasis, the young samurai is greatly impressed, and maintains his ties with The Country of the Tiger even after his departure from it. As the narrator sums up, "The rumour of 'The Tiger Country' became widely known among gamblers, thieves and outcasts . . . and there were those who thought of it as a kind of *Tōgenkyo*" (p. 325).

Compared to the monumental *Shifuku sennen* (The Millennium), "Tora no kuni" is a slight work, but it prefigures some of the most important themes in the two postwar Utopias I would like to examine. First, it is about a pastoral community which, although symbolically lost on the border of two provinces, defines itself through conscious opposition to the center in its laws and customs. It does carry on the Tokugawa tradition of martial arts, but the story's violence is never aggressive. Finally, despite being basically realistic, "Tora no kuni" has a fantastic flavor to it, as evidenced through the narrator's linking of it to the pastoral *Tōgenkyo* tradition.[16]

OUTCAST GODS?: ŌE KENZABURŌ'S *DŌJIDAI GĒMU* (THE GAME OF CONTEMPORANEITY)

Ōe Kenzaburō (1935–) has spent much of his career reworking the pastoral tradition in his own unique fashion. Many of his early works were set in a fantasy version of his own Shikoku village. These celebrations of nature and primitivism stood in contrast to the soiled and violent adult world. Frequently, his most sympathetic characters are victims of this outside world. These range from children, Koreans, and deserters to, in "Shiiku" (1958) (trans. "Prize Stock" (1977)), perhaps his most beautiful work, a captured black American soldier. A consistently anti-establishment writer, whose many causes include the mistreatment of the Korean minority and Hiroshima victims and the destruction of the environment, Ōe's basic vision might be called "anarchic humanism."

His pastoral settings have a dark side that initially comes from the outside world of military and centrist authority. Later on, as his vision grows more complex, Ōe introduces the reader to the dark side of the pastoral world itself, although he sees the violence it contains as potentially salvific. Another salvific power is the environment, in particular the invigorating and purifying effects of water, which is often seen as an avenue back to the self.

Ōe's 1979 novel *Dōjidai gēmu* (The Game of Contemporaneity), comments on the possibility of achieving Utopia in reality. This work takes all the previous elements of Ōe's pastorals – the uninhibited sexuality, the redemptive potential of violence, and the celebration of the outsider and the marginal – and overlays them with a complex theoretical framework derived from such critical theories as Bhaktin's (1968) emphasis on grotesque realism and Victor Turner's (1969) theory of liminality. The result is a dense textual forest where myth and allegory mix with deconstructionism to force the reader to play the game that Ōe has constructed.

The way into the forest is through water, for *Dōjidai gēmu* is the story of a group of outcasts who make their way upriver into the heart of the Shikoku wilderness where they found a "village = nation = microcosmos." Village legend has it that they are descendants of the "dark gods" who were expelled from heaven when the Sun Goddess Amaterasu (and by extension the Japanese imperial family whom Ōe condemns) ascended to power. Forced to assume earthly guise in the form of outcasts of the shogunate, the villagers create a community that defines itself through confrontation with the central Japanese authority.

The leader in these conflicts is a magical figure known as "*kowasu hito*" (The Destroyer), so called because he destroyed a large clump of rock that blocked the way of the escapees as they travelled up-river. His redemptive destructiveness and hostility to central authority reveal his nature as a trickster figure, an outsider who leads others to attack the establishment, as Michiko Wilson points out.[17] As was the case with Ishikawa's authority figures, however, The Destroyer is a very problematic savior. At times he seems to abandon his people completely, as at the opening of the book, where it is uncertain whether he is dead or alive.

Another problematic authority figure is the narrator, an enigmatic character who has been forced by his father, the village priest, to become the official historian of the village. He is thus the reader's representative in this other world and also the main commentator and interpreter of the village and its meaning. This is a meaning which at times can be quite obvious, as in the explicit equation of the village with the universe, forcing the reader to be consciously aware that the novel is expressing a message.

What is *Dōjidai gēmu*'s message? There is of course no single one, but the text, in true Utopian tradition, places the hidden village in a positive light in comparison with the damaged real world outside. This contrast becomes a direct confrontation in the "Fifty Days War" against what the narrator calls "the Great Empire of Japan." Although the village loses the war, it puts up a brave defense through various tricks and stratagems that humiliate the Japanese soldiers without causing too many losses on their own side. The soldiers defeat the rebels by threatening to burn down their forest, a sacrifice of the environment that the villagers cannot make.

The village's conduct of the war contains many elements that are in Utopian contrast to that of the central authorities. The village army is an aggressively egalitarian one that includes old people, women, and children. They humiliate the Japanese army rather than kill them. Although hardly pacifists, their violence is shown to be anarchic and cleansing, not imperialistic and oppressive. Their defeat is a noble one, based on their sacralization of the environment.

The villagers' refreshing iconoclasm, especially in relation to what Ōe sees as the typically Japanese attitude of unthinking acquiescence, is evident in their willingness to lampoon authority even after their defeat. In one scene, for example, the narrator's father, forced to lead the worship at the state-sponsored Mishima shrine, dresses up in a bizarre costume and leads the crowd in derisive laughter at the imperial ritual.

As the above scene suggests, *Dōjidai gēmu* parodies a number of contemporary events in Japanese history. The Mishima shrine incident is certainly an attack on the writer Mishima Yukio and his emperor-centered nationalism. The villagers, with their redemptive laughter and japery suggest the correctly cynical attitude to take toward what Ōe considers to be obscurantist chauvinism.

By defining itself so clearly in opposition to the center, however, the village contains violent aspects that make it a very radical form of Utopia. This is most apparent in a sequence in which the novel fantastically parodies the upheavals of the 1960s, through the tale of the "Great Upheaval:" Driven by a strange sound, the young people force the elders to leave their own houses and move into the homes of other villagers until the entire village is topsy turvy. This generational boundary crossing and transgressing of established hierarchies echoes the youth movements that occurred throughout both the West and East Asia in the 1960s.

The Great Upheaval's inversion of society has aspects that are both repressive and refreshing. Through being coerced into leaving their homes, families lose their traditional bonds and even marriage vows are broken. Somewhat as in "Tora no kuni" (The Country of the Tiger), people mate with whom they please after the upheaval. Indeed, one older woman, The Destroyer's wife, keeps many of the village young men in sexual thrall, adding to the omnipresent sense of chaos.

Although The Destroyer's wife is reminiscent of Mao's wife and the Gang of Four's depredations during the Chinese Cultural Revolution, the Great Upheaval also suggests the student–establishment clashes that disordered Japan in the 1960s. This period of near-anarchy (at least in the educational system) was a time which could be looked upon as either liberating or alarming depending on one's position in the political spectrum. In the case of *Dōjidai gēmu* such chaos is clearly viewed as a positive form of empowerment on the part of the formerly powerless.

Cutting back and forth between myth, history, and contemporary Japan, *Dōjidai gēmu* ultimately becomes an inverted history of modern Japan as seen from the periphery, and it is this valorization of the margins which is perhaps the most Utopian aspect of the novel. Ōe is not presenting this village as a perfect society in a rigidly Utopian sense. As Kurihara Akira says, "It is no more than a place deep in the mountains with trees and a bubbling stream summoning forth a community."[18] It is also violent, primitive, and anarchic but, in Ōe's vision, the disorder of nature and social anarchy are infinitely preferable to the monolithic, repressive world of modern Japan.

THE AGRARIAN UTOPIA: INOUE HISASHI'S *KIRIKIRIJIN* (THE PEOPLE OF KIRIKIRI)

Ōe's notion of an alternative marginal community in violent antagonism to the central Japanese authority and by extension, the consensus reality of modern Japan is echoed and amplified in Inoue Hisashi's long comic novel *Kirikirijin* (The People of Kirikiri) (1986). Less ambitious in intellectual scope than *Dōjidai gēmu*, *Kirikirijin* comments on Japanese history in its own humorous and colorful way. This richly detailed fantasy of a rural village that declares its independence from Japan shows, perhaps even more clearly than Ōe's novel, what modern Japan has lost.

This loss is most obviously expressed in terms of rural versus urban values and institutions. Inoue shares with Ōe a desire to validate the pastoral and the communal over the urban, fragmented worlds of contemporary Japan. He is also keenly aware of the loss of history and the folk tradition, although, again like Ōe, Inoue is not interested in official histories. Instead, he looks in history for the lost voices of the common people. Inoue, a comic writer and playwright, resembles Ōe and Miyazawa in that he comes from a rural background (in fact, both he and Ōe have written on Miyazawa),[19] and he shares Ōe's and Ishikawa's left-wing political attitudes.

Although Inoue's works lack Ōe's intellectual depth and complexity, they contain other narrative riches, one of them being a brilliant use of language. *Kirikirijin* is written almost entirely in rural Tohoku dialect and tells its story largely through dialogue, thus giving the novel an unusual freshness and immediacy. The language used encapsulates the difference between Inoue's Utopian village characters and the representatives of the "real world" who speak standard Japanese.[20]

The accomplished use of dialogue also allows the characters to seem strikingly and memorably three-dimensional. Inoue's most notable accomplishment, however, may well be his seamless blending of the fantastic and the quotidian, rendering the village of Kirikiri utterly believable and at the same time unarguably Utopian. It is not surprising that *Kirikirijin* won both the Yomiuri award and an award for best science fiction the year it was published.

As Ishikawa does in *Shifuku sennen* (The Millennium) Inoue posits a fictional "what would happen if . . ." situation. In this case the scenario involves what would happen if a small village in the northern Tohoku area of Japan decided to declare its independence. The novel begins on the borders of the little village named Kirikiri as hijackers stop a Tohoku-bound train carrying, among others, a middle-aged writer named Furuhashi who is in search of rumored buried treasure in the district.

The train is boarded by a group of people, including a small boy holding a rifle. They explain that the train has entered the independent country of Kirikiri and demand that the passengers present their passports. Since he, along with most of the passengers, is not carrying his passport, Furuhashi is led off to the Kirikiri National Jail and becomes a spectator and then a participant in the drama of Kirikiri independence.

Through his eyes we learn that Kirikiri is indeed an independent country with a president, a National Theater (formerly the strip show), various national treasures and even the Kirikiri National Anthem which is sung for the benefit of Japanese audiences in an NHK television interview. The singers include a number of civic leaders, including the hijackers of Furuhashi's train, who are led by Miss Abe Maria, the chief dancer of the Kirikiri National Nude Theater. The actual anthem comes as a surprise to their audience since it includes such lyrics as:

> The people of Kirikiri's eyes are tranquil
> Their noses and their hearts are straightforward
> Their foreheads and their resolve are firm
> Their lips and their manners are warm
> The people of Kirikiri's eyes are clear
> Their cheeks and dreams are full
> The men's organs and wishes are big
> The women's mounds and thoughts are glossy.
>   (pp. 178–179; my translation here and subsequently)

As should be clear by now, *Kirikirijin* is a clever satire on many of the conventions that modern Japan holds most dear. Through the mock seriousness of the National this and National that, not to mention the whole notion of cultural offerings controlled by a national establishment, Inoue pokes fun at the kind of pomposity involved in so many of the rituals of the modern Japanese state. But *Kirikirijin* is more than just satire, it also offers a genuine alternative to the society it parodies.

The most fundamental aspect of this way of life is what might be called agrarianism, a concept of salvation through working and living with nature, that Inoue shares with Ōe and Miyazawa. Inoue's attitude is closer to Miyazawa's than Ōe's, since his valorization of rural labor is reminiscent of Miyazawa's agricultural-cooperative-based view of the world, not the surreal primitivism espoused by Ōe.

Other aspects of Kirikiri society are both more imaginative and more unusual than in the other Utopian works discussed. Both men and women seem to participate fairly equally in society and politics. There is even an amusing sequence involving a male strip show, in which Furuhashi unwittingly and embarrassingly participates, that suggests not only equality of the sexes but sexual equality as well.

Another intriguing element of Kirikiri's new order is the parliament which consists of an old bus called the *kokkai gijidōsha* (a pun combining the Japanese word for parliament and vehicle). The *kokkai gijidōsha* moves throughout the village picking up whoever would like to participate in politics. Its core members consist of such personages as a woman poet, who later becomes Furuhashi's fiancée, the young boy who helped hijack the train, and a number of elderly farmers. Combining women, children, and the elderly, the *kokkai gijidōsha* is reminiscent of Ōe's ragtag army, with the added aspect of continuous motion. The bus thus becomes the quintessential symbol of an inverted society where outcasts are empowered and where there is no established center.

The rather dim-witted but ultimately tragicomic Furuhashi is the perfect representative from our real world to introduce the reader to Kirikiri. From a rural background himself, Furuhashi went to the city at an early age and became, almost accidentally, what the narrator terms a "hack writer." As the novel progresses Furuhashi becomes increasingly pleased to have broken his urban exile and to have found, in the congenial inhabitants of Kirikiri, the family that he never had possessed. It is no doubt significant that Furuhashi's only successful book is called *In Search of a Lost Memory*. The lost memory he finally discovers is his appreciation for the rural traditions of Kirikiri.

Furuhashi does more than observe. He is, in fact, forced to become an important part of the entire independence process. In quick succession he is given the Kirikiri National Poetry Prize, the Kirikiri National Fiction Prize and the Kirikiri National Essay Prize. Along with this metamorphosis into a national treasure, the end of the novel finds Furuhashi transformed by the advanced medical techniques of Kirikiri National Hospital into a female terrorist, who then becomes the president. As president, the unfortunate Furuhashi brings about the destruction of Kirikiri at the hands of the Japanese Self Defence Force through a typical slip of the tongue.

In some ways, the destruction of Kirikiri is thematically necessary. Inoue himself has said of the community he created that Kirikiri could not have continued without losing the very momentum and dynamism on which it was based, thereby necessitating another Kirikiri independence movement and then another and another.[21] Furthermore, even though the villagers are by and large positively portrayed – the authority figures are probably the most positive and least intimidating of any of the postwar works discussed here – the novel contains hints of a darker side to the society. The hospital where Furuhashi is transformed into a woman, for example, performs experiments on human beings of a bizarre and unpleasant nature.

Furuhashi's final transformation into a woman is also problematic. Although the notion of boundary and gender crossing can be seen as liberating, as we saw in our discussion of the alien in Chapter 4, it also suggests a dizzying and ultimately disturbing pace of change that hints at a world potentially out of control. Furthermore, although, on the whole, women come across quite sympathetically in Inoue's work, the notion of a woman as terrorist evokes the fundamental lack of sympathy or connection between male and female that, as we have seen, has become an important theme in postwar fantasy.

Kirikirijin also deals with capitalism in a somewhat ambivalent fashion. The very money that built the hospital and financed Kirikiri's independence movement is problematic. Although this money is actually the buried treasure that Furuhashi came to Tohoku to look for, and thus has an appealingly fairytale aspect to it, it plays a potentially subversive role in the agrarian economy on which the original Kirikiri is proudly based. And it is surely not an unconscious Freudian slip on the part of Inoue that he has the villagers hide the money in the sewers of the hospital, thus implicitly equating money with waste, something to be gotten rid of rather than treasured.

Despite these occasional shadows, however, *Kirikirijin* is perhaps the most effective Utopian novel to be written in modern Japan, for two reasons. The first reason is that, of all the works discussed in this chapter, it possesses a carefully worked out political philosophy at its heart, what might be called progressive agrarianism. This stands in important contrast to the works of Miyazawa, Ishikawa and Ōe, who are less concerned with the quotidian details of political institutions than they are with delineating the empowering or at least confrontational aspects of their respective philosophies. Moreover,

Inoue's agrarian philosophy is one that is vividly realized in the speech, actions, and vehicles (e.g. the *kokkai gijidōsha*) of his characters.

The second reason behind the success of Inoue's Utopian vision is that it leaves the reader yearning to visit the Utopian community realized on its pages. This is partly due to the extraordinary appeal and vividness of its remarkably three-dimensional characters. It is also due to its literally down-to-earth setting, as opposed to the classic Utopian novel which tends to dwell on the elite layers of society. In fact, both *Kirikirijin* and *Dōjidai gēmu* have been called examples of the "new" political novel, a novel which, according to Kurihara Akira, inverts the traditional political novel of the Meiji period, with its emphasis on the *kokka* or national polity, by turning it upside down, "submerging the state within daily life."[22] It is this daily life, albeit a rather unusual daily life in an alternative world, that Inoue presents so seamlessly.

Mentioning the genre of political novels has brought us full circle from the urban, technologically advanced, and politically centralized Utopias of the Meiji period to the pastoral, narratively open-ended fantasies of anarchistic outcasts that characterize the postwar period. *Setchūbai*'s prologue opened with the cannon's booming announcement of the 200th year of the Meiji state. To see how much the postwar idea of Utopia as changed, we might consider the parodic dance around the shrine by the priest in *Dōjidai gēmu* or the subversively funny Kirikiri national song. On a more agrarian note, one could consider Furuhashi's summing up of what Kirikiri is:

> In the country of Kirikiri the earth is a nostalgic color. Different from the whitish soil overstrewn with chemical fertilizers, this is a warm soft dark color, thanks to the droppings from stables and cow sheds and to human dung. This indeed is a place where human beings live.
>
> (p. 472)

These postwar Utopias subvert the consensus reality of modern Japan on a variety of levels. They largely reject the ideal of urban living and warn of the dangers of reliance on technology. They question the solemnity and rigidity of established institutions and undermine the notion of patriarchal authority. Most importantly, they offer sites of free play for the imagination and the soul, through humor, creativity, and psychic energy.

Of course, modern Utopias are more than simple reactions against the industrialized state. As I have said, these works also offer blueprints toward a better way of life. Sometimes these blueprints contain some surprising ideas.

Of these, one of the more surprising is that all of these works, despite their celebration of an older pastoral Japan and the generally suspicious attitude toward Western hegemony mentioned at the beginning of this chapter, delineate societies strongly open to international influences.[23] Miyazawa accepts these influences most uncritically in his joyous welding of Darwinism, Marxism, scientific theory, and the celebration of the natural world. But even Ishikawa, a confirmed lover of Edo culture and tradition, ultimately suggests that his protagonists in *Shifuku sennen* must seek their Utopias beyond the Tokugawa barrier in the promise of the Western Black Ships. Ōe and Inoue are even more explicitly international. Ōe begins *Dōjidai gēmu* in Mexico with his narrator mulling over the role of peripheral nations such as Mexico and Japan *vis-à-vis* the center.

Inoue goes furthest in this international alignment of non-central nations. Kirikiri hosts the Kirikiri International Table Tennis World Cup to which representatives of all the alternative communities around the world are invited, from members of the Quebec Liberation Front and the American Indian Movement to the founders of the "Republic of Frestonia," a squatter's town in London, and the leaders of the Scottish independence movement. Naturally, this "internationalization" is of a very different kind from what the Meiji leaders might have dreamed of, or what post-war Japan's political leaders are calling for today. Rather, it might be called an "alternative internationalization," a gathering together with foreign groups who also oppose the technological authoritarianism that Westernization and modernization have wrought.

In their celebration of liminality, marginality, and anti-technological attitudes, the postwar Japanese works have a good deal in common with other contemporary Western Utopianists, such as Ursula K. Le Guin. In particular, the valorization of liminality is a notion common to almost all contemporary Western Utopian literature in which "narrative stasis is overcome by ambiguity, contradiction and fragmentation."[24] Where once the state could promise Utopia, now only the antagonists to the state can hope to bring it about, and their Utopias inevitably exist in dynamic opposition to the central authority.

What is perhaps unusual about this emphasis is that it should be Japan, a notably homogenous country, which hosts writers who so consistently emphasize the marginal. This in itself may be a reaction against the very homogeneity that politicians such as former Prime Minister Nakasone are wont to celebrate. It also may be an implicit admission of Japan's own peculiar status in the contemporary world, a modern nation that is ultimately neither East nor West.

The anti-technological stance and the concomitant concern for the environment expressed in both Ōe's and Inoue's work are also common to contemporary Western Utopian writers. In the case of Japan, however, this message may have more urgency than elsewhere, because of the small size of Japan and the breadth of environmental disruption that has already occurred there.

Another similarity with contemporary Western writers is narrative technique, especially the use of fantasy or surrealism. Both Japanese and Western authors are increasingly willing to use the fantastic to make their Utopian points, unlike many authors of mainstream fiction. Again, this is most notable in Japan, which has less of a Utopian tradition and must also contend with the still powerful influence of the *shishōsetsu*.

Finally, unlike the traditional static Utopias, contemporary Utopias in both Japanese and Western fiction invariably revolve around process rather than goal. This is reflected not only in the aforementioned notion of constantly evolving Utopias that have become a staple of postwar literature, but also within the texts themselves by their consistent emphasis on movement and fluidity. Miyazawa's fantasy highlights the train and the fluidity of time and space. Ishikawa emphasizes flowing water, from the rivers of Edo to the Black Ships which symbolize both change and escape. Ōe privileges movement itself in the anarchic momentum of the Great Upheaval which forces villagers into different houses and positions in life, and in the continued pattern of The Destroyer's death and rebirth.

Inoue privileges movement within the community through the image of the constantly circulating *kokkai gijidōsha*, a genuine example of bringing politics to the people. He also highlights movement in general, most importantly through the use of the hijacked train that brings Furuhashi to Kirikiri. An inverted echo of Miyazawa's train that cuts across space and time, Inoue's train goes backwards into Japan's past, the agrarian village, and forward to the future, the newly independent, technically advanced Kirikiri.

It should be noted that Miyazawa's train brings his protagonist not only a vision of a better world but also the tools to build that world through education. Giovanni's "go-anywhere" ticket leads to a better future, as long as he is willing to work for it. By contrast, Inoue's train is finally more of a train to the past. Despite the high-tech aspects of the new hospital and the village's international visitors, Inoue is essentially celebrating the lost world of agrarian Japan. As Yamada Yuji says, "this tale is a scathing indictment of modern Japan's progress through abandonment of agriculture and it is also a call for a return to the original Japan."[25]

The impossibility of this return highlights a problem in the Utopian longings of both Ōe and Inoue. They cannot help but find Utopian aspects in a simpler past, but is such a yearning ultimately regressive rather than radical? In fact, Ōe and Inoue constantly and explicitly wrestle with the pervasive influence of *natsukashisa* (nostalgia). Ōe has tried to depersonalize and deconstruct *natsukashisa* through theoretical constructs which help him universalize his village = microcosmos.

But this attempted theoreticization also lessens the literary impact of *Dōjidai gēmu*, making it seem at times more like a political treatise than a novel. Interestingly, in 1986 Ōe published his mimetic *Natsukashi toshi e no tegami* (Letters to the Nostalgic Years), a work which deals with the attempt to build a Utopian community in a small Shikoku village. In this work Ōe accepts and even celebrates his own nostalgia, at the same time acknowledging its impossibility as a working method for society's salvation, thus, by extension, acknowledging the impossibility of creating a genuine Utopia.

Inoue accepts *natsukashisa* (nostalgia) and even plays on it. The title of his hero Furuhashi's only successful book refers not only to the protagonist's lost memory but to the lost memory of the Japanese people. Poignantly, the mysterious narrator of *Kirikirijin* turns out to be the ghost of a former peasant leader who rebelled against the Meiji polity. Like Ōe's Shikoku village, then, Inoue's community is ultimately constituted both through the positives of the rural Japanese community and the negatives of existing as an anti-establishment, anti-centrality, and anti-emperor community, a recovery of non-elite history. The inevitable destruction of this dynamic amalgamation of positives and negatives that constituted Kirikiri only underlines both its nostalgic quality and its unattainability.

The narrative movement and fluidity that these works share with other contemporary Utopian texts may be a product of the writers' implicit awareness of the dizzying rate of change in the modern world, especially Japan. In Miyazawa's writing change is positive. The swiftly moving galactic railroad brings about only improvement.

While the necessity for change is accepted in the works of the three other writers, their attitude toward change is sometimes ambivalent. Ishikawa's protagonists attempt to flee the immense changes that they themselves have helped to bring about. Ōe believes in process over progress, as shown in the voyage upriver and in the Great Upheaval. Inoue gives positive value to the people's movement, represented by the *kokkai gijidōsha*, but his symbol of technological progress, the hospital, is an ominous one. Even more problematic are the changes that Furuhashi, the everyman, is subjected to, from hack writer, to national treasure, to woman terrorist president. These dizzying but in some ways meaningless changes suggest a postmodern vision of a world with no center and no base.

The center is what the postwar Japanese Utopianists profess to despise, because the center and the establishment are not only repressive in themselves but are ultimately aligned with the emperor system. In fact, one of the commentators on *Shifuku sennen* suggests that Inoue's highlighting of water and fluidity is connected to the lack of anything besides the emperor as a center for Japanese culture.[26] Finding Japanese high culture empty, Utopian writers must turn to the people. Inverting the emperor system, they seek to find a new hope in the energy below. Whether they do or not remains unclear.

All these Utopias are surrounded by imagery of death. Miyazawa's train carries dead passengers, while *Kirikirijin*'s narrator is a ghost. Ishikawa's one truly "Christian" protagonist dies alone. Ōe's village is shaped like a gigantic coffin, one reason why the superstitious Great Japanese Empire left it alone for so long. Characteristically, Ōe inverts this notion of death into a positive one and has his narrator suggest that the powers of darkness are not only morally superior but will conquer the myth of the imperial center, just as The Destroyer will return once again. The dead being reborn is a truly Utopian notion, testifying both to the despair with which these writers view modern Japan and to the faith that they somehow manage to retain in the prospect of its rebirth.

A FEMINIST UTOPIA?: KURAHASHI YUMIKO'S *AMANONKOKU ŌKANKI*

Ishikawa's most overtly Utopian works were published in the 1950s and 1960s while the two novels discussed by Ōe and Inoue appeared in the late 1970s. Ōe's vision of a pastoral refuge continued through the 1980s in such mimetic works as the previously mentioned *Natsukashi toshi e no tegami* (Letters to the Nostalgic Years) (1986) and in his venture into science fiction *Chiryōto* (Tower of Healing) (1990). In general, however, the paradigm of a pastoral Utopia seems to have lost some of its appeal by the end of the 1980s as younger writers such as Murakami Haruki and Yoshimoto Banana increasingly turned toward dealing with the complexities of city life. Murakami, as we will see in the next chapter, does engage with the problems of Utopia and dystopia but his vision is far less revolutionary or all-encompassing than those of the older writers, and it is questionable whether they actually constitute a Utopia at all.

One writer in the 1980s who does present a form of Utopia, albeit with tongue in cheek perhaps, is Kurahashi Yumiko. I would like to end this chapter with a discussion of her unique Utopian novel *Amanonkoku ōkanki* (Record of a Voyage to the Country of Amanon). Kurahashi's work may be considered more a deconstruction of Utopia than a vision of an actual ideal place in itself, and as such is a particularly useful bridge to our next chapter, an examination of the anti-Utopia or dystopia in modern Japanese fiction.

Kurahashi's Utopian world differs from the others described above in a number of important ways: first, it is clearly an "Other" world, one reached by spaceship; second, it is highly urban and largely static, a throwback to the traditional Utopia; finally and most importantly, it is a world in which women are dominant. *Amanonkoku ōkanki* has in common with the other three post-war works a problematizing of the very notion of Utopia, but in this case the impossibility of Utopia is based almost solely on the problem of sexual difference.

The reasons for the lack of commonalities between Kurahashi's work and that of the other writers discussed in this chapter are worth speculating about. Her interest in female-dominated Utopia relations may have something to do with the fact that Kurahashi is the only female writer discussed in this chapter, although, as we have seen, male–female relationships have been a fruitful subject for virtually all the male writers examined in this book. At least as likely a reason for Kurahashi's uniqueness may also be due to her relative lack of ideological commitment in comparison to the other writers.

Although Kurahashi was considered at her debut to be indebted to Ōe, she is in fact far less overtly ideological than her presumed mentor and has always maintained a more jaundiced eye with regard to political action. She is a female writer who deals with politics, religion, and society, but she can be labelled neither Marxist nor feminist, choosing instead to play the astringent outside observer. In certain ways she is a metapolitical writer, concerned with politics and ideology but refusing to promote any particular program.

The complexity of Kurahashi's thought and attitudes is on full display in *Amanonkoku ōkanki*. This work creates what at first glance seems to be a feminist Utopia privileging a separatist female state in which women dominate and men are virtually invisible. As it turns out, the Utopian aspects of her fictional country of Amanon are highly suspect, and the reader is made to realize the impossibility of such simplistic Utopian gender reversal. In doing so the reader is forced to question a number of his or her assumptions, not only about sex roles, but about the possibility of Utopia in general.

Kurahashi leads the reader to these questions through her male protagonist P. This choice of protagonist is an intriguing one, for it is through P's highly chauvinistic gaze that the reader encounters Amanon. P is so chauvinistic, in fact, that for a long time he is incapable of recognizing that the leaders of Amanon are all female.

The novel begins in a way that is typical of the traditional Utopian fantasy:

> From early childhood P had dreamed of voyaging to unknown lands far away . . .
>
> Blessed with a generous inheritance upon his father's early death, P was allowed sufficient leisure to enjoy himself. After spending a lengthy time at university in the departments of medicine and engineering where he obtained the general expertise and medical knowledge required for adventuring overseas, he entered the Monokami Sect Collegio, as the training school for missionaries was called, expecting in the near future to become a member of a missionary expedition bound for the country of Amanon.
>
> (p. 7; my translation here and subsequently)

This slightly pompous opening situates the novel squarely within the Utopian paradigm of a journey to another country that will turn out to be spiritually and technologically superior to the voyager's own. Indeed, upon his arrival, P is favorably impressed by almost all aspects of Amanon. Compared to the vast barrenness of his own country of Monokamikuni, Amanon is a beautiful, peaceful, and humane land.

Even the food is better, as P learns through the countless banquets (described in detail) that punctuate his visit, for his hosts are a very hospitable people. Although Amanon has been closed off from other countries for hundreds of years, the elite of Amanon are tolerant of P's new religion and are also excited about the possibilities of what they call *intaka*, which is short for *intakōsu* (presumably a pun on the English "intercourse") and is used in relation to internationalization.

The only aspect of Amanon that gives P pause is its most important one. He discovers about mid-way through the novel that virtually everyone he encounters, from the so-called *peepu*, the elite, and their *sekure*, or secretaries, down to the lowly fisherfolk who discover him on arrival in Amanon, is female. Women have achieved this dominance through careful breeding techniques in which girl babies predominate and male babies are relegated to either an underclass or to a eunuch caste.

Judging only by this summary, Amanon seems to fit comfortably into the paradigm of Western feminist Utopias from *Herland* to *Woman on the Edge of Time*; small, separate communities based on principles of harmony and non-aggression in which women are either dominant or demonstrably equal.[27] Although Amanon is larger than most feminist Utopias, it can still be seen as a separatist state constituted in opposition to the center, if we take the center to be P's vast country of Monokamikuni. Furthermore, as is typical with feminist Utopias, sexual relationships (exclusively between women, in this case) are gentle and tender, as opposed to the implied brutality and danger of male–female relationships.

As it turns out, P is indeed dangerous, although in a more subtle and complex way than the Manichean dichotomies of purer feminist dystopias would dictate, and it is with P's increasingly active function within the narrative that *Amanonkoku ōkanki* begins to reverse the typical dynamics of a Utopian work. For P, unlike the traditionally passive Utopian protagonist, brings his own agenda to Amanon. This agenda consists of the promotion of what he calls "*osu kakumei*" (male revolution) in the name of Monokamiism. P promotes this revolution through a surprisingly open series of moves: he sets himself up in Tokio, the capitol of Amanon, with a eunuch adviser and a beautiful *sekure* named Himeko, and begins a campaign to go to bed with as many women as possible.

The campaign is outrageously successful. Far from being disgusted by his advances, as one might expect the inhabitants of a feminist Utopia to be, the *peepu* actually go out of their way to solicit sexual contact with P. In a short time, P ends up as master of ceremonies on a live television sex show called "Monopara" (short for "Monokami Paradise") complete with hired believers, a shamaness, and a special guest with whom he engages in sex in front of a live audience. Both audience and partner are invariably delighted by this display and "Monopara" becomes the most highly rated show in Amanon.

Its success is short-lived, however. The country of Amanon starts to undergo a series of earthquakes, volcanic eruptions, and other cataclysms, leading scientists to predict the country's ultimate destruction. P decides to flee back to Monokamikuni, taking with him his *sekure* Himeko and a select group of *peepu*. The last textual description of him places him asleep in his flying saucer, apparently heedless of the destruction around him.

In the novel's epilogue we finally learn the real secret of Amanon and its destruction. It is P himself, it turns out, who has brought about the catastrophe, but he has done it with the willing compliance of the country's own elite. For Amanon is not actually a place, but a body, a female body belonging to a certain "Mrs. Amanon," as the novel's epilogue makes clear. Its final scene consists of the birth of a baby to "Mrs. Amanon," the product, presumably, of P's efforts inside her body. *Amanonkoku ōkanki* is thus the portrait of a Utopia which self-destructs, and the reasons for this self-destruction revolve around the issue of sexual difference.

From the beginning the text gives some very overt hints concerning Amanon's true nature. P's voyage to the country is described in the following memorable (and in retrospect, obvious) manner: In a wrenching departure, P is shot into space along with hundreds of his comrades, each encased in small saucer-shaped vessels, that go bursting into air. Arriving in the vicinity of Amanon, P's vessel penetrates with great speed and force a gelatinous barrier, and enters a long tubelike passageway in which P loses consciousness, just as he senses that he is approaching a large central cavity.

Anyone familiar with Woody Allen's film *Everything You Always Wanted to Know About Sex But Were Afraid To Ask*, in which Woody Allen plays a sperm, can probably understand the full implications of P's journey. But P is not only sperm he is also "penis," and it is the introduction of this sexual difference into Amanon that inexorably brings about the country's demise. This is obvious from P's very first encounter with the inhabitants of Amanon, a group of fisherwomen who find him washed up unconscious on the beach.

P awakens in a mood of quiet contentment surrounded by caressing images, a warm breeze, the gentle regularity of the ocean, evocative of existence in the womb. This comforting imagery changes abruptly when P finds himself surrounded by a dozen naked female legs. He knows that they are female because, even though he cannot see the owners' faces, his peculiar vantage point (on his back looking up) allows him to focus on their most "feminine part." Stimulated by this view, P's body reacts automatically, causing the owners of the legs, the fisherwomen, to scream in consternation, probably because the sight is a totally unfamiliar one.

Not only is P's anatomy unfamiliar to them but his language is as well. When P tries to speak to them, using polite, old-fashioned Amanon dialect, they don't understand. Giving up in disgust, one of the women says, "This person must be mad," whereupon another disagrees: "Person, this is not a person. This is a man!" (p. 16).

This first encounter between the women and P forecasts the basic dynamics of the rest of the novel. Neither side can understand the other and end up labelling each other as different species. Language thus becomes yet another means of enforcing difference.

Of even more importance is the shift from the gentle womblike quality of P's awakening to his immediate metamorphosis into mature sexual awareness upon seeing the women's genitals. If Moylan is correct, and all Utopias are quests for home, then P awakens into "home," literally the womb, the place of the imaginary before the constitution of difference, according to Lacan. But he is unable to accept this return to the womb and his sexuality rends the imaginary by forcing difference in three significant areas: first, through the signifying power of P's genitals, which frightens and confuses the women; second, through his male gaze, which morselizes the women into "their most feminine part," and finally, through language, which both he and the women fight to control.

Throughout the novel P uses all three methods to forward his "male revolution." His sexual organ is the most obvious and most immediately successful of his weapons, for, with the crucial exception of his *sekure*, Himeko, the women of Amanon all enjoy their initiation into heterosexual activity. Although much of this activity is described in a lighthearted fashion, the underlying theme is deadly serious. As Foucalt points out, "[Sex] is an especially dense transfer point for relations of power,"[28] and the power struggle that P and the women engage in is one that ultimately destroys Amanon.

But P's destructive power is not only of the genital variety. His gaze is also an important factor, a particularly intrusive one in a world that supposedly constitutes a feminist Utopia. The fact that the novel is constructed only through P's perspective allows the reader to vicariously participate in his consistent morselization of the female body. Kurahashi plays on the reader's normal desire to identify with the main character, a temptation that was easy to give in to with such works as *Ginga tetsudō no yoru* (Night Train to the Stars) or *Kirikirijin*. But, P's inability to see women as a whole can be fundamentally disturbing to the reader who sees through his eyes. Furthermore, it aligns with the third strategy of control in P's agenda, the contest for domination of the language.

What P brings to Amanon is the word of the father, Monokamiism, which literally means "One Godism" but is obviously phallogocentrism. This is made clear both through P's aggressive and invasive actions and through his explanation of how writing is considered the highest value in Monokamiism. It is the phallus as pen which controls the word, the realm of language which all humans are eventually forced to enter, away from the realm of the imaginary, the Utopian union with the mother.

But if the phallus controls the word in Monokamikuni, the situation is more fluid in the country of Amanon. For example, although the women do not write histories, they do produce romances. And at the climax of *Amanonkoku ōkanki* a woman takes it upon herself to control the phallus. This woman is Himeko, P's young *sekure* and the only woman who has spurned his advances. Seemingly changing her mind, Himeko agrees to appear with P on his television show as a sex partner but, when the actual moment comes, she attempts to castrate him with a knife. In a Lacanian sense, Himeko has decided to write her own story, refusing to accept P's domination over her.[29]

Himeko is apparently unsuccessful, although P does bleed copiously (the only real violence in the novel). Moreover, P makes no attempt to punish Himeko but instead takes her with him as he flees Amanon. In many ways, she is the only woman he really cared for throughout his sojourn in the country.

And yet, P and Himeko's fundamental inability to connect en-capsulates the problem of difference which *Amanonkoku ōkanki* deconstructs. Unlike the other works discussed here (with the possible exception of *Kirikirijin*), *Amanonkoku ōkanki* is essentially a tragedy. Its bleak message seems to be that male and female together can create only problems, ruining any hope of a genuine Utopia.

Although the Utopia limned in *Amanonkoku ōkanki* has serious limitations, and in many ways could be considered more a satire on modern-day Japan than a genuine idealized state, it is still a peaceful and harmonious society, clearly superior to the fierce, brutal land of Monokami (which has obvious echoes of the West, especially Ameri-ca)[30] from which P comes.

The tragedy of Amanon is not entirely P's fault. In a final grotesque twist, the creature that "Mrs. Amanon" gives birth to is so horrific that the doctors cannot bear to look at it, and the text makes it clear that it is a product of both P and Mrs. Amanon. In fact, some of the most surprising scenes in the novel show the wholehearted enthusiasm with which the women of Amanon greet P's sexual overtures.

In the long run, however, all the characters in *Amanonkoku ōkanki*, both male and female, are fighting for power, since the elite hope to manipulate P as much as he plans to use them. It is this struggle, endemic to humanity in general, which also characterizes the impossi-bility of Amanon's continuation. In this regard it is important that the ultimate site for this fight for power is the womb. As Patricia Waugh says, "the female body is an area where the struggle for control is likely to be enacted because it has come to signify the threat of incorpora-tion and the loss of identity."[31]

This "threat" may be the real reason why P insists on his male revolution despite his genuine admiration for Amanon and his initial enjoyment of his womblike state. P's insistence on departing the womb is an interesting contrast to Inoue's and Ōe's two postwar Utopias which are clearly searches for *Heimat*, albeit a different form of home than that with which the establishment has presented them. Inoue and Ōe also valorize history, as long as it is from the margins, while Kurahashi implicitly problematizes it as something exclusive to men, in comparison with the romances which women write. And yet Kurahashi, Inoue, and Ōe all share a certain pessimism as to the possibility of achieving an actual Utopia for any real length of time. Ōe and Inoue at least show their characters working for its achievement while Kurahashi suggests that human nature is such that Utopias will always be an impossibility.

Just as the thing which emerges from Mrs. Amanon's body is a product of both male and female, so is the often grotesque world of reality which Kurahashi brilliantly defamiliarizes in the novel. Through her writing, Kurahashi is able temporarily to take over the language of the father to create for a brief fictional space the Utopian world of Amanon. That she destroys it, is, like Inoue's destruction of Kirikiri, a tribute to her willingness to go beyond Utopian day-dreams and squarely confront dystopian reality.

The works examined in this chapter have described alternative worlds which, if not perfect, are at least potentially better places. Although differing widely from one another, these "better places" have a number of key elements in common: First and foremost they provide a sense of community, even, in the case of P in *Amanonkoku ōkanki*, a literal "womb" to which to return. As an alternative to the real Japan's increasing urbanization and attendant alienation, Inoue and Ōe suggest a nostalgic rural "hometown" which offers comfort, connection, and escape. Ishikawa's "Tora no kuni," although set in the Edo period, envisions a mountain refuge safe from the central hierarchy. The ending of the prewar *Ginga tetsudō no yoru* (Night Train to the Stars) offers hope that Giovanni's father will return and that the family will be happily reconstituted.

The reconstitution of the family and the community is related to another important aspect of contemporary Japanese Utopias, their valorization of history as a means to increase community connections and to develop a sense of identity. This history is rarely state-inspired, however. Indeed, it could be called an "alternative history," one that privileges the margins and rural roots over the dominant contemporary Japanese ideology which offers a rhetoric of economic growth based on continuous urbanization and technological advancement. At the same time, however, although the Utopias are usually based on indigenous folk values, they are remarkably open to international influences, with the key exception, in the later works, of Western technology.

This changing attitude toward technology brings me to some of the important changes in the development of the Utopian imagination in twentieth-century Japan. This chapter has traced what might be called a downward trajectory of Utopia in twentieth-century Japanese fantasy, from the limitless spaces of Miyazawa's Milky Way to Kurahashi's pseudo galaxy in *Amanonkoku ōkanki*, which is actually the claustrophobic interior of a diseased womb. Along this trajectory a number of important changes can be discerned. The optimism about the potential for Utopia on earth in *Ginga tetsudō no yoru* has turned to skepticism and doubt in Ishikawa's and Ōe's works and to a pervasive sense of tragicomedy in *Kirikirijin* and *Amanonkoku ōkanki*, as the novels' respective authors create Utopias only to destroy them.

The role of the West has also undergone similar alterations. From being a site of Utopian inspiration in the Meiji period and in Miyazawa's works it becomes another example of the regressive center which must be escaped in Ōe's and Inoue's novels. Most negative of all is the vision of the West in Kurahashi's *Amanonkoku ōkanki*, where it is seen as an enforcer of hegemonic domination on every front, from the intellectual to the sexual.

Finally, the attitude toward technology has changed drastically from being almost entirely positive in Miyazawa's work to becoming largely negative in the works of Ōe and Inoue. While Miyazawa's train brought visions of movement and progress, Inoue and Ōe concentrate on the destructive powers of technology. In one explicitly anti-technological (and anti-Western) scene in *Kirikirijin*, for example, the villagers discover that their lake has been poisoned by chemicals manufactured by Dupont – the first attack by the established powers which are massing against them. Far from being empowering, technology, in these later Utopian works, is seen as both dehumanizing and despoiling.

The Utopian imagination still exists in the Japan of the 1990s, as is evidenced in the frequent use of the word "*yutopia*" in everything from novel titles to advertisements, but it is a tempered vision. Compared to the limitless possibilities that the Meiji period seemed to promise, the idea of Utopia is a more constrained one in a contemporary Japan, increasingly aware of its limits. It is not surprising that Utopian visions in the 1980s and 1990s are fewer and less all-encompassing. Furthermore, as we shall see in the next chapter, it is the dark side of Utopia, the dystopian imagination, which is increasingly coming to the fore.

NOTES

1   *Webster's Seventh New Collegiate Dictionary*, 1987, p. 978.
2   C. Gluck, 1985, p. 18.
3   Gluck, 1985, p. 21.
4   F. Manuel and F. Manuel, 1979, p. 1; and K. Kumar, 1987, p. 19. See also D. Plath, 1971, Introduction.
5   Two other common Utopian forms which the Manuels mention and which are also present in Japanese culture are the "Euchronia" (the good time), usually a golden age, and the "Eupsychia" (the good mind), referring to an ideal spiritual state. The Euchronic impulse is, if anything, more common in East Asia than in Western thought since, from the time of Confucius, Chinese philosophy has looked back to a better time. The Japanese continued this Euchronic vision up until the Meiji Restoration, justifying all attempts at reform under the rubric of returning things to a previous, better condition. The Restoration itself, of course, was justified under the fundamentally Euchronic assertion of *restoring* the Japanese Emperor to his proper place. In contemporary literature, not surprisingly, the conservative backward-looking Euchronia is virtually absent (with the possible exception of Mishima's privileging of prewar militarism). What is perhaps more surprising, given the fascination with modernity and progress on the part of Japanese society, is that neither can I find many examples of any future Euchronias.
    The Eupsychia is also an important aspect of East Asian thought, appearing in the Buddhist notion of Nirvana or nothingness. It is also arguable that the aesthetic Utopia, based on an individual's artistic accomplishments, is an example of Eupsychia. In contemporary Japanese fantasy Murakami's novel *Hard Boiled Wonderland and the End of the World*, with its vision of a "perfect" world inside the protagonist's brain, may be seen as a problematic example of a Eupsychia.
6   Y. Kimyoshi 1984, pp. 24–25. Obviously, Japanese history contains its share of rebellions and wars, but it is true that, compared to many countries, it also had a remarkably long period of peace – the 250-year stretch of the Tokugawa period. Unlike China, where the Mandate of Heaven theory implicitly allowed for change of government or the post-Enlightenment West with its doctrine of individual rights, Japan seems to have had less of an explicit tradition of radical change from outside the established order. Indeed, when radical change was finally brought about in the Meiji Restoration it was justified by a tortuous combination of conservative philosophies, both neo-Confucianism and the nativist *Kokugaku* or national learning school, neither of which, with the possible exception of the neo-Confucianist, Chu Hsi, showed more than tangential concern with anti-authoritarian sentiment. For discussion of premodern Japanese political philosophy see Maruyama Masao, 1974. The *Kokugaku* philosophers and neo-Confucians were of course all from the elite samurai class. For a discussion of a possible merchant-class movement towards a more egalitarian system during this period see T. Najita, 1987.
7   Nakamura Shinichiro, 1984, p. 25.
8   Hino Tatsuo, 1977 pp. 4–9.
9   A. Delprat, 1985.

10 Yura Kimyoshi, 1982, p. 17; my translation.

11 Miyazawa Kenji, quoted in Ueda Makoto, 1983, p. 209.

12 S. Strong, 1991, p. 121. This quote is taken from the introduction to Strong's translation (Miyazawa, 1991), which she has entitled *Night of the Milky Way Railway*. Elsewhere, quoted material is my own translation of the Japan edition (Miyazawa, 1986).

13 Kurihara Akira, 1987, p. 53.

14 Ueda, 1983, pp. 186–187. For another discussion of Buddhist influences on *Night Train to the Stars* see Strong, 1991, pp. 130–131.

15 W. J. Tyler, 1990, p. xiv.

16 A more overtly fantastic story by Ishikawa which also contains references to a pastoral Utopia is his novella *Shion monogatari* (1956) (trans. *Asters* (1961)). In this densely textured historical work Ishikawa describes a community "on the other side of the mountains" in which "there are only good things ... people drink, sing, dance and enjoy themselves after a long day of hard work" (Donald Keene's translation, p. 141). Although this community is less ideologically realized than "Tora no Kuni" it is clearly related to the myth of the *Tōgenkyo* in its pastoral simplicity, peace, and isolation.

17 M. Wilson, 1986, pp. 116–117.

18 Kurihara, 1987, p. 53.

19 Ōe has an interesting discussion in English on Miyazawa's relation to "people's literature" (Ōe, 1989, pp. 212–213).

20 Miyoshi comments on this distinctive dialogic style as follows:

> What is important is the work's rejection of standard bureaucratic Japanese that serves merely as a transmitter of messages. The marginal and deformational zu-zu-drawl [Tohoku dialect] deflects the reader from the neutral flow of communication to the language of writing itself.
>
> (M. Miyoshi, 1991, p. 27)

21 Inoue Hisashi in "Umi," March 1982, quoted T. Imamura, 1982, p. 126.

22 Kurihara, 1983, p. 52.

23 In this regard they make an interesting contrast to what one might call the aesthetic Utopias of such (mainly) prewar writers as Kawabata and Tanizaki who, in such works as *Snow Country* or *Bridge of Dreams*, created private aesthetic and erotic worlds that were highly traditional, even self-consciously "Japanese," and untainted by any foreign influence whatsoever.

24 M. Cummings and N. Smith, 1989, p. 161.

25 Yamada Yusaku, 1988, p. 90.

26 Kawamura Minato, 1988, pp. 220–221.

27 Feminist Utopias have existed for over a century in the West but it is only since the 1970s that they have become a major part of contemporary Utopian writings. Indeed, many scholars credit the feminist movement of the early 1970s with bringing about a resurgence in Utopian writing in general. For more information on specifically feminine Utopias see, N. Albinski, 1988; L. Armitt, 1991; and S. Lefanu, 1988.

28 M. Foucault, 1984, p. 103.

29 In many ways the relationship of P and Himeko is reminiscent of the hero of *The Tale of Genji* and his young ward Tamakazura. In fact, *Amanonkoku ōkanki* as a whole contains many similarities to *The Tale of Genji*, a work

with which Kurahashi is intimately familiar. Both works privilege what are essentially Utopian worlds of women in which aesthetics, material enjoyment, and erotic play are foregrounded while the savage struggles for power to maintain this attractive life make up the subtext, as Norma Fields and Haruo Shirane (1987) have pointed out. Also like *The Tale of Genji*, Kurahashi's work revolves around a male protagonist's obsessive pursuit of a variety of women, although in this regard there is a crucial difference. In the Japan of *Genji*, difference was at least as much based on class as on sex. The high-class Genji was therefore not an intruder into this Utopian world. In contrast, P is and must remain an outsider. Genji, in fact, ends up contributing to the Utopian quality of the novel by gathering all his female partners around him in one more or less happy family, thus establishing for himself the *Heimat* that had eluded him since the death of his mother. P's narrative journey, on the other hand, begins in the womb and ends in his self-induced expulsion from it, another reason why I consider *Amanonkoku ōkanki* an essentially tragic novel.

30 In fact, on a superficial level, *Amanonkoku ōkanki* could be read as a satire on present-day Japanese relations with the West. Western imperialism and exploitation are clearly associated with Monokamikuni while the feminine, materially prosperous, and peaceful Amanon is equated with Japan in a number of obvious ways. *Amanonkoku ōkanki* can therefore also be interpreted as a satire on the West's failure to understand Japan, but I believe its deconstruction of male–female relationships is more central to the novel. For a more obvious and truly savage critique of western imperialism see Kurahashi's short story "Ōgurokokutokōki" (An Account of a Voyage to the Country of the Ogres) (1985).

31 P. Waugh, 1989, p. 175.

6　The dystopian imagination
From the asylum through the labyrinth to the end of the world

All negative Utopias are indictments of progress.
> (S. K. Vohra, *Negative Utopian Fiction*, p. 42)

From that point on there was no hometown for me. Nowhere to return to. What a relief! No one to want me, no one to want anything from me.
> (Murakami Haruki, *A Wild Sheep Chase*, p. 88)

As discussed in the Introduction, modern Japan has contained both Utopian and dystopian aspects, not only in the eyes of its citizens, but in the eyes of the West as well. Exotic, even larger than life, Japan seemed in the twentieth century to be constituted in extremes. From Meiji through the prewar period, its military and technological successes brought its citizens pride at the same time as the price of industrialization proved to be rural poverty and urban ferment in the 1920s. In the 1930s the government ventured abroad on increasingly blatant military adventures under the impressively titled Greater East Asia Coprosperity Sphere, a vision which promised, if not a Utopia, then at the very least a new world order. This vision faded as the war ground down and ended completely with the nuclear bombings of Hiroshima and Nagasaki, a defeat which made Japan temporarily an archetype of a devastated Third World nation.

This bleak image changed drastically only a few years after the war. In the postwar period Japan's economic advances in the 1960s once again impressed the rest of the world, although at the same time they brought about legendary pollution problems in land and water. For a time in the 1970s, however, Japan seemed to regain the Utopian high ground after scholars, politicians, and business professionals flocked to learn its secrets of industrial policy and social interaction.

In the 1980s this image of Japan as a technological and social Utopia came increasingly under attack from both inside and outside.

Trade tensions made some Westerners demonize the country they had formerly lauded. Images of the Japanese as "robots" or "terminators" become common currency in the Western press. An infamous quote from a European Community diplomat described the Japanese as a nation of worker bees living in rabbit hutches.

Surprisingly, while many Japanese took pride in Japan's increasing economic power versus what they perceived as a decadent Western model, others agreed with at least some of the West's negative assessments. Concern about certain of the problematic aspects of the vaunted Japanese educational system, such as the national epidemic of *ijime* (bullying) or the increasing numbers of disillusioned young dropouts from the system, drew national attention. Younger Japanese, echoing the "rabbit hutch" quote, complained about their crowded and unappealing living conditions and questioned the value of endless sacrifice for the company. The so-called "new religions," which had initially seemed to offer a sense of community to displaced city dwellers were frequently exposed as cynical shams preying on their naive adherents. A growing number of Japanese, both young and old, took to questioning the motives and ethics of the conservative politicians who, along with business and government bureaucrats, had ruled Japan since the end of the Occupation in what seemed an unbreakable combination.

Finally, in July 1993, the unthinkable happened. A combination of new parties and centrist older parties preaching genuine political reform ousted the Liberal Democratic Party which had been constantly in power since 1955. Experienced or cynical observers predicted that the new government would have problems keeping a majority against the extraordinarily well funded LDP. They were correct. In March of 1994 the new government was brought down by a previously unimaginable political alliance of the right-wing LDP and the left-wing socialists, old enemies now united only in their opportunistic interest in power.

It is against this complex background of success, failure, hope, and cynicism that I wish to discuss the development of the dystopian imagination in twentieth-century Japanese fantasy. Unlike the previous chapter which described a number of clearly delineated Utopian visions, this chapter deals with a dystopian imagination which is both more diffuse and more all-pervasive, encompassing everything from urban alienation to nuclear disaster. The dystopian imagination also cuts across a wide variety of genres, including pure literature, science fiction, live action film, and, perhaps most intriguingly, *manga* (comic books and animated films).

The works discussed in this chapter will therefore include film and *manga* as well as prose examples ranging from "pure literature" to science fiction. Although differing widely from one to the other in style and genre, these do share some important commonalities. Even more than Utopian fiction, dystopian literature is "message fiction," and the message is one of alarm and warning. Most of the works to be examined in this chapter are what Constance Penley (1989) calls "critical dystopias," works which critique contemporary life by exaggerating certain elements already existing within the modern world.[1] Rather than departing from consensus reality by offering alternatives, these fantasies drill into the real, transmogrifying it into a grotesque version of itself.

At the same time, however, the dystopian visions explored here are importantly related to the Utopian worlds discussed in the previous chapter. We remember that the majority of the Utopias previously discussed were animated by a desire or a search for a lost *Heimat*. In the anti-Utopian works to be considered here, Akutagawa Ryūnosuke's *Kappa* (1927) (trans. *Kappa* (1974)), Abe Kōbō's *Dai yon kampyō-ki* (1958) (trans. *Inter Ice Age 4* (1970)), Murakami Haruki's *Hitsuji o meguro bōken* (1982) (trans. *A Wild Sheep Chase* (1989)) and *Sekai no ōwari to hādo boirudo wandārando* (1985) (trans. *Hard Boiled Wonderland and the End of the World* (1991)), and Ōtomo Katsuhiro's *Akira*, it is the absence of any real "home" which is a paramount feature. The shadow of a homeland may still linger as a largely unattainable object of desire, but its existence seems increasingly unrelated to the lives of the protagonists.

Movement, which we saw as an important aspect of the Utopias, is also privileged here, but it now contains very different ideological and emotional connotations. As with many Western dystopias, motion in order to escape some threatening form of entrapment is often a key feature. In these largely nihilistic dystopias, however, the escapes are often futile. Even more ominously, as in *Kappa*, the escaped protagonist discovers that he wishes to return to the presumed dystopia.

Another literary device that is inverted is the quest. When a search is enacted, the object of the search is either a highly problematic one, such as the Kappan double in *Kappa*, or else absurd, as in the magical sheep in *A Wild Sheep Chase*. Guidance, if it comes, is often wrong or mistaken. Authority figures are difficult to find and usually of a suspect nature.

Instead of help, both protagonist and reader are given what are essentially "burned out maps," to borrow a title of Abe Kōbō's, ineffective charts of worlds that offer nothing beyond dark visions of a failed humanity or, sometimes, a failed Japan. History, which we saw as

being reshaped and rediscovered in the Utopian chapter, is now noticeable by its absence, or, even worse, as something to be escaped. Technology is now totally sinister and oppressive, and internationalization has
only brought about the empty world of consumer products described
in Murakami's works.

A universal element of all dystopian fiction is the utter bleakness of
the worlds delineated. Far from the highly colored Edo of Ishikawa,
Kurahashi's bountiful Tokio (sic), or the idealized villages of Miyazawa, Ōe, or Inoue, these worlds tend to be depressingly urban. Distorted paradigms of progress, such as ominously labyrinthine hospitals
and laboratories, characterize these dystopias. Nature is almost totally
absent, a particularly noticeable phenomenon when one considers
the importance of nature as a Utopian refuge in much of twentieth-
century Japanese literature.

The marginal location of Utopias is often replaced by a dystopian
centrality. Thus, Akutagawa's Kappaland is a macro-satire of an entire
country, the Japan of the Taishō period, centered in its capital city,
while Abe's novels are located in large cities and concern an established elite of science or medicine. Murakami takes on the complex
interrelations between corporations and the central government in
Hard Boiled Wonderland and the End of the World and *A Wild Sheep
Chase*; his vision even extends downwards to the sewers and subway
systems of downtown Tokyo. Most brilliantly realized of all is the
exceptional image of the decaying post World War III capital of
twenty-first-century "Neo-Tokyo," created by Ōtomo Katsuhiro in
Akira. Here the city itself, from the sewers to the skyline, becomes at
least as important a character as the protagonists within it.

Japanese dystopias share their visions of an absurd quest, a problematization of history and technology, and bleak urban imagery with
much postmodern and dystopian literature in the West.[2] There are
some important differences, however, which may be related to the
respective roles of dystopia in Western and Japanese literature in
general. To understand the role of dystopia in Japanese literature
it is helpful to understand the major importance of dystopias in
general in modern thought.

THE DYSTOPIAN TRADITION

It is virtually a truism that the twentieth century has been the age of
the anti-Utopia or dystopia.[3] In the past satirical critiques existed,
such as the writings of Marcus Aurelius or Jonathan Swift, whose
Gulliver's Travels contains both Utopian and dystopian elements. The

Christian notion of hell is as dystopian as heaven is Utopian. But neither premodern satirical visions nor the inferno fully embody the notion of dystopia with which the twentieth century has become familiar: this contemporary concept of dystopia usually expresses itself in two reinforcing visions – technology run amok and a repressive totalitarian government able to exploit that technology. Both these elements are inextricably linked to the modern world.

Other reasons for twentieth-century ascendance may have to do with the fact that, as the term "anti-Utopia" suggests, the anti-Utopia exists only in reaction to Utopia, and it was in the nineteenth century that Utopian thought particularly flourished. The great anti-Utopias of twentieth-century Western literature, such as Zamyatin's *We*, Orwell's *1984* or Huxley's *Brave New World*, can and have been seen as more or less explicit written reactions to the Utopian dreams of Marxism and socialism, or else to the belief in technological progress first espoused in the early works of H. G. Wells and exemplified in contemporary American culture. By showing Utopia-as-nightmare, these works question the belief in a better future that Utopian fiction was founded upon.

Japan too, as was chronicled in the previous chapter, was caught up in a form of Utopianism in the nineteenth century, although the Meiji program of "Civilization and Enlightenment" owed much more to Spenser's social Darwinism and to the Victorians' idea of technological progress than it did to Marxist ideology. The Japanese were also avid readers of Western science fiction writers such as Jules Verne, Conan Doyle, and especially H. G. Wells whose early visions of a roseate future, argues Mark Hillegas (1967), contain "many of the central as well as the peripheral images in the (later) anti-Utopias."[4]

Despite this common background, however, prewar Japanese literature seems relatively devoid of dystopias in the sense of the classic totalitarian governments brought chillingly to life by Zamyatin and Orwell. Initially, this lack seems surprising since, as in the West, the tradition of satire, the forerunner of dystopia, was strong in premodern Japan, beginning with the visual satires of Heian period scrolls and reaching its greatest height in the Edo period humour of writers such as Hiraga Gennai and Ihara Saikaku. Furthermore, although the Shinto religion contains little in the way of a complex hell, a topos which is usually cited as the initial model for dystopias in the West, Buddhism brought to Japan in the medieval period a rich and highly colored vision of a variety of hells.[5]

A number of explanations are possible for this relative lack of totalitarian dystopias: one may simply be censorship. By the time the dystopian tradition was becoming established in the West (*We*, arguably the first modern dystopia, was published in 1920), the Japanese government was becoming increasingly concerned with politically suspect fiction. Although anti-establishment proletarian literature survived into the 1930s, its descriptions of repressive landlords and capitalists were severely dealt with. Presumably, descriptions of repressive governments bearing any likeness to the contemporary Japanese situation would have been treated even more harshly.[6]

Another possible reason for the absence of dystopian visions of a totalitarian government may have been the paradoxical influence of the *shishōsetsu* ("I"-novel) on formerly politically committed writers. Politics, particularly communism or socialism and their disillusionments, has often been the primary inspiration for anti-Utopian fiction. Anarchist movements existed in the prewar period and were a prime excuse for the repressive government measures. The Japanese intellectuals of the prewar period were often strongly committed to a wide spectrum of radical ideologies but, upon becoming disillusioned with them, the writers' first impulse was to create a *shishōsetsu* type of work treating his or her own personal life, rather than a fantasy world delineating a repressive political state. Thus, there exists a considerable number of so-called *tenkō shōsetsu* or apostasy novels concerning a writer's giving up his or her faith in Marxism, but these are told from a totally personal point of view after the writer's reconversion, and have little discussion of ideology itself.[7]

Finally, the prewar Japanese were still used to a relatively more authoritarian government than most Western writers who reacted with such horror to the excesses of Nazi Germany or the revelations of the Soviet Union under Stalin. The authoritarian and patriarchal tradition of the Tokugawa shogunate was far from entirely broken by the Meiji state. Although a constitution, modelled on the Prussian one, was eventually "given" to the Japanese people, the Western liberal emphasis on individual rights and freedoms was not a key element in Meiji statist thought. As was illustrated in the so-called *seiji shōsetsu* (political novels), the Utopian (or at least futuristic) elements of the new state were not so much its philosophy but its emphasis on modernization, in short, creating a state of industrial capitalism with an educated work-force to sustain it.

It is not surprising, therefore, that the modern Japanese dystopian tradition is less concerned with the crushing of the individual will, a narrative element which is a major feature of Western dystopias (although there are exceptions, most notably in Abe Kōbō's postwar works, as we will see). At the same time, however, the modern Japanese anti-Utopias do tend to conform to what is one of the other most important Western categories of the dystopia, the technological nightmare. If anything, the Japanese works highlight this aspect even more, emphasizing not simply the general failure of technology but also the dark interlocking nexus between industry, science, and the military.

It is also not surprising, therefore, that some of the earliest Japanese dystopias appear in popular culture films and magazines, or that science fiction, a genre eagerly embraced by the Japanese, became a major showcase for dystopian works.[8] Indeed, dystopias and science fiction have long been interrelated in all modern cultures. Not only is science fiction, with its explicit concern with technology, a particularly appropriate vehicle for dealing with both the problems and potential of modernity, but it is also a genre that is peculiarly part of the twentieth century as is dystopian literature. Or, as Jameson puts it, "[science fiction serves to] defamiliarize and restructure our experience of our own *present* and to do so in various ways distinct from all other forms of defamiliarization."[9]

In regard to this, the quotation from Vohra at the beginning of this chapter, "All negative Utopias are indictments of progress," is relevant. Although Vohra is commenting on Western dystopias, his remark is even more apt for Japan, especially from the 1920s through the 1990s during which time the Japanese "present" went from being characterized as hopelessly technologically backward to becoming by the 1960s a world-renowned success story based on "progress." Science fiction in general and the dystopian novel in particular are able to tell the other side of that success story, to defamiliarize it so that "progress" may be seen in a more complex and ambiguous light.

An ambivalent attitude toward progress is hardly unique to Japan, as Vohra's statement makes clear, but there is another aspect of technological progress which is specifically Japanese. This is the fact that, until recently, technology in Japan came from an alien source, the West. Thus, "industrialization," "progress," and even "science" itself were all indissolubly linked with "Westernization" in the Japanese consciousness until the economic boom of the 1960s. Furthermore, initially at least, science and technology were held in relative contempt as simply useful tools to be exploited, rather than as cultural products in themselves; an attitude summed up in the nineteenth-century slogan, "Eastern Ethics and Western Technology."

With the passage of time the Japanese found that technology brought with it a new way of life and thought which eventually infiltrated much of Japanese culture, and the emptiness of this slogan was realized. As Najita puts it, the prewar Japanese considered that

Technology as a system of knowledge and production belonged to
the Western Other, and had been directly imported into the native
historical stream rendering much of that history artificial.[10]

Najita's statement raises two important aspects of technological
progress: its negative effect on history and its "Otherness." I will discuss the role or rather the absence of history from modern Japanese
dystopias later on, but for now I would like to concentrate on the sense
of "Otherness" which technology brought to Japanese culture. Perhaps because technology was so overtly Other, not only fantasy and
science fiction but modern Japanese fiction in general was quick to
emphasize the dehumanization brought by it. Najita goes on to describe how Sōseki, for example, described the modern Japanese as "a
crippled personality," incapable of independent thought or action.[11]

If history is "artificial" and personality is "crippled" in the Japanese
confrontation between culture and technology, it is hardly surprising
that many Japanese dystopias concern a search for something lost;
searches are often identified with madness or dreams. It is also appropriate that the first fictional descriptions of dystopias appeared at the
same time as Japan's first major efforts at industrialization were beginning to succeed in transforming both country and city.

Paradoxically, the very success of Meiji modernization laid the
grounds for critiques from all ranges of society. As Najita puts it,
"Beginning in 1910, we detect a wide range of critiques against the
previous transformational synthesis of the Meiji era that subordinated
culture in relation to the new knowledge of Western technology."[12] As
Najita's essay goes on to suggest, however, the "defense" of culture
was an increasingly rearguard action, as intellectuals became more and
more aware of the overwhelming power of technology and industrialization sweeping their world.

Thus, the equation of modern industrial life with an anti-human
world began to flourish in the prewar fiction of the late Meiji and
particularly the Taishō periods. Taishō was a time when the roseate
dreams of Meiji were beginning to show a nightmare side with the rise
of unemployment, the spread of the factory, and the increasing depend-
ence by both urban and rural populations on the outside economic
factors that made up the "take-off stage" in the developing Japanese
capitalism. It is against this bleak "consensus reality" which dystopian
literature was reacting.

The critique of Meiji's dark side was not confined to popular culture. The most articulate commentary on the problem of modernization in general occurs in the works of Natsume Sōseki. In his famous

essay "The Civilization of Modern-day Japan" Sōseki compared the modern Japanese to someone undergoing a nervous breakdown in an attempt to change on so many levels at the same time.[13] In his mimetic 1912 novel, *Kōjin* (trans. *The Wayfarer* (1969)), Sōseki becomes more specific and clearly links technological advance to madness. In one memorable scene in *The Wayfarer* the protagonist goes so far as to state categorically that:

> Man's insecurity stems from the advance of science. Never once has science, which never ceases to move forward, allowed us to pause. From walking to ricksha, from ricksha to carriage, from carriage to train, from train to automobile, from there on to the dirigible, further on to the airplane, and further on and on, no matter how far we may go, it won't let us take a breath. How far it will sweep us along, nobody knows for sure. It is really frightening.
>
> (p. 285)

Sōseki's hero articulates one of the major themes of the works in this chapter, the obsession with constant movement that leads nowhere in combination with a fear of technological advancement. An even bleaker example occurs in Sōseki's experimental 1908 work *Kōfu* (trans. *The Miner* (1988)). In this novel the protagonist leaves the city to move literally downward into what a fellow worker calls "the gates of Hell" (p. 104), the copper mines whose brutal conditions became infamous during this period. The journey which had led to hope in the Utopian novels now becomes a futile descent into a labyrinth.

While Sōseki's visions of hell occurred in primarily realistic settings (with the exception, of course, of his nightmare psychological hells in *Ten Nights of Dream*), other near-contemporary writers explored fantasy worlds in which mental illness met with modern urban technology. Of these, the extraordinary and unfortunately untranslated works of the popular writer Yumeno Kyūsaku deserve special note. Yumeno Kyūsaku's most important novel, written in 1935, *Dogura magura*, is set in a hospital in Kyushu where the amnesiac protagonist attempts to discover his identity through psychotherapy and finally unearths both an hereditary genetic problem and an ancient family curse.

This complex work is a fascinating mazelike mystery story that suggests an extremely grim view of Taishō culture. As Imaizumi Fumiko (1991) points out, the "modern" red-brick asylum which the protagonist characterizes as the "bottomless crazy hell which extends on the other side of modern culture" is not simply the insane asylum but the "modern city itself."[14] *Dogura magura* is perhaps Kyūsaku's most extensive statement on the horrors of modern life but, throughout

Kyūsaku' work, deranged, amnesiac, and sexually ambivalent characters move through nightmare settings that finally suggest the entire twentieth-century world to be an insane anti-Utopia.[15]

Not only fiction writers shared this implicit equation of modernity and madness. In 1926 a Japanese film director, Kinugusa Teinosuke, directed a film entitled *Kurutta ippeiji* (*A Page of Madness*), a landmark avant-garde work set in an insane asylum. A complex exploration of reality, memory, and fantasy written in collaboration with Kawabata Yasunari, *A Page of Madness* climaxes in an asylum riot in which the inmates one by one remove their masks, a scene which could be interpreted either as a search for identity or else, perhaps, as an abandonment of the search for identity.

A Page of Madness was well received at the time but only recently has it been rediscovered and hailed for its sophisticated ability to "*play on the codes*"[16] of Western cinematic art. In fact, Noel Burch goes so far as to say that Kinugusa's film was slightly "ahead of its time,"[17] and although he is referring to the sophisticated narrative techniques of montage and free floating signifiers which the film displays, I might suggest that it was Taishō Japan itself that was "ahead of its time," in its concatenation of technological, industrial, and social upheaval.

Particularly because so many of these changes were imported,[18] the period can be seen as a nexus of modernity. Lack of control over one's fate, a sense of omnipresent powers, and the increasing awareness of technology's dehumanizing effects, achieved an intense encapsulation. The mental asylum became a central image for the era. The concept of trying on different roles and the interpenetration of reality and fantasy are aspects both of the mental asylum and the Taishō period itself.[19]

THE FIRST JAPANESE DYSTOPIA: AKUTAGAWA AND TAISHŌ JAPAN

Yumeno Kyūsaku's and Kinoshita's nightmare visions of Taishō Japan also came to be shared by the well-known "pure literature" writer Akutagawa Ryūnosuke, especially in his later works. His posthumously published short story "Haguruma" (1927) (trans. "Cogwheels" (1965)) discussed in Chapter 4 is a particularly bleak example of madness inside an urban labyrinth. The title itself evokes a demonic technological force. In fact the "Cogwheels" are merely apparitions that appear in front of the desperate protagonist's eyes (and indeed may have links to real mental diseases), but the surreal image of constantly moving mechanical objects is an excellent topos for a vision of incipient collapse.

Akutagawa also uses images of the train and airplane as fearsome alien forces in "Cogwheels." Undoubtedly, some of these visions are personal ones (his brother-in-law committed suicide beneath a train), but his dislike of technology seems to have been part of a more general attitude characteristic of the Taishō period. Even non-fantastic writers used the cultural instrumentalities of nascent capitalism in their work to capture the bleakness of a society lost in the turmoils of modernization.

Miriam Silverberg has traced the poet Nakano Shigeharu's use of such topical imagery as trains and prisons to a culture of "reproduction" that was just taking off in the Taishō period. According to Silverberg, Nakano's work emphasizes the "constant repetitive movement of capitalist society" in its attempts simultaneously to offer presumed innovation that actually "concealed the repetitive and non-progressive aspects of social and economic reproduction."[20]

While poets and writers were attacking the commodification of culture in the cities, folklorists and anthropologists such as Yanagita Kunio were abandoning urban areas to search for a genuine folk "identity" in the countryside. Implicit in this search, Harootunian suggests, was the "real problem," which was "the confrontation between city and countryside which, it was generally acknowledged, had already inflicted irreparable damage on the latter in the interest of developing the former."[21]

Japan's first full-blown dystopian novel, *Kappa* (1927) (trans. *Kappa* (1974)), appeared during this period. Written by Akutagawa, whose aforementioned "Cogwheels" played on the theme of the nightmarish industrial city, *Kappa* is a problematic novel because it seems to combine aspects of the confessional *shishōsetsu* within a clearly fantastic genre inspired by both Swift's *Gulliver's Travels* and Samuel Butler's *Erewhon*.[22] Thus, Japanese literary criticism of it has tended to be divided between those interested in tracing Akutagawa's own private agony (he said that "*Kappa* was born out of my disgust for many things, including myself"), and those who appreciated the work's clever and far-reaching evisceration of Taishō Japan.[23]

For our purposes, it is not necessary to resolve the debate, but it is useful to note that the personal aspect of *Kappa* is not unique in dystopian literature. Most of the great satirists and dystopian critics have been animated by some sort of deep and negative emotion, perhaps one reason why dystopias tend to be read longer than the often blander Utopian fiction. Thus, most of the writers discussed in this chapter also have invested personal experiences and emotions into their fictional creations.[24]

But it is through this investment that Akutagawa was able to satirize contemporary Japanese society in general. He accomplishes this by telling the archetypal dystopian/Utopian story of an everyman journeying in an alien land, but at the same time incorporating specific elements of Taishō Japan including its culture of reproduction. The alien country Akutagawa envisions is Kappaland, peopled by Kappas, or Japanese water sprites. The way into Kappaland, intriguingly, is through a hole in the bucolic mountain wilderness of Nagano, an unconscious reminder, perhaps, that it is impossible to escape modern industrial society even in the countryside.

Kappa's first line sets its ominous tone: "This is the story of Patient No. 23 in one of our mental homes" (p. 435). The narrative, therefore, is already calling attention to its suspect and even fantastic nature at the same time as it sets the bleak and disturbing tone for the rest of the work. The actual description of the asylum is brief, however, and most of the remainder of the work is devoted to "Patient No. 23"'s narration of his adventures. One "ordinary summer's day" while hiking in the mountains, the narrator becomes lost in the mist and ends up taking shelter on a river bank. Happening to glance at his watch, the narrator then notices a "fleeting reflection" (p. 49) in the watch glass, that of a "weird eerie face" (p. 49). He jumps up to pursue the Kappa (for that is what it is) for many minutes only to lose him finally in a clump of grass. However, the narrator continues, "But I was not to know that there was some sort of hole just there. I was just getting the tips of my fingers on his glassy slippery back when I suddenly found myself toppling headlong, deep into a pitch black abyss" (p. 50).

In its opening vision *Kappa* thus brilliantly evokes some of the basic contemporary dystopian tropes, the culture of reproduction in the Kappan double, the mountain retreat which is no longer safe, and finally the descent underground, into the abyss. Even the image of the Western watch is interesting, an import through which the Japanese protagonist reconstructs himself as a Kappa. Written in the year of Akutagawa's suicide (as was "Cogwheels"), *Kappa* is a sometimes uneasy amalgam of fantasy and black-humored grotesque. The fall into Kappaland echoes *Alice in Wonderland*, while the Kappa figure itself comes out of traditional folklore where, as mentioned in Chapter 4, it plays a kind of "trickster" role, as a half-amusing, half-malicious water sprite.

Kappa is far from a children's fantasy, however. Rather, it is a savage parody of Akutagawa's world, a "reproduction" that is exaggerated on every level. Thus, the narrator awakens far from the sylvan setting where Kappans are traditionally expected to be found, to discover that he is in a street, "which for all I could see, looked just like Ginza, the main street in Tokyo" (p. 52). Contemporary readers no doubt discovered similarities between Kappaland and Taishō Japan almost immediately, as they followed the protagonist on a guided tour of Kappan life and society.

Kappa parodies virtually all aspects of Japanese society but its main targets are familiar to most dystopian fiction.[25] For example, some of Akutagawa's most savage critiques are aimed at the collusion between capitalists and the military exemplified by the grossly obese Kappa Gael, "a capitalist to end all capitalists" (p. 81), according to the narrator. The work also anticipates Aldous Huxley's *Brave New World* and other satires on scientific tinkering with humans, not to mention fascism itself, in describing the Kappan government eugenics campaign to "eradicate evil heredity" by having "all hale and healthy kappas marry unsound and unhealthy kappas"(p. 63).

Other targets include a brilliant and extremely mordant satire on art and artists personified by the pathetic poet, Tok, who commits suicide but returns in a seance to find out about his posthumous reputation. On a level more specific to modern Japan, the work also includes an accurate and extensive critique of the Japanese fascination with modern Western trends, parodied in the novella as "Modernism" or "Viverism."

Sometimes the parallel between Kappan and Japanese society is drawn rather heavy-handedly. For example, the protagonist is shocked to discover that unemployed workers in Kappaland are slaughtered and used as meat. When he protests at the barbarity of this practice, his friend Gael merely replies, "Tell me, isn't it true that, in your country, the daughters of the fourth class are sold into prostitution?" (p. 84).

Some of the novella's most telling points focus on the notion of technology overpowering culture. The narrator finds himself "astonished by the advanced state of mechanization in the industries of Kappaland" (p. 82). He is particularly impressed by the new method of Kappan book production: "simply pouring paper, ink and a grey-looking powder into a funnel mouth machine" (p. 82) will produce a book in five seconds. The material used for the books is ass-brain, a satirical swipe no doubt aimed at Akutagawa's fellow authors, but also, perhaps, at his readers as well.

The relationship between technology and mass culture is exemplified in the novella's description of the mass production, not only of books, but of art and music as well. Indeed, the narrator discovers that "in an average month Kappaland sees the invention of as many as seven or

eight hundred new devices of this kind" (p. 83), but there is no comment on the quality of these "devices." Furthermore, this technological "progress" is also seen as responsible for the rise in unemployment,
leading to the aforementioned appropriately technological solution of
grinding the unemployed workers into meat.

Somewhat more unusual for prewar dystopian fiction, and more
specific to Japan, is *Kappa*'s dissection of the Japanese family system
and the family in general. One especially vivid image of the family
system occurs when the narrator relates how a male Kappa "who was
still quite young, was staggering along the street, gasping desperately
for breath; draped around his neck were seven or eight Kappas, including two who looked like his mother and father" (p. 66).

This scene is reminiscent of "Cogwheel"'s surreal fantasy of being
pursued by one's brother-in-law/double, but adds a few more bodies
for comic and grotesque effect. Ironically, however, the narrator strives
to find something "admirable" in the young Kappa's self-sacrifice
which makes him, as a Kappan friend comments derisively, "a good
citizen of our Kappaland, as well as your own country" (p. 66).

Other scenes in *Kappa* show the family in an even darker light,
without allowing any of the above rationalizations. Perhaps the most
memorable of these is the birth scene where the Kappan fetus refuses
to be born because he does not want to inherit his father's insanity and
he also believes Kappan existence to be evil.

This scene can and has been read on many levels, most prominently
as a straightforward echo of Akutagawa's own personal preoccupation
with insanity, due to his fear of inheriting his mother's madness. Related to this, a more general interpretation sees the fetus' rejection of
the world as tied to Akutagawa's own state of disgust with life when he
was writing *Kappa*.

We might also point out, however, that the fetus's rejection of his
father anticipates a rejection of the family, the past, and of history that
will become a major element in postwar dystopian fantasies. Furthermore, the notion that Kappan/human existence is "evil" borders on
the total nihilism that becomes an increasing element in postwar fiction as well.

Kappa ends on a typically Akutagawan twist, one which intensifies
the bleakness of its vision even more. This twist is the problematic role
of the insane asylum and the relationship of fiction/fantasy to reality.
It transpires that the narrator decides to escape back to the "real
world" of modern Japan. Once he has returned home, however, he
succumbs, like Swift's Gulliver, to loneliness for his previous Other
world. Unlike Gulliver, however, *Kappa's* protagonist ends up in a

mental asylum where he insists on telling his tale to anyone who will listen, at the same time insisting that his Kappan friends come to visit him often. The last scene includes the narrator "reading" a poem (actually a "tattered telephone directory") which goes as follows:

> In the palm flowers, among the bamboo
> Buddha long went fast asleep
>
> With the withered fig tree by the roadside,
> Christ, too, is already dead.
> But we all need our rest –
> Even in front of the stage set
>
> When you look behind the set,
> You find only patched canvas.

(p. 141)

Kappa plays extensively with the interlocking problems of language, fantasy, and perception as the image of the "patched canvas" stage set suggests. In terms of language, the madman's "delirium," as Foucault has pointed out, has traditionally taken on special significance in the West as a "cycle of non-being" presented in confrontation to the discourse of reality.[26] But Patient No. 23 is attempting to replace reality with his own version of "non-being." He does this by telling his tale to the unnamed first narrator, thereby attempting to give himself a past, a history that will provide him with a rationale and an identity, albeit a clearly manufactured one. The fact that his tale is suspect is overshadowed by the realization that he prefers it, "the stage set," to the reality of his own grim existence.

In fact, Patient No. 23 makes attempts to escape back to Kappaland, also echoing Swift's Gulliver in his aversion to humanity following his own travels. It is interesting to compare the ending of *Kappa* with that of *Gulliver's Travels*. In the case of Gulliver, we are left with the impression of a man and a narrator in control of his plot and his identity, who, although he despises his fellow humans as "yahoos," at least has the memory of a superior civilization to comfort him. Furthermore, Swift's protagonist is left alone and tolerated by his family and friends. Far from being considered "mad," he is said to live in "good esteem among his neighbours."

Incarcerated in his asylum, Akutagawa's protagonist drifts off into poetry and fantasies of his Kappan friends coming to him. Escape through language, art, or narrative acts is now his only hope, but these are all seen as acts of madness. In Akutagawa's vision, however, these are the only possible acts in an increasingly insane world.

To make this point even clearer, the last lines of the novella concern a Kappan friend of the narrator who "went quite out of his mind. Someone told me that he's now in a mental hospital in Kappaland. If only the doctor in charge would give his consent, it would be nice to go and visit him. But . . ." (p. 141).

Kappa thus ends in a hall of mirrors where vision is constantly doubled or revised. Its vision is less of the apocalyptic kind that we see in some dystopias and more a dark excoriation of contemporary life in general, typical of the "critical dystopia." Akutagawa's dystopia is not set in the future, nor is it really set in another world. Instead, it is reproduced all around him and, as such, there is no escape except through the transforming powers of the literary imagination or madness.

THE INTERWAR YEARS: FROM CENSORSHIP TO THE DECADENTS

A few months after *Kappa* was written, Akutagawa committed suicide, leaving a note which said in part that he was killing himself because of "a vague anxiety about the future." This vague anxiety was, of course, a personal one, but it seemed to many Japanese intellectuals at the time to encapsulate their own feelings about the future as well. As it turned out, Akutagawa's uneasiness was highly prescient. The Japan of the next decade, the 1930s, became an increasingly unfriendly place for writers of any kind as militarism and censorship mounted in parallel fashion. Except for formulaic boys' fantasy tales involving the glorious Japanese empire conquering the rest of the world, very little fantastic literature was produced during this time.

With the end of the war and the relaxation of censorship, a more imaginative form of literature began to be written but, initially, dystopias *per se* were few. The reasons behind this absence are perhaps obvious, since the Japanese in 1945 did not have to look very far to find the opposite of a Utopia; it was all around them in the rubble of Tokyo and the ashes of Hiroshima. Perhaps the closest thing to dystopian fiction might be found in the writings of the so-called decadents or *buraiha* such as Sakaguchi Ango or Ishikawa Jun. These writers exaggerated the already ghastly environment around them to produce nihilistic portraits of a society gone mad and whose values have been totally turned upside down. To make their points, writers such as Sakaguchi attacked some of the most obvious and long-cherished values of the prewar Japanese culture. Sakaguchi's "Sakura no mori no mankai no shita" (Under the Forest of Cherry Trees in Full

Bloom) (1956), for example, is a bitter parody of the Japanese fetish for cherry blossoms, alleging that far from beautiful or lyrical, cherry blossoms are ominous and sinister and connected to madness.

The theme of omnipresent madness and horror is also dealt with in Ishikawa Jun's "Yakeato no Iesu" (Jesus of the Ruins) (1946), in which a young boy upsets the black market by his impish or perhaps even demonic activities. Ishikawa's work later went on to produce notably Utopian visions as well, some of which I have discussed in the previous chapter, but in 1953 he also created a novel which contains certain clearly dystopian elements. This work, *Taka* (The Hawk) (1953), is a surreally grim fantasy containing such typically dystopian elements as an underground revolutionary movement united in a dream of a "new order," fighting against a vast conglomerate of uniformed enemies. It also uses the topos of the prison cell with grim effectiveness: by suggesting the shadow of a hawk on the wall of the protagonist's cell, it sets freedom and energy against a grey world of uniformity.

POSTWAR DYSTOPIAN VISIONS

Ishikawa's bleak vision is offset somewhat by his images of freedom and escape. This tension between entrapment and freedom is maintained in the works of other writers who became famous in the 1950s and 1960s but, by the 1980s, even such relative optimism seems largely to disappear. The reasons behind this are related to both the writers' personal experiences and their respective places in postwar Japanese history. Thus, the writers who dominated the 1960s and 1970s such as Abe Kōbō, Ōe Kenzaburō, and even the popular science fiction author Komatsu Sakyō, all grew up during the war and undoubtedly its destructive shadow influenced their often apocalyptic visions. At the same time, however, the values taught by the prewar period and even the Occupation authorities gave these older writers some moral base from which to propound their ideas. Even if, as in the case of Abe and Ōe, they disagreed with the prewar emperor system, the writers still tended to have some moral center in their works and described characters willing to fight against the dystopian worlds created by the authors.

While the older generation of postwar writers still held on to some ideals even as they described the alienation and materialism of modern Japan (although Abe, in particular, became increasingly nihilistic by the end of his life), the most recent generation of dystopian writers are notable for their lack of any moral center. Thus, Murakami Haruki creates a world of materialism and corruption where the only basis for moral authority is in the individual. Ōtomo Katsuhirō is even more bleak; his world contains no heroes, only villains and victims of a vast military industrial conspiracy. The works also contain few descriptions of attempts to subvert these bleak worlds. Resistance, if any, is on the level of individual escape.

The three older writers still seem to be grounded in an ideological system which suggests the possibility of a moral center somewhere. Abe expressed Marxist beliefs throughout much of his life, while Ōe is still a strongly left-wing humanist. Komatsu is more conservative; his works often privilege a lost world of Japanese culture. In contrast, the most recent Japanese dystopias highlight a world in which tradition, be it elite or folk, and moral values are totally lost, and this loss is seen as a release rather than a tragedy.

INTO THE LABYRINTH: ABE KŌBŌ'S JOURNEY FROM HOPE TO APOCALYPSE

Disappointment and a highly ambivalent longing for "home" are two of the key elements in the works of Abe Kōbō, whose extraordinarily imaginative and consistently dark visions have made him arguably the greatest writer of dystopias in modern Japan. One of Japan's most internationally renowned writers, Abe's examinations of humanity entrapped in a meaningless existence, unable to escape from others or themselves, seem to have struck a responsive chord throughout the world. Critics have found the influence of Kafka, Camus, and Sartre in his work, while his early overtly Marxist ideology made him highly accessible as well. At the same time, Abe is an exceptionally original and highly personal writer using certain recurring metaphors, situations, and themes in his work to create one of the most consistently dark and surreal fictional worlds of any writer, Japanese or Western. What Todorov says of Kafka's technique is appropriate for Abe as well: "we are ... confronted with a *generalized fantastic* which swallows up the entire world of the book and the reader along with it."[27]

Abe's rather unusual background is worth mentioning at this point, since it provides some clues both to the particular themes he explores and also, perhaps, to why his works seem so internationally accessible. Unlike virtually all of the other writers considered here, Abe grew up outside of Japan in the Japanese colony of Manchuria. No doubt because of his essential rootlessness, Abe's works, although they often show his protagonists searching for an elusive "home," usually show that "home" to be unattainable, in important distinction to his peers such as Ōe and Inoue. Also unusual for a writer, when he did return to Japan at the age of sixteen he studied medicine, instead of literature, at Tokyo University. Not surprisingly, Abe's writing has sometimes strayed toward the science fiction genre and even his more clearly fantastic works are informed by a coldly logical scientific mentality.

Abe's works often deal with scientific questions in relatively sophisticated form, at the same time as he is also one of Japanese literature's most articulate critics of the alienating aspects of technology on human beings. In his insistence on the dangers of technology, Abe is of course hardly alone among writers, either Japanese or Western, but it is interesting to note that the years in which his works achieved their greatest success in Japan, the 1960s, were also the decade when Japan achieved both double-digit economic growth and the beginning of technological preeminence in many industries. Conversely, Abe's works began to lose their following in the late 1980s when Japan's preeminence in technology became increasingly accepted and valued by the younger generation of Japanese.

Abe's double outsiderhood of medicine and Manchuria, may help to account for the distinctiveness of his vision, but his dystopian worlds also share important commonalities with the rest of the dystopian fiction examined in this chapter. Like *Kappa*, his work concerns doubling and the search for identity, as well as often exploring the gap between illusion and reality. Also like *Kappa*, Abe's work problematizes the family system, though in ways that are more obviously avant-garde. Abe's works also often deal with madness (or at least what would be considered madness from some socially based norm), although Abe locates the sites of madness no longer in the mental asylum but among institutions that might be expected to be citadels of responsible and rational behaviour – the labyrinthine corridors of universities, laboratories, and hospitals.

Indeed, Abe's work falls collectively within a genre that in film criticism is known as "paranoid horror," the sense of the individual being alone in an ominous, threatening world where a friendly face often hides an enemy.[28] Conspiracies abound and the individual is usually left with no way to escape. The feeling of paranoia is one typical to the dystopian genre, but Abe carries it further than most. Thus, in the first of his novels to be considered, *Dai yon kampyō-ki* (1958) (trans. *Inter Ice Age 4* (1970)), the protagonist's enemy turns out to be himself.

Inter Ice Age 4 is a landmark novel in a number of ways. It is genuinely classifiable as science fiction, although it was written by a practitioner of *junbungaku* or "pure literature." The two genres were considered quite separate at the time. It is also a detailed, thorough, and believable vision of a dystopian future in which technology overwhelms all aspects of life. In fact, *Inter Ice Age 4* is actually set in two futures, the very near and the very far. The very near future occupies most of the narrative space of the novel and consists of an alienating urban world familiar from much of Abe's fiction.

In this near future a team of scientists headed by the novel's protagonist, Professor Katsumi of the Institute for Computer Technique, develop a computer which can predict future events. Attempting to substantiate some of the computer's predictions, Katsumi becomes involved in a murder, apparently accidentally. He discovers that the murder victim has been dealing in aborted fetuses at about the time that his pregnant wife undergoes a bizarre experience: She is lured to a hospital and forcibly aborted, after which she is paid three thousand yen.

A second strange event occurs at this time which is a series of warning phone calls to the professor from an anonymous person whose voice sounds strangely familiar. Mixing elements of mystery and science fiction, *Inter Ice Age 4* eventually arrives at a brilliant and provocative conclusion in which all is revealed: The professor is the victim of a conspiracy on the part of his colleagues who have used the computer to predict the future and found that it foresees a time when global warming will cause the seas to rise and cover the land. To prepare for this, the scientists are attempting to develop a race of "aquans," human beings with gills attached to them so they can live safely under water. The professor's aborted baby will become one of them.

Furthermore, it turns out that his colleagues have also used the computer to produce a computer simulacrum of the professor himself. It is this computer personality who is the mysteriously familiar voice on the other end of the phone. Unfortunately for the professor, the computer has also predicted that the professor will betray the conspiracy should he discover it, so his colleagues sentence him to death. The computer Katsumi is unsuccessful in saving the real Katsumi, and the professor continues his investigations until he is found out and duly sentenced. Before his execution, however, he is granted one boon: he is allowed to witness a computer simulation of the future so that he can see how his son will live.

It is a disturbing vision of the future. The aquans are highly intelligent but they seem without emotions, perhaps because they have no tear ducts. A few real humans are left, living in underwater "museums" for the edification of the aquans. The professor's final vision of the future is an ambiguous one: a young aquan climbs back onto land to feel the wind on his skin and dies there.

In his afterword to the novel, Abe insists that he is not trying to be definitively optimistic or pessimistic about the future, but it is hard to avoid the overtly dystopian and specifically anti-technological elements in *Inter Ice Age 4*. I have already mentioned the fear of conspiracy which surrounds the novel, a paranoid horror element which, when linked with the computer, is a distinctive feature of many technological dystopias. The revelation that the conspiracy is perpetuated by his other self in the form of a computer is a particularly appropriate twist, redolent not only of twentieth-century technological paranoia but also evocative of earlier fantasy and horror archetypes of the demonic *doppelgänger*. The "museum" life of the remnants of humanity also suggests a final twist on a culture of reproduction.

Inter Ice Age 4 contains another feature common to Western dystopian literature but relatively absent from most Japanese visions of anti-Utopia. This is what Krishan Kumar in *Utopia and Anti-Utopia in Modern Times* (1987) has dubbed the so-called Grand Inquisitor scene, based on the legend recounted in Dostoevski's *The Brothers Karamazov* of Christ's return to the world at the time of the Inquisition.[29] In this scene the Grand Inquisitor explains to Christ that it is the Church's mission to care for the people rather than to give them freedom, because human beings do not actually want freedom. The conflict between freedom of thought and an all-powerful, all-knowing elite is one of the most important tropes of Western dystopian fiction. The particulars of this scene may change, from O'Brien and Winston Smith in *1984*, to the Savage and Mustapha Mond in *Brave New World*, but the dystopia's underlying message is always the same: human beings lose their freedom of thought once they either join with or accept the domination of those who "know better."

In the case of Abe's protagonist the scene occurs at the end of the novel when, just as predicted, Katsumi balks at the aquan project. The professor speaks first: "I can't approve of any of this." His colleagues respond:

> It's prejudice. It's quite undeniable that living creatures evolved as a result of their struggle with nature ... However, the human species has ultimately subjugated nature. Man is liberated from his natural state. Should he not ultimately reconstruct himself?
>
> (p. 192)

Katsumi answers, "But accepting aquans like that is denying one's self, isn't it? Humans on land live as inheritors of the past" (p. 193).

Katsumi's arguments are futile. Indeed, in his own case, his "self" has already been "denied" and reconstituted as part of the computer.

Moreover, his erstwhile colleagues are consciously working to reject the past, rather than to inherit it.

Abe's works in the 1960s and 1970s continue to show protagonists searching for themselves, and for their freedom to choose, against a background that increasingly denies the validity of any past, personal or cultural. Thus, in his 1962 novel *Suna no onna* (1962) (trans. *The Woman in the Dunes* (1972)), Abe, unusually, posits a rural dystopia, a village at the bottom of a sand pit which can only survive by having the villagers constantly shovel the all-encompassing sand back out. To help them in their work, the villagers occasionally need to entrap people from outside; the narrative framework of *The Woman in the Dunes* consists of the entrapment of one such hapless man and his frantic and ultimately futile attempts to escape.

As the above summary suggests, *The Woman in the Dunes* is more an allegory, an extended variation of Sisyphus, than a fully realized dystopian critique. But its problematizing of the traditional village social structure, with its intense pressures and obligations, is interesting in comparison to the widespread myth of the pastoral Utopia which we have seen reworked in such novels as *Kirikirijin* (The People of Kirikiri) (1980). *The Woman in the Dunes* also echoes *Kappa* in an interesting way in terms of freedom of choice and the human need to construct one's own life. This occurs at the end of the novel where the protagonist is finally given a chance to escape but decides not to, resolving instead to stay on and putter with various contraptions for creating water and trapping birds.

Like the insane protagonist of *Kappa*, Abe's hero prefers, finally, to construct his own reality. His ties to the outside real world have grown increasingly weak as his memories have faded and the reader is given to understand that his former life was, in any case, not very satisfying. Whether, like *Kappa*'s protagonist, he too is insane or not, the text leaves to the reader to decide. As in *Kappa*, however, the vision afforded the reader of the "real world" is dark enough to make the hero's decision to reject it seem reasonable.

The real world becomes steadily darker and more inundated by horror as Abe's fiction continues into the 1960s and 1970s. No longer set in the far future or in a remote rural area, his novels increasingly limn a dystopian now that not only cannot be ignored but that actually starts to invade perceived reality. Thus, his 1967 play *Tomodachi* (1967) (trans. *Friends* (1977)) satirizes the Japanese notion of communal solidarity by describing a family who force themselves into an unfortunate man's apartment and never leave. Before they finally murder him, an action which they feel was forced upon them by the man's ungrateful behaviour, the family manage to get the man in trouble with the police (who refuse to evict his smiling, wholesome-looking "friends") and contrive to break off his engagement to his fiancée, all the while insisting that "You might say we're knitting a fabric, not out of yarn but out of people" (p. 97).

Friends essentially takes *Kappa*'s image of a man with the weight of his family literally around his neck and spins an entire surreal tragedy out of it. The play's dialogue chillingly and accurately skewers the clichés and homilies that support the ideology of a cozy communal existence which still suffuses Japanese society today. Thus, the family insists that the man's desire to be alone is neurotic and pathetic and, as is true in the best dystopian fiction, their arguments in favor of their superior knowledge and authority are frighteningly persuasive. In the end, the man's death while crouching in a cage is made to appear as a welcome escape from an increasingly oppressive and incomprehensible world.

The total nihilism of *Friends* is typical of the direction taken by Abe's later fiction. The earlier, *Inter Ice Age 4*, although grim, at least allowed the reader some psychological comfort in its notion of a pan-determined conspiracy that had a final point to it, even if it was the creation of an aquan race.[30] Although the novel's sense of dark conspiracy is of course threatening, at the same time the discovery that there is a controlling presence in the novel is almost reassuring, compared to Abe's later works where society has descended into total chaos.

In such novels as *Mikai* (1977) (trans. *Secret Rendezvous* (1980)) or *Hakobune Sakuramaru* (1984) (trans. *The Ark Sakura* (1989)), the world's insanity becomes steadily more aggressive and the attempts by Abe's everyman protagonists to combat the horror seem more and more feeble. Indeed, there is an increasing sense of complicity between protagonist and insane world, prefigured, perhaps by the smooth-talking computer, Professor Katsumi's "other self," in *Inter Ice Age 4*. Gone is the sense of any rational response and there are no more Grand Inquisitor scenes, no moral opposition to the insanity around the characters.

Kathryn Hume has suggested that many dystopian satires "derive much of their power from some central image of violence."[31] In fact, the central image in most of Abe's novels is often even more disturbing: after a long series of aborted movements, searches, escape attempts, etc., the protagonist is usually seen motionless, a passive observer to his own fate, often quite literally. Thus, Professor Katasumi is allowed one final look at the aquans, while the protagonist in *Secret Rendezvous* is forced to watch the woman he presumes to be his wife copulating with other men and is last seen squatting in the sewers. In *Suna no onna* (1962) (trans. *The Woman in the Dunes* (1972)) the protagonist is left trapped at the bottom of a sand pit. Sometimes the image of entrapment is vegetative rather than technological, as in "Dendorokakaria" (1949) (trans. "Dendrocacalia" (1991)) where a man is slowly and inexorably turned into a plant. The central image of final inertia is an important and pervasive one, in distinction to the fruitful movement privileged in the Utopian fiction we have discussed.

If, as is often argued, Abe's novels concern protagonists searching for a lost homeland or a lost identity, his later works increasingly acknowledge the uselessness of such a search. Isoda Kōichi in an article tracing Abe's lack of cultural identity, speaks of Abe's "loss of home" which exists simultaneously with a "thirst for home."[32] Isoda also mentions a revealing change over a twenty-year period in Abe's writing in which the lack of a home now becomes acknowledged. Isoda gives an example of this development by comparing the first edition of Abe's first novel, *Owarishi michi no shirube ni* (The Sign at the End of the Road) (1948), with later editions. The first edition contained the sentences, "A hometown is necessary, for pain, for laughter, for living. A hometown is sublime forgetfulness." In the later edition of this work, these sentences are excised, to be replaced by the following: "Therefore I decided to be always leaving, like running water."

Abe's works span a number of important generational shifts in modern Japan. His earlier stories, written in the 1950s when Marxism still seemed like a genuine alternative to capitalism, showcase the spirit of individual resistance against government, business, or technology, or the three combined. His later writings increasingly show the individual acquiescent, beaten down by a variety of factors, usually including a vast, faceless, and ultimately insane conspiracy which is often abetted by an increasingly incomprehensible and sophisticated technological base.

Abe's writings also seem implicitly to reflect a generational change in the Japanese attitude toward technology from the immediate postwar period, when technological supremacy was still tacitly ceded to the West, and was therefore still "Other." By the 1980s, however, this formerly alien technology had, as Najita puts it, "come to be articulated as . . . expressive of a distinctive culture within."[33] For the younger generation of Japanese, technology was no longer distinctively "Other," it was part of the indigenous cultural fabric.

Thus, Abe's later works show protagonists who are no longer fighting technology as in *Inter Ice Age 4*, so much as acknowledging its preeminence as in *Secret Rendezvous* and *The Ark Sakura*. But with that acknowledgement comes an acknowledgement of other negative forces, the lack of a moral center and the uselessness of a search for identity in a world where identity is fragmented or dissolved. Increasingly, an apocalyptic tinge sets in. Thus, in his late dystopian novel, *The Ark Sakura*, Abe's bizarre protagonist, Mole, is depicted as hiding in an underground cavern trying to construct a refuge out of the flotsam of civilization that will somehow protect him against the coming end of the world through nuclear disaster.

Inevitably, Mole's asylum is invaded by outsiders, including a couple of criminals and an eerie group of senior citizens known as the Broom Brigade (the latter an amusing satire on Japan's increasing number of elderly). The outsiders force Mole out of his hideaway and our last vision of him is as he confronts the unreal city he had tried to leave behind. Technology is now seen as so overwhelming that little can be done to escape it, except for a few pathetic attempts to save the individual. The Mole himself is so bizarre and unattractive a figure that there seems little reason to save him in any case. The lunatics have taken over the asylum in Abe's frighteningly nihilistic world, and there is no sane voice left.

In the 1970s and 1980s other writers besides Abe also turned to issues of dystopia and apocalypse. Ōe Kenzaburō, in his 1973 novel *Kōzui wa wagatamashi ni oyobi* (The Floodwaters Have Come Unto My Soul), also tackles the idea of refuge from the apocalypse, in this case a cataclysmic flood his protagonist expects will accompany imminent nuclear disaster. Ōe's protagonist rebels against his dystopian reality, however, finally sacrificing himself in an apocalyptic shoot-out with what seems to be the entire Japanese military–industrial establishment.[34]

Ōe's most recent writing continues to revolve around apocalypse and dystopia but this time, unusually for a writer of "pure literature," in a science fiction context. His 1990 novel *Chiryōto* (Tower of Healing) is set in a full-blown future dystopia complete with such science fiction touches as starships and a search for immortality. The dystopian aspects are also chillingly realized in such touches as having AIDS sufferers wear yellow stars, as the Jews did under Hitler. Typical for Ōe, however, *Chiryōto* privileges the idea of escape from the urban dystopia into a pastoral haven in mountainous Nagano. This small Utopian haven seems far more peaceful than Ōe's groundbreaking village in *Dōjidai gēmu* (The Game of Contemporaneity) (1979), and the novel ends on a relatively optimistic note, suggesting that Ōe at least, still hopes to find some way out of dystopia.

Other writers of the 1970s and 1980s are not so sure. Even in popular science fiction, writers such as Tsutsui Yasutaka and Komatsu Sakyō are almost consistently bleak in their imaginative explorations of technology and the future. Tsutsui's short story "Tatazumo hito" (1974) (trans. "Standing Woman" (1989)) evokes Abe's imagery of a passive, impotent protagonist in a fantasy describing a future government's ability to turn dissidents into pieces of vegetation. Komatsu's work shows humans meddling with technology only to destroy themselves. Thus, in his short story "Hokusai no sekai" (The World of Hokusai) he depicts a couple from the future returning to the past to have a look at Mt. Fuji, the mountain itself having been destroyed in the devastating technological fighting of the twenty-third century.

CONTEMPORARY DYSTOPIAS: MURAKAMI HARUKI'S SEARCH FOR IDENTITY AT THE END OF THE WORLD AND ŌTOMO KATSUHIRŌ'S VISION OF APOCALYPSE

Needless to say, there are other contemporary writers such as Hoshi Shinichi or the creators of the popular *Gundam* robot series who see the future and science in a more positive light, confirming a more technology-friendly consensual world view. On the whole, however, even in popular culture, the trend is largely negative. Starting in 1953 with the enormously popular movie *Godzilla*, which played on the understandable nuclear paranoia of that period, popular culture images of dystopia and apocalypse have become ever more sophisticated, emphasizing the increasing alienation of humans from their environment and from society in general. Perhaps the most interesting recent writer who deals with the notions of dystopia, technology and in his own distinctive way, the end of the world, is Murakami Haruki.

Murakami's works have become bestsellers in Japan, earning him the dubious distinctions of being known as a "phenomenon" and being looked down upon by critics and scholars as "too popular." Initially, however, Murakami was considered a "pure literature" writer and hailed by many of these same critics, usually of the older generation, as a fresh and important voice. In part the older generation of writers are incensed by what they feel is Murakami's lack of moral responsibility, his refusal to confront head-on the ills of industrial capitalism which Abe and Ōe, among others, consistently treated in their fiction. Miyoshi Masao encapsulates this view of Murakami's novels as "all sophisticated stylizations of trivia, flying over the boredom and irritation of everyday life."[35]

In fact, as I will try to demonstrate, Murakami does deal with political and social issues, albeit in a more elliptical way and without either the moralistic vehemence of Ōe or the embittered nihilism of Abe. In this more equivocal attitude, Murakami emblematizes a new, younger generation of Japanese, those who grew up during the riot-torn, but economically successful 1960s and who saw the inexorable destruction of those 1960s' ideals by both political outside forces and by the needs of the individual. When pressed on these issues, Murakami's stock explanation is that "we lost" (the ideological battle of the 1960s). In fact, however, certain of these ideals still exist in his works, although in fairly subtle form.

Furthermore, in his straddling of the gap between pure and popular, Murakami seems to encapsulate much of where Japanese literature is going. It is increasingly international, and increasingly fantastic. At the same time, however, Murakami's works have a moral core, albeit on an individual rather than an ideological basis, which takes them outside the purely postmodern genre. This "traditional" aspect may be another reason behind their popularity.

Popular or not, Murakami's works are exceptionally interesting from the point of view of the fantastic and in relation to contemporary Japanese notions of Utopia and dystopia. By using a few fantastic touches, Murakami creates extraordinarily vivid "other worlds" characterized by dreams, ghosts, and magic that still speak eloquently of contemporary Japan. Much of his work is Utopian or escapist but of his novels *Hitsuji o meguru bōken* (1982) (trans. *A Wild Sheep Chase* (1989)), contains clearly dystopian touches, while *Sekai no owari to hādo boirudo wandārando* (1985) (trans. *Hard Boiled Wonderland and the End of the World* (1991)) is a fascinating work which problematizes the question of both Utopia and dystopia within a high-tech information-driven society.

Quoted at the beginning of this chapter, *A Wild Sheep Chase* is a quest story with clearly fantastic elements concerning a young advertising company worker's search for what can only be called a magic sheep. The work's dystopian elements are not confined to the essential meaninglessness of the quest itself, but include a vivid portrait of the menacing right-wing "boss" whose interest in the sheep is what forces the protagonist on his quest. A shadowy figure with influence in both the corporate and the political world of contemporary Japan, the "boss" is an unusual character to find in Japanese literature, for much of Japanese fiction tends to be apolitical. The detailed description of the boss and his henchmen's rise to power in postwar Japan is also an unusual and particularly chilling one, since it seems to support the stereotype of Japan as an apolitical submissive society.

But the most interesting aspect of the story of the "boss" is that it is actually based on a real person, the infamous right-wing figure Kodama Kazuo, as Kawamura Minato suggests.[36] Thus, despite its overtly fantastic elements (the magic sheep is posited as the cause of the boss's rise to power), the narrative of *A Wild Sheep Chase* deals directly with some very real aspects of Japanese society, notably the collusion between politicians, business, and implicitly, organized crime, aspects of Japanese society which have only recently become widely known.

Another unusual and fascinating aspect of *A Wild Sheep Chase* is the problematic importance of history in it, both on the individual level and on the level of national culture. On a personal level, history seems to be important for its absence. Thus, the protagonist, his girlfriend, and his friends all seem desperately trying to escape their history. In a revealing early episode, for example, the protagonist's ex-wife returns home and goes through their photo albums, cutting out the part of every picture in which she appears.

As for the narrator himself, his attitude is summed up in the quotation at the beginning of this chapter in his apparent pleasure at having "no hometown" and "no one to want me." The narrator has escaped the constraints of the Japanese family system so graphically delineated in *Kappa* and *Friends*. Like Abe's protagonist in *Owarishi michi no shirube ni*, Murakami's characters seem to be "always leaving."

And yet, paradoxically, it is the protagonist of *A Wild Sheep Chase* who becomes involved with a rediscovery of history on a national level through his search for the sheep. Some of this history is highly negative. His investigations into the boss's interest in the sheep, for example, lead him to knowledge of both the Japanese Empire's prewar activities in Manchuria and to the postwar collusion between government, industry and the right wing at home. These are aspects of recent Japanese history which few younger Japanese deal with. As such, they give *A Wild Sheep Chase* a richer and more disturbing tone than much recent fiction, as Japan's national identity is reconstituted in a less than glowing light.

But there is another, more positive side of history which the narrator also discovers, again through his search for the sheep, a search which takes him to Hokkaido, the northernmost district in Japan and the one most recently settled. In finding out about the history of the area where the sheep was said to be most recently living, the narrator learns a great deal about another little-known and more heroic aspect of Japanese history, the colonization of Hokkaido by desperately poor tenant farmers who had to fight not only a hostile environment but the oppressive levies of government tax collectors. In his rediscovery of marginal history, the protagonist of *A Wild Sheep Chase* seems to be performing a Utopian act, similar to the narration of history by Ōe's protagonist in *Dōjidai gēmu* (The Game of Contemporaneity) (1979) or Furuhashi's rediscovery of rural life in *Kirikirijin*.

The history of the right-wing bosses in Manchuria and the settlement of Hokkaido initially seem to come from different ends of the political continuum; but, as Kawamura points out, both Hokkaido and Manchuria were "new worlds" for the Japanese in the nineteenth and twentieth century, offering hope and dreams of a new life to many people.[37]

A Wild Sheep Chase ends, in fact, on quite a Utopian note. The protagonist not only finds the sheep and also the ghost of an old friend; he even manages to destroy the dead boss's evil henchman in an episode whose satisfying closure may be another reason behind Murakami's popularity. The individual may not be able to do much in Murakami's world, but there is a sense at the end of the novel that, though the quest may have been absurd, some small thing has been accomplished.

Murakami's novels have been described as having their dominant tone be one of "nostalgia," and indeed, much of his work does seem to be populated by ghosts, memories, or people who are soon to be ghosts and memories. And yet, *A Wild Sheep Chase* goes beyond nostalgia to confront history both aggressively and imaginatively. Not only does it paint in a corner of Japanese history which many would prefer to forget, but it also brings to light an example of struggle and fortitude by an outcast group which would not be out of place in the works of Inoue or Ōe.

In Murakami's *Hard Boiled Wonderland and the End of the World* the issues of history and identity are again problematized but on a level that is at the same time both more personal and more overtly dystopian than in *A Wild Sheep Chase*. This is accomplished through the book's construction: it consists of two separate but ultimately interlocking narratives, which encompass two different worlds, respectively, the "Hard Boiled Wonderland" and "the End of the World" of the title. While *A Wild Sheep Chase* contains definite dystopian elements within a satirical quest narrative, *Hard Boiled Wonderland and the End of the World* creates an entire dystopian world, or perhaps even two dystopian worlds, depending on the reader's final judgement.

The "Hard Boiled" narrative is the more clearly dystopian side of the novel, set in a near-future Tokyo where two information organizations, the corporate conglomerate known as the System and the illegal data Mafia known as the Factory, battle each other for power in the form of data. "Hard Boiled"'s nameless protagonist (hereinafter referred to as "Watashi" or I) is a footsoldier in these battles, a specialized human data-processor for the System known as a Calcutec. At the novel's beginning, "Watashi" is assigned a special task shuffling data for an eccentric scientist, known only as the "old man," whose laboratory is underneath the Tokyo subway system hidden behind a waterfall. The scientist's hiding place is a good one because it is guarded by fearsome creatures known as INKlings (more appropriately translated as "Darklings") who haunt the subway system after it closes down at night.

Soon, "Watashi" begins to suspect that the task is more involved than he had realized, and he eventually ends up getting involved with sinister representatives from the Factory, with whom he has a comically violent falling out. As he begins to investigate the relationships between System and Factory in more detail he discovers that the two are actually intertwined to produce a functioning economy, or as the Factory goons put it, "Is Japan a totally monopoly state or what? The System monopolizes everything under the info sun, the Factory monopolizes everything in the shadows."

As the above description hints, the "Hard Boiled" side of Murakami's novel is a pastiche, but a brilliant one, of various popular culture genres. The eccentric scientist, who also has an attractive, empathetic granddaughter, is clearly a refugee from 1950s generic science fiction. At the same time the shadowy System and its equally shadowy opposite number the Factory correspond to the genre of paranoid horror mentioned in our discussion of Abe, while the high-tech information war that gives the work its narrative impetus has echoes of 1980s cyberpunk fiction such as Gibson's *Neuromancer*. The wisecracking loner protagonist, on the other hand, has strong connections with the hard-boiled detective genre, while the actual narrative structure of the entire novel is a well-worked-out, almost classic, form of mystery.

The vision that animates the "End of the World" side of the novel also has clear popular culture antecedents, but this time from the realm of fantasy. The End of the World is actually a town, seemingly structured like a medieval European village, complete with an Old Bridge, a Clocktower and, most important, a Wall that entirely encircles it. The unnamed protagonist of The End of the World (hereinafter referred to as "Boku," the informal male pronoun for "I" which he uses) has arrived from outside the Wall but has no memories of his life before the Town. His memories, it turns out, have been consigned to his shadow, whom he surrendered before entering the Town. Once in the Town, "Boku" discovers that his assigned task is that of Dream

Reader. His eyes slit, he sits in the Town Library every evening and reads dreams from the skulls of unicorns, huge herds of which die every year outside of the Town.

The narrative suspense in the "End of the World" side of the novel is provided by the protagonist's shadow which lingers just outside the Town, plotting to be reunited with its owner and escape. In classic Utopian fashion, the shadow plays the part of the rebel, the alien agent who can potentially escape the tentacles of dystopia. In Murakami's original vision, however, the shadow is a highly complex entity. The shadow, it turns out, is the "mind" or heart of "Boku," a mind which is being slowly killed off in the static perfection of the town. With the help of the protagonist, the shadow does eventually escape, but "Boku" himself decides to stay on in the Town rather than return to the world of memory.

The real narrative suspense of *Hard Boiled Wonderland and the End of the World* does not lie in either of the parallel stories, however, but in their complex and brilliant interrelationship. For, as both "Watashi" and "Boku" discover at the end of their respective stories, the Town is actually the mental creation of "Watashi," the protagonist of the "Hard Boiled" part of the narrative. It exists inside his own brain unbeknownst to him, having been developed based on his memories and fantasies by the eccentric scientist known only as the old man. The only purpose for the Town was as an instrument to facilitate data-shuffling. Its code name is The End of the World.

The Calcutec "Watashi" might never have known of the End of the World's existence except for an unfortunate error on the part of the scientist who forgot to put an override circuit in "Watashi"'s brain. Because of this failure, "Watashi"'s surface mind or consciousness is slowly but irrevocably switching over into his unconscious, the End of the World. Because the scientist's laboratory has been destroyed by Factory technicians, he is unable to override the system; "Watashi" is consequently literally about to lose his mind, or his surface consciousness at least. Although his body may go on functioning, his mind will permanently enter the End of the World mode.

Unlike the novel's generic antecedents, *Hard Boiled Wonderland and the End of the World* does not provide a conventional happy ending. Instead, it leaves both protagonists in uncertainty. "Watashi" of "Hard Boiled," knowing that he will probably never regain consciousness, uses his final twenty-four hours of life in dining at a good Italian restaurant, sleeping with his recently acquired girlfriend and lying in a park drinking beer. Eventually he drives to a pier and waits quietly for the cessation of consciousness, listening as Bob Dylan sings "A Hard Rain's A-Gonna Fall," over and over.

As was described earlier, "Boku" in the "End of the World" decides not to escape with his shadow (thereby mirroring the loss of mind in Hard Boiled), and walks back to the Town realizing that, "I am alone at the furthest periphery of existence. Here the world expires and is still" (p. 400).

Hard Boiled Wonderland and the End of the World is an intriguing novel in many ways. One of its most interesting aspects, especially in comparison to much postmodern literature, is its almost classical symmetry based on a range of obvious dualisms. These dualities can be interpreted in a variety of ways and the novel provides many clear clues.[38] Obviously, "Watashi" and "Boku" are each other's *alter egos*, but they are not opposites in the Jekyll-and-Hyde sense of the *doppelgänger*, or even the coldly logical computer persona of Professor Katsumi in *Inter Ice Age 4*. Instead, they are clearly symbiotic; we are not surprised to find that the intelligent, solitary Calcutec would have an elaborate and in some ways equally solitary fantasy world at the under-layer of his consciousness. In a certain way it makes him more human rather than less.

There is, nevertheless, a troubling aspect to "Boku"'s decision to remain within his own unconscious, at least for any reader who hopes to find a commitment to change in the real world in Murakami's works. Is his decision to remain there an "escapist" or "Utopian" one, an abandonment of his responsibilities in the real world?

In many ways, one would have to say yes, but the novel itself suggests a more complex answer. This brings me to the problem of dystopia in the novel, specifically, is the "Hard Boiled" side of the novel the only dystopia depicted? At first glance, the novel seems to be divided into a classic dystopia versus Utopia mode. The "Hard Boiled" chapters delineate an almost textbook dystopian world of vast underground conspiracies, metonymically reflected in the subterranean wanderings of the protagonist and the fearsome scurryings of the INKlings.

At its best, this anti-Utopia offers some material and sensual satisfactions such as the excellent Italian restaurant where "Watashi" has his final dinner, but the overall picture of near-future Tokyo is of a bleak and alienating city, a world based on mindless consumption of products that range from Italian food to data information. Technology is seen as out of control and fundamentally dangerous, as evidenced not only in the goons from the Factory, for whom technical information becomes simply a reason for violence, but in the character of the eccentric scientist (who claims to be only interested in pure science) and his inability to correct the failure of his own experiment. Finally, the collusion between the state and criminals evidenced in the inter-relationship between System and Factory suggests a world where the citizenry are oppressed and unaware, a world, in fact, not unlike the present state of government and business relationships in contemporary Japan.

In comparison, "The End of the World" seems an almost perfect traditional Utopia. It is static, comfortable, and peaceful, since everyone has lost their memories and therefore their minds. Each person knows his place and is taken care of accordingly. As "Boku"'s neighbour, the Colonel, explains,

> The Town is fair in its own way. The things you need, the things you need to know, one by one, the Town will set these before you. Hear me now: this Town is perfect. And by perfect, I mean complete. It has everything. If you cannot see that, then it has nothing. A perfect nothing.
>
> (p. 86)

The Town's perfection is such that "Boku" eventually succumbs to it, despite his initial desire to escape with his shadow. In the climactic final scene of the "End of the World," his shadow tries to convince him to escape together by telling him that "your rightful world is there outside." But "Boku" replies,

> I have responsibilities ... I cannot forsake the people and places and things I have created. I know I do you a terrible wrong. And yes perhaps I wrong myself too. But I must see out the consequences of my own doings. This is my world. The Wall is here to hold *me* in, the River flows through *me*, the smoke is *me* burning. I must know why.
>
> (p. 399)

It would be impossible to deny that with this extraordinarily solipsistic statement "Boku" seems to be abdicating all sense of political and social engagement. Indeed, we appear almost to have come full circle back to the mental hospital of *Kappa* where Patient No. 23 happily exists in *his* world responsible only to himself and his creations.[39] And yet, just as *Kappa* becomes an even more savage indictment of Taishō Japan simply by presenting insanity as the only reasonable response to an insane world, so "Boku"'s decision to remain inside the End of the World is also a form of social criticism. Of course in comparison to Ōe's protagonist in *Kōzui wa wagatamashi ni oyobi* (The Floodwaters Have Come Unto My Soul) (1973), who leaves his refuge to die in battle against the military–industrial establishment, it is a choice that seems frankly lacking in courage or at least in romance. Still, "Boku"'s concern with "responsibilities" might be seen as in some ways admirable, rather than only self-serving, emblematic of a generation which realizes that to change the world one must start with oneself.

Furthermore, as in *Kappa*, the problematic nature of the choice – a retreat into the unconscious – is also a form of social criticism. Kappaland itself, as the reader has been shown, is far from a Utopia, and the world of the Town is perhaps even more problematic than Kappaland. In fact, its static, hierarchical nature echoes traditional Japanese society more than the brash consumer culture of "Hard Boiled."

The Town's mindless inhabitants subsume what desires they have left in such work as endless hole-digging, a kind of task that promotes group harmony without providing any sort of meaning for the individual's life. Also like traditional Japanese society, people are defined by roles such as "Dream Reader" rather than by their given names. The people of the Town live in smug unconsciousness of others, their former shadows, the wood folk, etc., who live outside the wall, another implicit critique at the hermetic nature of Japanese society.[40] The fact that "Boku" chooses this rather grim world is another indication of how unappealing is his other world.

Moreover, it should be noted that "Boku" intends to stir things up a bit at the End of the World. In the course of the narrative he develops a relationship with the Librarian and becomes interested in helping her find her own identity, a suggestion, perhaps, that he will not be a passive observer of his own unconscious but intends to delve more actively into the past. It is this awareness of the past that is perhaps the most potentially subversive aspect of the novel. *Hard Boiled Wonderland and the End of the World* does not privilege the past the way *A Wild Sheep Chase* does, but in its implicit problematization of those who lose their shadows, their past, it suggests one of the central aspects of life in modern Japan, a world where "shadows" of the past are increasingly ignored.

The people of the Town have tradition without memory of a past, or even a reason for their traditions. The "Hard Boiled" inhabitants, on the other hand, have memories but no tradition. Perhaps "Boku"'s choice to stay and search for the past in the Town might be seen as an attempt to reweave the two strands.

The absence of a past is an important aspect of our last text to be discussed in this chapter, Ōtomo Katsuhiro's *manga* or comic-book epic *Akira*. *Akira* is a work which begins with the end of history, the destruction of Tokyo by a nuclear blast in 1989, and ends with at least the potential for a very real end of the world. In between this lies a complex and violent saga of life in twenty-first-century Neo-Tokyo, a world which is a truly nightmarish form of dystopia. This critical dystopia, like *Kappa*, exaggerates and builds on a number of obvious problems in contemporary Japanese society.

It should be mentioned at the outset that since *Akira* is a *manga*, or comic series, it is not a work of literature, even in the sense of such popular writers as Tsutsui or Komatsu.[41] I feel justified in including it here, however, in that its dystopian themes are so well worked out. Furthermore, whether we lament the trend or not, it cannot be ignored that the *manga* are increasingly elbowing out all forms of literature as the preeminent reading matter of choice on the part of the young generation of Japanese. In fact, perhaps because of their very reliance on drawing and special effects, *manga* are often at the forefront of contemporary visions of dystopia and apocalypse, presenting their readers/viewers with exceptionally vivid realizations of grim future worlds, of which *Akira* is the most brilliant.

Akira is also an interesting comparison with Murakami's works, in that to some extent it is reaching the same audience, at least in terms of age (teenagers and those in their twenties). This is less true in terms of gender, since Murakami's fans tend to be female, while *Akira* appeals particularly to young males. The movie version of *Akira*, however, was the most popular film in Japan in the year of its release, suggesting a wider appeal than at first might be expected.

Ōtomo and Murakami share an audience that has been characterized as the *shinjinrui*, the "new people" who grew up in a postwar Japan and whose culture seemed to be based on an endless economic success story of double-digit growth followed by increasing international recognition. Ōtomo and Murakami are not themselves members of this generation but, born in 1956 and 1949 respectively, they are certainly part of the postwar baby boom and were clearly shaped by the turmoil of the 1960s. Thus, these dystopias are truly speaking to a very different Japan, one that at first glance seems far more successful than either the nerve-racked Taishō period or the bleak postwar years. And yet Murakami's vision is hardly celebratory, while Ōtomo's vision is perhaps the grimmest of all the works discussed in this chapter.

It is worth asking what the young Japanese find in *Akira* to make it so popular. One possible explanation is that *Akira* exists as a thoroughgoing rejection of the hierarchical, careerist, and consumerist ideology of the older generation. *Akira*, along with a wide variety of other contemporary dystopian *manga* series is almost unremittingly bleak in both setting and story.

The Neo-Tokyo the film and comic describe is a corrupt, decayed state where the politicians seem ineffective pawns of a sinister military–industrial establishment led by an enigmatic figure known only as the Colonel. It is this establishment that was responsible for the destruction of "Old Tokyo" in 1989 through scientific experiments attempting to harness a group of children's psychic energies. The experiments were essentially successful in that they unleashed huge psychic energies. These energies were at the cost of the children's personalities, however, and of the world war that began as a result of the initial blast.

The complex narrative action of *Akira* follows the destinies of the mutant children into the twenty-first century, especially that of Akira, the most powerful child of all. The mutants become involved with three other groups, a cadre of revolutionaries, a new religion led by the enigmatic Lady Miyako, and finally, and most importantly, a group of outcast young bikers led by two boys, Tetsuo and Kaneda. Tetsuo and Kaneda first encounter the mutants at the vast bombed-out crater that was old Tokyo, and Tetsuo's own psychic energies are stirred up. Much of the remaining six volumes of the series is devoted to the increasing violence wrought by Tetsuo and by Akira, including the destruction of the Moon.

Some of the work's most stunning visual images are concentrated in Tetsuo's extraordinary series of metamorphoses as his powers increasingly begin to take on a life of their own. The narrative ends with Tetsuo's powers going out of control and his being sucked into the powerful entity which is Akira. Their struggle lays waste to most of Neo-Tokyo. Along the way the story satirizes a number of targets that are part of contemporary Japanese life today, a school system that is increasingly incapable of containing juvenile violence, the problematic power of the new religions, and, of course, the two-edged aspect of ever more powerful technology.

Perhaps the work's central image is the aimless riding of the young bikers as they roar violently through Neo-Tokyo.[42] In this image of aimless motion against a superbly realized background of huge and barren cityscapes, *Akira* parodies the whole notion of a quest for meaning or intensity in life. The pictures of the motorcycles themselves are beautifully executed, suggesting the excitement and grace of technology at its best. In the long run, however, the constant imagery of movement recalls Sōseki's hero quoted at the beginning of this chapter, "Never once has science, which never ceases to move forward, allowed us to pause." Technology brings motion but it cannot give these young men direction.

In their riding, the bikers do find something, the mutants, but it is questionable whether this discovery, which ultimately leads to the destruction of much of Neo-Tokyo, does anything positive for the youths. Rather, in its privileging of narrative movement simply for the sake of movement, and metamorphosis simply for the sake of change, *Akira* seems to fit well into the postmodern genre, a genre which suggests that identity is in constant fluctuation.

Related to this is the loss of history in *Akira*. This loss is exemplified visually in the image of the huge empty crater of old Tokyo, a literal black hole whose image dominates the first part of the text. It is also exemplified in the ironic use of a rebuilt version of the old Yoyogi Olympic stadium, which becomes a staging ground for the work's most climactic battles. The absence of history is also seen on a personal level in the fact that most of the young protagonists are orphans, either literally (Kaneda and Tetsuo) or metaphorically (the mutant children abandoned to the state for scientific experimentation).

In Chapters 2 and 3 we saw how the traditional image of a protective, all-embracing mother figure increasingly disappears in post-war works, even as a fantasy figure, but *Akira* goes even further in its almost celebratory privileging of the wholesale destruction of family and society. With the possible exception of the ambiguous Colonel, there are no positive authority figures and no moral center. In fact, *Akira* contains no refuge of any sort. The action leaps from the ruins above the ground to a vast and forbidding network of tunnels below the city.

The last image of the work is a particularly arresting one. The few young people who are left in the rubble-strewn city insist on expelling all the invaders, claiming that "Akira still lives." As the bikers begin one last ride through the city, ghosts of their friends appear riding bikes on either side of them. And, as the group rides on, the city reconstitutes itself, the rubble seems to rise up and re-form in front of the reader's eyes. Is it a dream or a new tomorrow? The text leaves the answer up to the reader but the final view is of an immense and glorious city, toward which the bikers speed with all their power, swept up in a world which cannot stop.

Akira is not alone in its nihilism. Indeed, as this chapter has shown, a deeply pessimistic view of modernity has been part of Japanese culture almost since the inception of modernization. Many of its images, of labyrinthine tunnels, of vast far-flung conspiracies, are also central to the other novels discussed previously. And yet, *Akira* remains one of the most memorable of all the dystopian works examined in this chapter, paradoxically because of the very detailed quality of the destruction presented in it.

This chapter has traced a somewhat different trajectory than our Utopian chapter because the dystopian vision is inherently a bleak one. Some significant developments do exist between the prewar and the postwar mode, however. One particularly interesting one is the notion of insanity. This was a powerful, virtually all-encompassing metaphor in the fantasy of Taishō Japan, and remained an important notion in the postwar works of Abe Kōbo. In the two most recent dystopias discussed here, however, insanity is no longer an issue. Neo-Tokyo world is a dark and frightening place in *Akira* but it is one whose citizens behave logically, given the magnitude of their problems. In the same way, *A Wild Sheep Chase* and *Hard Boiled Wonderland and the End of the World*, while containing more than their fair share of eccentric characters, provide rational motivations for all of them.

The attitude toward technology has changed somewhat as well. In Akutagawa's "Cogwheels" we saw the protagonist feeling pursued by alien machines. In the 1960s Abe's work intensified this sense of paranoia by showing technology as totally overwhelming the helpless individual. By the 1980s, however, technology is no longer so one-dimensionally ominous.

While *Akira* begins with the hoary horror story theme of scientific experiments run amok, it ends with an image of bikers speeding through the surreal cityscape that is truly beautiful, though bleakly inhuman. Murakami's work questions technology in the fate of "Watashi," who becomes a pawn in a scientific game between System and Factory, but it also implicitly suggests that, in entering the End of the World, the Calcutech may ultimately find himself.

Mention of the End of the World brings me to another important difference between recent and earlier dystopias. This is the increasingly apocalyptic aspect of the postwar dystopias. This aspect is obviously related to Japan's wholesale defeat in World War II, and the nuclear bombings of Hiroshima and Nagasaki which gave the Japanese who lived through them a close-up glimpse of genuine apocalypse. Thus, Ōe, Abe, and Komatsu, who were all born before the war, tend to write obsessively of wholesale destruction, not only of a world but of a culture as well.

The apocalyptic aspect of the most recent dystopias is fascinatingly different, however. Murakami's novel explicitly highlights "The End of the World" but this "End" is a personal one and to some extent the protagonist's choice. Compared to the chaotic shoot-outs of Ōe's and Abe's work, it is an end that is remarkably controlled.

Akira's apocalyptic vision is perhaps even more unsettling since it is such an exhilarating one. The film version in particular almost seems to celebrate wholesale destruction as a combination of visceral and aesthetic thrills. In this no-holds-barred enjoyment of fluidity and chaos, it is reminiscent of Tsutsui's story "Kaomen hōkai." Both of these works share an attitude toward destruction that may well be termed postmodern.

This postmodern state is not unambiguously celebratory, however. It is as if the very success of modern Japan seems to beg its own demise, as the citizenry becomes more and more enervated by a plethora of material goods and technology which does not take the place of a lost community or history. Written throughout the 1980s, *Akira* seems both to emblematize these problems and to forecast some of the social and political problems that became more apparent in the 1990s. The harmonious facade that still constitutes modern Japan seems increasingly to be cracking.

Surprisingly, however, the cracks in the facade may not be entirely negative. By acknowledging the price paid for its successes, modern Japanese culture now allows for a richer, more all-encompassing vision. It is also a vision which is notably more universal. The popularity of both *Akira* and Murakami's works in the West suggests that they are reaching beyond the traditional strongholds of Japanese literature, the university, and the art house cinema, to reach and influence a wider, genuinely international audience.

Ironically, these works are using the very cultural instrumentalities they excoriate, such as mass marketing and technology, to achieve this success. At first glance, this may seem hypocritical on the part of the writers. Viewed another way, however, it may simply suggest how much the younger generation of Japanese has changed. They may condemn the modern world of technology, but they are also at ease with it, able to satirize it, criticize it, and ultimately able to exploit it for the purposes of their messages.

As the prewar and immediate postwar generation fades from the scene it is possible to suggest that modernity is no longer being subverted so much as coopted. The present generation of Japanese fantasy writers no longer look for departures from consensus reality. Instead, they seem to be intent on creating their own realities.

NOTES

1 As Penley puts it, "[the critical dystopia] tends to suggest causes rather than reveal symptoms" (C. Penley, 1989, p. 122).

2 A particularly good discussion of the dystopia and the absurd quest in postwar American fiction can be found in J. Kuehl, 1989, pp. 119–208.

3 See K. Kumar, 1987, especially pp. 380–424. As Kumar pithily expresses it, "The problem with all utopian strivings of the time was that they struggled against the overwhelming anti-utopian character of world events" (p. 386).

4 M. Hillegas, 1967, p. 5.

5 Buddhism also brought to Japan the notion of *mappō* or "the latter days of the Law," a form of millenarianism which posited a degenerate age in the eleventh and twelfth centuries. This apocalyptic vision is one that has to some extent returned in some of the newer Japanese religions and it may even be influential in some of the more apocalyptic of Japanese *manga*.

6 For an in-depth discussion of prewar Japanese writers and their up-and-down relationships with government censors see J. Rubin, 1984.

7 For a discussion of *tenkō* literature see D. Keene, 1984, pp. 846–905. For a translation of the "consummate *tenkō shōsetsu*" (conversion novel), see Brett de Bary's translation of "Mura no ie" ("The House in the Village"), in De Bary, 1979 pp. 19–73.

8 For more information on Japanese science fiction, see R. Matthew, 1989. Matthews mentions, among others, two clearly dystopian works, Kizu Tora's "Hairo ni bokasareta kekkon" (The Wedding Shrouded in Grey) (1928), which details a future world whose atmosphere has been destroyed by gas poisoning, and Unno Juza's "Jūhachiji no ongakuyoku" (The Music Bath at 1800 Hours) (1937), which describes the efforts of a future totalitarian government to force its population to work harder by having the citizenry sit in a mind-controlling "music bath" every day. Unno's work also includes a varied group of other science fiction elements, including androids, video-phones, and atom bombs, all used for sinister purposes by a totalitarian government, often equated with the Soviet Union. Unno was not a simplistic anti-communist, however. A scientist himself, he understood science's Janus face, even writing that, "This is a time when people are both showered with the blessings of science at the same time as they are threatened by the nightmares of science" (quoted in *kokubungaku* 1975, p. 159).

9 F. Jameson, 1982, p. 152.

10 T. Najita, 1989, p. 11.

11 Najita, 1989, p. 11.

12 Najita, 1989, p. 10.

13 N. Sōseki, 1992, pp. 280–282.

14 Imaizumi Fumiko, 1991 p. 78.

15 Critics are increasingly finding the dark side of the Taishō period. Even some of the works of the relatively optimistic Miyazawa Kenji have been held up as an example of this bleak aspect. Commenting on such works as Miyazawa's clever satire "Chumon no ōi ryōriten" (The Restaurant of Many Orders) (1924), in which two *nouveau riche* hunters are threatened with being cooked and eaten by animals in a fancy woodland

restaurant, Kawano points out that this is a "fearsome tale" and goes on to suggest "One cannot help but believe that [such works] show that on the other side of the social reality of this period was a dark and gloomy undercurrent" (Kawano Tsuneaki, 1975, pp. 155–156).

16　N. Burch, 1979, p. 132; Burch's italics.

17　Burch, 1979, p. 128.

18　As an example of both the pervasiveness and the style of imported culture during this period, one might offer the three-word slogan which defined the roaring twenties part of Taishō, "*ero guro nansensu,*" Japanizations of "eros", "grotesque," and "nonsense." For an interesting discussion of eroticism and the West see Rubin, 1993, pp. 236–238.

19　Interestingly, Kawabata's original setting for the screenplay was a circus. It would be enlightening to know why Kinugusa changed it.

20　M. Silverberg, 1990, p. 141.

21　H. D. Harootunian, 1990, p. 104.

22　Akutagawa was familiar with both books, as well as with a great many other Western fantastic novels of the nineteenth and early twentieth centuries.

23　See Miyasaka's discussion of the critical history of *Kappa*, in Miyasaka Satoru, 1985, pp. 110–111.

24　Gilbert Highet, in his discussion of Swift's dystopian satire on the Irish question, "A Modest Proposal," sums up the satirist's feelings as "irony, scorn, and desire," all words which would be highly applicable to Akutagawa as well. See G. Highet, 1962, p. 59. Or as Makoto Ueda puts it, "[Akutagawa] had too clear a view of human bestiality" (M. Ueda, 1976, p. 123).

25　It is interesting to note that the aforementioned film, *A Page of Madness*, also includes a scene in which children imitate the actions of the asylum inmates, another example of doubling and grotesque parody.

26　M. Foucault, 1988, p. 93.

27　T. Todorov, 1975 p. 174; italics in original.

28　For a discussion of the paranoid horror genre in film, see A. Tudor, 1989, pp. 185–210.

29　See Kumar, 1987, pp. 120–124.

30　Todorov considers pan-determinism to be an important aspect of the supernatural, and of psychoanalysis, and defines it as follows: "[it] is a generalized causality which does not admit the existence of chance and which posits that there are always direct relations among all phenomena, even if these relations generally escape us" (Todorov, 1975, p. 161).

31　K. Hume, 1984, p. 112.

32　Isoda Kōichi 1974, p. 32.

33　Najita, 1989, p. 13.

34　For further discussion of *kōzui* in relation to technology and apocalypse, see S. Napier, 1987, pp. 536–40.

35　M. Miyoshi, 1991, p. 235.

36　Kawamura Minato, 1989, pp. 174–81. Kawamura also mentions other models for the "boss" such as the former prime minister Tanaka Kakuei and the industrialist Sasakawa Ryoichi, all of whom were known as "controllers" with strong but often hidden ties to Japanese business and politics and whose stories have become part of the "legend" of the high-growth economic years of the sixties, seventies and eighties, (pp. 176–177).

37 Kawamura, 1989, pp. 177–178.
38 In his discussion of *Hard Boiled Wonderland and the End of the World*
    Suzumura sums up its dualities as follows: Thought (End of the World)
    and Reality (Hard Boiled), Death and Life, Stasis and Dynamism, Quie-
    tude and Action, Purposelessness and Purposefulness, (I have some
    doubts about that distinction), and finally, The World of the Novel, and
    the World of Novelistic theory (Suzumura Kazunari, 1987, pp. 21–22).
39 In fact, the Town bears more than a passing resemblance to a genuine
    mental asylum in another of Murakami's books, his bestselling realist
    novel *Noruwei no mori* (Norwegian Wood) (1987). This novel is far from
    being a fantasy but the asylum described in it is a surprisingly peaceful
    and appealing place. Situated far from the urban world on top of a high
    mountain, its inmates seem quietly happy doing their assigned tasks and
    are fearful of ever returning to the "real world." Like the asylum in *Kappa*
    or the Town at "the End of the World," then, this is a dangerously seduc-
    tive place, a Utopia for the elect who either desire or are driven to retreat
    from reality.
40 One of my former students, Isolde Standish, has suggested that the "Hard
    Boiled" side of the novel is the "metaphorical representation of an alien
    Western Other" (basing her argument on the clearly alienating aspects of
    technology in that part of the book), while the End of the World repre-
    sents modern Japanese society. Although I believe this to be an extremely
    provocative idea, I would question whether the dualities are based on lines
    of nationality, especially in regard to the "Hard Boiled" section of the
    novel. While I agree that technology is obviously alienating in "Hard
    Boiled," I question whether it is any longer as obviously alien (i.e. West-
    ern) as in the prewar period. As mentioned in my discussion of Abe, the
    interpenetration of technology into modern Japan is so widespread and so
    taken for granted that it would be difficult now to see technology as clearly
    Western.
41 For further discussion of *Akira* in relation to popular culture and the
    notion of history, see S. Napier, 1993.
42 As with many of the dystopian images of *Akira*, the bikers' aimless and
    violent wanderings are an increasing part of contemporary Japanese life.
    For a discussion of the role of the biker in Japanese culture see Sato
    Ikuya, 1991.

7 Conclusion

Is there a "Japanese" fantastic?

This book has traced the themes of the Japanese fantastic over the course of the twentieth century, demonstrating Japanese literature's dynamic involvement with a range of alterities, from other worlds to other identities, altered states of being that consistently probe and question Japanese modernity. The question remains, however: "Is there a distinctively Japanese fantastic?"

My answer would have to be an extremely qualified "yes," but only in a matter of degree, rather than indicating any essential dissimilarity between Japanese and Western literature. Obviously, certain themes and images are more emphasized in Japanese fantasy than in that of the West, but this study has found no one specific theme that is unique to Japan. Individual authors and specific periods give rise to particular uses of the fantastic, but it would be reductive to say that these treatments are somehow uniquely "Japanese."

On a general level, we can say the fantastic in Japanese literature exists as a site of difference. It shares this *raison d'être* with the fantastic in other twentieth-century cultures, although it may well be that difference is a more highly charged issue in Japan than elsewhere. This site of difference is one that privileges the alien, the illusory, and the irrational in contrast to a vision of modernity that subsumes all difference under a bland rubric of homogeneity, materialism, and rationality.

We have seen, for example, the importance of the countryside in Japanese Utopias, as a magical place of escape and of difference, in direct rejection of the "real" world that is urban Japan. This privileging of the pastoral has been paralleled by a concomitant unease with technology in all but the most recent Japanese dystopias. Both of these tendencies suggest a very different Japan from the Western stereotype of a thoroughly industrialized country at home in the world of high technology.

We have also seen how the role of women in Japanese fantasy has become increasingly problematic. Women have gone from being clearly agents of wish-fulfillment in fantasies of escape and cultural retrenchment to becoming aligned with the dark side of modernity, representatives of a world which entraps and destroys the male. In fantasies by women writers female characters are often seen as attempting their own form of wish-fulfillment, the creation of a world without men. These changes seem to parallel both the increased alienation that modernity has brought and the multiplicity of identities now offered to Japanese women.

Finally, we have seen how the modern concept of the self *vis-à-vis* others has been a major issue in Japanese fantasy. Here again, we come across a surprising variation from the stereotype of modern Japan as a homogeneous nation. While in prewar and early postwar fantasy the self is often viewed as alien and oppressive, the fantastic literature of recent decades celebrates difference in the form of a dizzying variety of selves.

Another overall development in Japanese fantasy that may be traced is a general tendency for the fantastic genre itself to cross boundaries and insinuate itself more and more into the real world. Thus, the prewar fantastic tended to be clearly delineated: it existed in Sōseki's dreams, in Kyōka's hidden valleys, in Akutagawa's retellings of traditional stories or the marginalized world of the asylum in *Kappa*, or in Tanizaki's aesthetic and erotic memories. This form of fantastic was an implicit rather than overt challenge to modernity, an alternative that was offered but not insisted upon.

In the writings of such postwar writers as Abe, Ōe, Nakagami, and Tsutsui the fantastic breaks down the barriers. Abe's lunatics are now directing the asylum in *Secret Rendezvous*, while Ōe's ghosts and monsters are now confronting and even battling the establishment in *Dōjidai gēmu* (The Game of Contemporaneity) and *Pinchrunner Memorandum*. Tsutsui's "Kaomen hōkai" (Collapsing Face) (1978) leaps out of the page and challenges the reader to look away. Perhaps most subversive of all is Nakagami, whose writing directly deconstructs the turn-of-the-century fantasies of Kyōka, forcing the reader to acknowledge the disappearance of that earlier world in which the fantastic was safely confined to the romantic genre.

Contemporary Japanese fantasy explodes out of any single genre to take on what is perhaps the central myth of modern Japan. This myth is that Japan is a purely hierarchical, stable society in which all know their place and authority figures know what is best. The Japanese fantastic, from pure literature to popular *manga*, subverts this myth on every level. Inoue's *Kirikirijin* inverts the conservative and elitist Japanese political system in its image of the *kokkai gijidōsha* driven by a group of marginals and outcasts. *Akira* celebrates change and fluidity in a dazzling series of metamorphoses. Even Murakami, whose fantasies are among the most classic and controlled of any contemporary writer, still insists on the primacy of the individual will and uses ghosts, monsters, and humor to challenge a too oppressive reality.

The fantastic in contemporary Japan is also breaking down barriers in other ways. In modern Japanese literature it is far from a marginal genre. Indeed, it could be said that it has also infiltrated and subverted mainstream realism. Ghosts and telepathy appear in the *shōjo* (young girl) novels of Yoshimoto Banana, while Ōe Kenzaburō, generally known as a master of "grotesque realism," has recently written two science fiction novels. As we saw in Chapter 4, *Scandal* by Endō Shūsaku, a writer known for his historical realism, is an extraordinary mix of the Todorovian fantastic combined with questions of faith and apostasy.

In Endō's work the fantastic is both a place of difference and of darkness. The protagonist's depraved *doppelgänger* forces him to confront unknown aspects of himself, and the experience is a terrifying rather than a liberating one. *Scandal* ends with a telephone's sinister jangling, a voice from outside consensus reality insisting that the dark side of the self can be neither escaped nor ignored.

The fantastic is not always dark in modern Japanese literature. Other writers, as we have seen, have found in the fantastic a territory where they can play with the notion of the real. Akutagawa's "Shūzanzu" (1921) (trans. "Autumn Mountain" (1972)) and "Ryū" (1919) (trans. "The Dragon" (1952)) remind us that uncertainty and irrationality can sometimes be more liberating than belief in an absolute truth.

Other writers have continued this tradition of implicitly questioning the notion of the "real." Perhaps the most prominent of these was Tanizaki, whose *The Bridge of Dreams* and *The Reed Cutter* are replete with clues suggesting that reality is never so easily knowable. Even more than Akutagawa, Tanizaki's texts suggest the joy and playfulness of this kind of fundamental uncertainty.

In recent years, Murakami might be considered another practitioner of the "joys of uncertainty" mode. Unlike Tanizaki or Akutagawa, his novels such as *A Wild Sheep Chase* and *Hard Boiled Wonderland and the End of the World* do provide satisfying examples of closure on the level of narrative structure. At the same time, however, they weave tantalizing and unexplainable bits of fantasy into the narrative itself, suggesting a world rich in possibilities, if the self can but choose to explore them.

Perhaps Japanese writers are more comfortable with this sort of playful attitude toward the real than Western writers who come from a Judeo-Christian tradition of absolutes. It should be pointed out, however, that by the twentieth century this celebration of the lack of an absolute truth is hardly unique to Japan. The fantastic in the West has also increasingly delighted in the presence of ambiguity and the lack of a moral center. Latin American writers such as Cortazar, Marquez, and Borges have forced readers into an awareness of the falseness of evidence and the dangers of memory, while such European writers as Italo Calvino and Flann O'Connor have delighted in presenting a variety of fictional worlds designed to subvert the reader's belief in one simple, knowable reality.

It is possible to suggest that the Japanese have had a longer tradition of this subversion of reality, going back at least to the Chinese philosopher Chuang Tzu (369–286 BC) and his famous dream in which he could not tell whether he was a man dreaming he was a butterfly or a butterfly dreaming he was a man. At the same time, however, it should be remembered that not all modern Japanese writers have celebrated this uncertainty. We remember the *hijiri*'s anguished search for salvation in the form of a woman who was not there in Nakagami's Kenji's "The Immortal," and his final bloody revenge on the uncertainty of existence. Abe Kōbō's most nihilistic work seems sometimes to distill down only to a profound certainty of life's gaping void, while Tsutsui's characters often seem to be frantically trying to escape from uncertainty through violence or anti-social sexuality.

Indeed, another aspect of Japanese fantasy that should be mentioned is its frequently nihilistic tone. Although this too may be more an aspect of twentieth-century culture than something unique to Japan, it is certainly clear that Japanese fantasy, even at the popular level of the *Akira* comics, is far from simple escapism. From the turn of the century to the present, the fantastic visions presented are far more likely to be disturbing, even horrific, than they are to be soothing.

Rosemary Jackson has pointed out concerning modern Western fantasy that, "from about 1800 onwards, those fantasies produced within a capitalist economy express some of the debilitating psychological effects of inhabiting a materialistic culture. They are peculiarly violent and horrific."[1]

If anything, this statement is even truer of twentieth-century Japanese fantasy. While guardedly optimistic works such as Miyazawa's

Ginga tetsudō no yoru (Night Train to the Stars) and Inoue's *Kirikirijin* do exist, the tone of much Japanese fantasy, from Sōseki's claustrophobic *Ten Nights of Dream* to Kanai Mieko's equally claustrophobic and far more horrifyingly bloody "Rabbits," is often one of terror and despair. Murakami's works are notably concerned with death, while *Akira* is a highly colored tapestry of images of destruction.

Sōseki's dark fantasy worlds at least contained a sense of history, even if this history was growing ever harder to recover. Writers of the immediate postwar generation such as Ōe and Inoue have consciously attempted to recover and even reshape history through creating fantasy collectivities. Recent Japanese fantasy, however, seems increasingly set in a world with no past and little future.

No longer do contemporary Japanese search for guardian gods in the trees of their garden. The garden is conspicuously absent in contemporary fantasy, replaced by Kanai's rabbit hutch or Murakami's and Abe's dark labyrinthine sewers, where all sense of past and present vanishes. Characters in contemporary Japanese fantasy seem to exist in a world where constant consumption of material goods, such as Tetsuo and Kaneda's shiny new motorcycles, is the only way they can mark time.

Murakami's protagonists at least are aware of the emptiness of their lives. But their obsessive searches for dead friends and lovers usually leave them alone and forlorn. As with Nakagami's phantoms, the ghosts they raise have little power beyond marking absence.

But even the delineation of absence can be a form of challenge to the oppressiveness of modern reality.[2] Japanese fantasists have also located hope in what Jackson calls the "other and unseen," the dark places of traditional Japanese culture. From Kyōka's hidden supernatural forces to Ōe's and Inoue's privileging of the rural, or even Nakagami's somewhat desperate attempt to raise the ghosts of premodern Japan, Japanese fantasy has also continued to supply those "tabooed images of freedom" which Moylan suggests are part of the Utopian strategy of the fantastic. Perhaps it is finally these "tabooed images" which are the most distinctive aspects of the Japanese fantastic, a subversion of modernity which offers a variety of unique alternatives in its place.

NOTES

1. R. Jackson, 1981, p. 4.
2. Jackson, 1981, p. 179.

Bibliography

JAPANESE FICTIONAL WORKS CONSULTED IN ENGLISH

Abe, Kōbō (1970). *The Face of Another*. London: Penguin Books.
—— (1970). *Inter Ice Age 4*. New York: Alfred Knopf.
—— (1972). *The Woman in the Dunes*. New York: Vintage Books.
—— (1977). *Friends*, in Howard Hibbett (ed.) *Contemporary Japanese Literature*. New York: Alfred Knopf.
—— (1980). *The Ruined Map*. New York: Perigee Books.
—— (1980). *Secret Rendezvous*. New York: Perigee Books.
—— (1986). "Song of a Dead Girl," in Makoto Ueda (ed) *The Mother of Dreams*. New York: Kodansha.
—— (1989). *The Ark Sakura*. New York: Vintage International.
—— (1991). "The Crime of S. Karuma," in *Beyond the Curve*. Tokyo: Kodansha International.
—— (1991). "Dendracacalia," in *Beyond the Curve*. Tokyo: Kodansha International.
Akutagawa, Ryūnosuke (1952). "The Dragon," in *Rashomon and Other Stories*. Tokyo: Tuttle Books.
—— (1952). "In a Grove," in *Rashomon and Other Stories*. Tokyo: Tuttle Books.
—— (1952). "The Martyr," in *Rashomon and Other Stories*. Tokyo: Tuttle Books.
—— (1952). "The Nose," in *Rashomon and Other Stories*. Tokyo: Tuttle Books.
—— (1961). "The Hell Screen," in *Short Stories by Ryunosuke Akutagawa*. New York: Liveright Publishing Co.
—— (1965). "Cogwheels," in *Chicago Review*, Vol. 18, No. 2.
—— (1972). "The Autumn Mountain," in Ivan Morris (ed.) *Modern Japanese Stories: An Anthology*. Tokyo: Charles E. Tuttle.
—— (1974). *Kappa*. Tokyo: Charles E. Tuttle.
Enchi, Fumiko (1983). *Masks*. New York: Vintage.
Endō, Shūsaku (1988). *Scandal*. Tokyo: Charles E. Tuttle.
Ishikawa Jun (1961) "Asters," in Donald Keene (ed.) *The Old Woman, the Wife, and the Archer*. New York: Viking.
—— (1990). *The Bodhisattva*. New York: Columbia University Press.
Kanai, Mieko (1982). "Rabbits," in Phyllis Birnbaum (trans.) *Rabbits, Crabs etc.* Honolulu: University of Hawaii Press.
Kawabata, Yasunari (1956). *Snow Country*. New York: Knopf.

—— (1970). *House of the Sleeping Beauties*. New York:Ballantine Books.

—— (1970). *Sound of the Mountains*. New York: Knopf.

—— (1970). "One Arm," in *House of the Sleeping Beauties*. New York: Ballantine Books.

—— (1988). "Snow," in *Palm of the Hand Stories*. Tokyo: Tuttle Books.

—— (1988). "Immortality," in *Palm of the Hand Stories*. Tokyo: Tuttle Books.

Kyōka, Izumi (1956). "A Tale of Three Who Were Blind," in Donald Keene (ed.) *Modern Japanese Literature*. Tokyo: Tuttle Books.

Mishima, Yukio (1959). *The Temple of the Golden Pavilion*. Tokyo: Charles E. Tuttle.

Miyazawa, Kenji (1991). *Night of the Milky Way Railway* (trans. Sarah Strong). Armank, NY: M. E. Sharpe.

Murakami, Haruki (1988). *Dance, Dance, Dance*. New York: Kodansha International.

—— (1989). *A Wild Sheep Chase*. New York: Kodansha International.

—— (1991). *Hard Boiled Wonderland and the End of the World*. New York: Kodansha International.

—— (1993). "The Little Green Monster," in *The Elephant Vanishes*. New York: Knopf.

Nakagami, Kenji (1985). "The Immortal," in C. Van Gessel (ed.) *The Shōwa Anthology*. New York: Kodansha International.

Nakajima, Ton (1962). "The Tiger Poet," in Ivan Morris (ed.) *Modern Japanese Stories: An Anthology*. Tokyo: Tuttle Books.

Natsume, Sōseki (1969). *The Wayfarer*. Tokyo: Charles E. Tuttle.

—— (1971). *Light and Darkness*. Honolulu: University of Hawaii Press.

—— (1974). *Ten Nights of Dream*. Tokyo: Charles E. Tuttle.

—— (1978). *And Then*. Batan Rouge, La.: Louisiana State University Press.

—— (1986). *I Am a Cat*. Tokyo: Charles E. Tuttle.

—— (1988). *The Miner*. Tokyo: Charles E. Tuttle.

—— (1992). *Kokoro and Selected Essays*. New York: Madison.

Nosaka, Akiyuki (1977). "American *hijiki*," in Howard Hibbett (ed.) *Contemporary Japanese Literature*. New York: Knopf.

Ōe, Kenzaburō (1968). *A Personal Matter*. New York: Grove Press.

—— (1977). "Agwhee the Sky Monster," in Howard Hibbett (ed.) *Contemporary Japanese Literature*. New York: Alfred Knopf.

—— (1977). "The Day He Himself Shall Wipe My Tears Away," in *Teach Us to Outgrow Our Madness*. New York: Grove Press.

—— (1977). "Prize Stock," in *Teach Us to Outgrow Our Madness*. New York: Grove Press.

—— (1994). *The Pinchrunner Memorandum*. Armonk, NY: M.E. Sharpe.

Ohba, Minako (1982). "The Smile of a Mountain Witch", in Lippit and Selden (eds.) *Japanese Women Writers*. Armonk, NY: M.E. Sharpe.

Saikaku, Ihara (1963). *The Life of an Amorous Man*. Tokyo: Charles E. Tuttle.

Satō, Haruo (1972). "The House of a Spanish Dog," in Ivan Morris (ed.), *Modern Japanese Stories*. Tokyo: Charles E. Tuttle.

Tanizaki, Junichirō (1957). *The Makioka Sisters*. New York: Knopf.

—— (1963). "Portrait of Shunkin," in *Seven Japanese Tales*. New York: Knopf.

—— (1977). *The Bridge of Dreams*, in Howard Hibbet (ed.) *Contemporary Japanese Literature*. New York: Alfred Knopf.

—— (1984). *In Praise of Shadows*. Tokyo: Tuttle Books.

—— (1993). *The Reed Cutter/Captain Shigemoto's Mother.* New York: Alfred Knopf.

Tsutsui, Yasutaka (1982). "Such Lovely Ladies," in Ellery Queen (ed.) *A Japanese Golden Dozen.* Tokyo: Charles E. Tuttle.

—— (1989). "Standing Woman," in John Apostolou and Martin H. Greenberg (eds.) *The Best Japanese Science Fiction Stories.* New York: Dember Books.

—— (1990). *What the Maid Saw.* New York: Kodansha International.

Ueda, Akinari (1974). "House Among the Thickets," in *Ugetsu Monogatari.* Tokyo: Tuttle Books.

FICTIONAL WORKS IN JAPANESE

Abe, Kōbō (1972). *Owarishi michi no shirube ni,* Vol. 1 of *Abe Kōbō zenshū.* Tokyo: Shinchōsha.

Akutagawa, Ryūnosuke (1971). "Kamigami no bishō," in *Akutagawa Ryūnosuke zenshū,* Vol. 3. Tokyo: Chikuma Shōbō.

Hiraga, Gennai (1932). *Furyū shidōkenden,* Vol. 2 of *Hiraga Gennai zenshū.* Tokyo: Gennai sensei kenshukai.

Inoue, Hisashi (1981). *Kirikirijin* (vols. I, II, and III). Tokyo: Shinchōsha.

Ishikawa, Jun (1980). "Yakeato no Iesu," Vol. 1 of *Ishikawa Jun zenshū.* Tokyo: Iwanami Shoten.

—— (1980). *Taka,* Vol. 4 of *Ishikawa Jun zenshū.* Tokyo: Iwanami Shoten.

—— (1980). *Shifuku sennen,* Vol. 8 of *Ishikawa Jun zenshū.* Tokyo: Iwanami Shoten.

—— (1980). *Tora no kuni,* Vol. 1 of *Ishikawa Jun zenshū.* Tokyo: Iwanami Shoten.

Izumi Kyōka (1981). *Kōya hijiri,* Vol. 5 of *Izumi Kyōka zenshū.* Tokyo: Iwanami Shoten.

—— (1981). "Kechō," Vol. 3 of *Izumi Kyōka zenshū.* Tokyo: Iwanami Shoten.

—— (1981). *Yashagaike,* Vol. 11 of *Izumi Kyōka zenshū.* Tokyo: Iwanami Shoten.

—— (1982). *Tenshu monogatari,* in *Kyōka shōsetsu gikyokusen,* Vol. 12. Tokyo: Iwanami Shoten.

Komatsu, Sakyō (1983). *Nippon chinbotsu* (vols I and II). Tokyo: Tokuma Bunko.

Kurahashi, Yumiko (1985). "Banpiru no kai," in *Kurahashi Yumiko no kaikishohen.* Tokyo: Shinchōsha.

—— (1985). "Aporon no kubi," in *Kurahashi Yumiko no kaikishōhen.* Tokyo: Shinchōsha.

—— (1985). "Ōgurukoku tokōki," in *Kurahashi Yuniko no kaikishōhen.* Tokyo: Shinchōsha.

—— (1986). *Amanonkoku ōkanki.* Tokyo: Shinchōsha.

Miyazawa, Kenji (1986). *Ginga tetsudō no yoru.* Tokyo: Kadokawa Bunko.

Ōe, Kenzaburō (1973). *Kōzui wa wagatamashi ni oyobi.* Tokyo: Kodansha.

—— (1979). *Dōjidai gēmu.* Tokyo: Shinchōsha.

—— (1986). *Natsukashi toshi e no tegami.* Tokyo: Kodansha.

—— (1990). *Chiryōto.* Tokyo: Iwanami Shoten.

Sakaguchi, Ango (1956). "Sakura no mori no mankai no shita," in *Sakaguchi Ango senshū,* Vol. 4. Tokyo: Sōgensha.

Shiba, Shirō (1885–1887). *Kajin no Kigū*, in Yanagida Izumi (ed.) *Meiji shōsetsushū*. Vol. 1. Tokyo.

Sōseki, Natsume (1952). "Maboroshi no tate," in *Rondontō Maboroshi no tate*. Tokyo: Shinchōsha.

Suehiro, Tetchō (1966). *Setchūbai*, in Yangida Izumi (ed.) *Meiji seiji shōsetsushū*, Vol. II of *Meiji bungaku zenshū*. Tokyo: Chikuma Shobō.

Tsutsui, Yasutaka (1982). "Kaomen hōkai," in *Uchueiseihakuankai*. Tokyo: Shinchōsha.

—— (1982). "Mondai gekka" in *Uchueiseihakurankai*. Tokyo: Shinchōsha.

—— (1982). "Poruno wakusei no sarumonera ningen," in *Uchueiseihakurankai*. Tokyo: Shinchōsha.

Yanagita, Kunio (1948). *Nihon mukashibanashi meii, Vol. 196*. Tokyo: Nihon Hōsō Shuppan Kyōkai.

SECONDARY WORKS IN ENGLISH

Albinski, Nan Bowman (1988). *Women's Utopias in British and American Fiction*. London: Routledge.

Alexander, Marguerite (1990). *Flights from Realism: Themes and Strategies in Postmodernist British and American Fiction*. London: Edward Arnold.

Armitt, Lucy (ed.) (1991). *Where No Man has Gone Before*. London: Routledge.

Auerbach, Nina (1982). *Woman and the Demon: The Life of a Victorian Myth*. Cambridge, Mass.: Harvard University Press.

Bargen, Doris (1991). "Twin Blossoms on a Single Branch: The Cycle of Retribution in *Onnamen*," *Monumenta Nipponica*, Vol. 46, No. 2, 1991.

Bhaktin, Mikhail M. (1968). *Rabelais and His World*. Cambridge, Mass.: MIT Press.

Bronfen, Elisabeth (1992). *Over Her Dead Body: Death, Femininity and the Aesthetic*. London: Routledge.

Bruno, Giuliana (1990). "Ramble City: Postmodernism and *Blade Runner*," in Annette Kuhn (ed.) *Alien Zone: Cultural Theory and Contemporary Science Fiction Cinema*. London: Verso.

Burch, Noel (1979). *To the Distant Observer: Form and Meaning in the Japanese Cinema*. Berkeley, Calif.: University of California Press.

Cummings, Michael and Smith, Nicholas (eds.) (1989). *Utopian Studies II*. Lanham, Md.: University Press of America.

Davis, Winston (1980). *Dojo: Magic and Exorcism in Modern Japan*. Stanford, Calif.: Stanford University Press.

deBary, Brett (1979). *Three Works by Nakano Shigeharu*. Cornell University East Asia Papers No. 21, Ithaca, NY.: Cornell University.

Delprat, Adrienne (1985). "Forms of Dissent in the Gesaku Literature of Hiraga Gennai (1728–1780)," unpublished doctoral thesis, Princeton University, Princeton, NJ.

DeVos, George (1985). "Dimensions of the Self in Japanese Culture," in Marsella, DeVos and Hsu (eds.) *Culture and Self: Asian and Western Perspectives*. New York: Tavistock Publications,, pp. 141–184.

Dijkstra, Bram (1986). *Idols of Perversity: Fantasies of Feminine Evil in Fin-de-Siècle Culture*. Oxford: Oxford University Press.

Foucault, Michel (1980). *The History of Sexuality*, Vol. 1. New York: Vintage Books.

—— (1988). *Madness and Civilization: A History of Insanity in the Age of Reason.* New York: Vintage.

Fowler, Edward (1988). *The Rhetoric of Confession: Shishōsetsu in Early Twentieth-Century Japanese Fiction.* Berkeley, Calif.: University of California Press.

Gessel, Van C. (1993). *Three Modern Novelists.* Tokyo: Kodansha.

Gilbert, Sandra (1983). "Rider Haggard's Heart of Darkness," in George Slusser, Eric Rabkin, and Robert Scholes (eds.) *Coordinates: Placing Science Fiction and Fantasy.* Carbondale, Ill.: Southern Illinois University Press.

Gluck, Carol (1985). *Japan's Modern Myths: Ideology in the Late Meiji Period.* Princeton, NJ.: Princeton University Press.

Grixti, Joseph (1989). *Terrors of Uncertainty: The Cultural Contexts of Horror Fiction.* London: Routledge.

Harbison, Mark (1985). "Introductory Note" to "The Immortal," in Van C. Gessel (ed.), *The Showa Anthology,* Vol. II. Tokyo: Kodansha.

Harootunian, H.D. (1990). "Disciplinizing Native Knowledge and Producing Place: Yanagita Kunio, Origuchi Shinobu, Takata Yasuma," in J. Thomas Rimer (ed.) *Culture and Identity: Japanese Intellectuals During the Interwar Years.* Princeton, NJ.: Princeton University Press.

Heilbrun, Carolyn (1981). "Introduction," to Heilbrun and Higgonet (eds.) *The Representation of Women in Fiction.* Baltimore, Md.: Johns Hopkins University Press.

Heller, Terry (1987). *The Delights of Terror: An Aesthetics of the Tale of Terror.* Urbana, Ill.: University of Illinois Press.

Herndl, Diane (1993). *Invalid Women.* Chapel Hill, NC.: University of North Carolina Press.

Highet, Gilbert (1962). *The Anatomy of Satire.* Princeton, NJ.: Princeton University Press.

Hillegas, Mark R. (1967). *The Future as Nightmare: H.G. Wells and the Anti-Utopians.* Carbondale Ill.: Southern Illinois University Press.

Hume, Kathryn (1984). *Fantasy and Mimesis: Responses to Reality in Western Literature.* New York: Methuen.

Inouye, Charles (1991). "Water Imagery in the Work of Izumi Kyoka," *Monumenta Nipponica,* Vol. 46, No. 1, pp. 43–68.

Irwin, W. R. (1976). *The Game of the Impossible: A Rhetoric of Fantasy.* Urbana: University of Illinois Press.

Ito, Ken (1991). *Visions of Desire: Tanizaki's Fictional Worlds.* Stanford, Calif.: Stanford University Press.

Jackson, Rosemary (1981). *Fantasy: The Literature of Subversion.* London: Methuen and Co.

Jameson, Fredric (1982). "Progress versus Utopia, or Can We Imagine the Future?" *Science Fiction Studies,* Vol. 9.

—— (1990). *Signatures of the Visible.* London: Routledge.

Keene, Donald (1984). *Dawn to the West: Japanese Literature of the Modern Era.* New York: Holt, Rinehart & Winston.

Kellner, Douglas (1992). "Popular Culture and the Construction of Postmodern Identities," in Scott Lash and Jonathan Friedman (eds.) *Modernity and Identity.* Oxford: Basil Blackwell, pp. 141–177.

Kramer, Peter (1993). *Listening to Prozac.* New York: Viking.

Kuehl, John (1989). *Alternate Worlds: A Study of Postmodern AntiRealistic American Fiction*. New York: New York University Press.

Kumar, Krishan (1987). *Utopia and Anti-Utopia in Modern Times*. Oxford: Basil Blackwell Ltd.

Lefanu, Sarah (1988). *In the Chinks of the World Machine: Feminism and Science Fiction*. London: Women's Press.

—— (1989). *Feminism and Science Fiction*. Bloomington, Ind.: Indiana University Press.

Malti-Douglas, Fedwa (1991). *Woman's Body, Woman's Word: Gender and Discourse in Arabo-Islamic Writing*. Princeton, NJ.: Princeton University Press.

Manuel, Frank and Manuel, Fritzie (1979). *Utopian Thought in the Western World*. Cambridge, Mass.: Harvard University Press.

Matthew, Robert (1989). *Japanese Science Fiction: A View of a Changing Society*. London: Routledge.

Mayer, Fanny Hagin (1986). *The Yanagita Kunio Guide to the Japanese Folk Tale*. Bloomington, Ind.: Indiana University Press.

Miller, Karl (1987). *Doubles: Studies in Literary History*. Oxford: Oxford University Press.

Miyoshi, Masao (1991). *Off Center*. Cambridge, Mass.: Harvard University Press.

Moylan, Tom (1986). *Demand the Impossible: Science Fiction and the Utopian Imagination*. New York: Methuen.

Mulhern, Chieko (1977). *Kōda Rohan*. Boston, Mass.: Twayne Publishers

Najita, Tetsuo (1987). *Visions of Virtue in Tokugawa Japan*. Chicago, Ill.: Chicago University Press.

—— (1989). "On Culture and Technology in Postmodern Japan," in M. Miyoshi, and H.D. Harootunian (eds.) *Postmodernism and Japan*. Durham, NC.: Duke University Press, pp. 3–20.

Napier, Susan J. (1987). "Brave New Worlds(?): Technology in Japanese Fiction," *Bulletin of Science and Technology*.

—— (1993). "Panic Sites: The Japanese Imagination of Disaster from *Godzilla* to *Akira*," *Journal of Japanese Studies*, Vol. 19, No. 2, pp. 327–351.

Nash, Christopher (1987). *World Games: The Tradition of Anti-Realist Revolt*. London: Methuen & Co.

Natsume, Sōseki (1992). "My Individualism," in *Kokoro and Selected Essays*. Lanham, NY: Madison Books.

Ohnuki-Tierney, Emiko (1987). *The Monkey as Mirror: Symbolic Transformations in Japanese History and Ritual*. Princeton, NJ.: Princeton University Press.

Penley, Constance (1989). "Time Travel, Primal Scene and the Critical Dystopia," in James Donald (ed.) *Fantasy and the Cinema*. London: British Film Institute, pp. 196–212.

Poulton, Cody (1993). "Supernatural Naturalism: Self and Nature in Izumi Kyoka," in Kinya Tsuruta (ed.) *Nature and the Self: Proceedings*. Vancouver: University of British Columbia.

Powell, Bill (1992). "Don't Write Off Japan," *Newsweek*, No. 919, p. 48.

Rabkin, Eric S. (1976). *The Fantastic in Literature*. Princeton, NJ.: Princeton University Press.

Rabkin, Eric S., Greenberg, Martin H., and Olander, Joseph D. (eds.) (1983a). *The End of the World*. Carbondale, Ill.: Southern Illinois University Press.

—— (eds.) (1983b). *No Place Else: Explorations in Utopian and Dystopian Fiction*. Carbondale Ill.: Southern Illinois University Press.

Rimer, Thomas (1990a). "The Move Inward," in Thomas Rimer (ed.) *Culture and Identity: Japanese Intellectuals During the Interwar Years*. Princeton, NJ: Princeton University Press, pp. 3–6.

—— (ed.) (1990b). *Culture and Identity: Japanese Intellectuals During the Interwar Years*. Princeton, NJ.: Princeton University Press.

Roden, Donald (1990). "Taishō Culture and the Problem of Gender Ambivalence," in Thomas Rimer (ed.) *Culture and Identity: Japanese Intellectuals During the Interwar Years*. Princeton, NJ.: Princeton University Press, pp. 37–55

Rose, Mark (1981). *Alien Encounters: Anatomy of Science Fiction*. Cambridge, Mass.: Harvard University Press.

Rosenberger, Nancy R. (ed.) (1992). *Japanese Sense of Self*. Cambridge: Cambridge University Press.

Rubin, Jay (1984). *Injurious to Public Morals: Writers and the Meiji State*. Seattle, Wash.: University of Washington Press.

—— (1993). "The Other World of Murakami Haruki," *Japan Quarterly*, pp. 490–500.

Sakaki, A. (1993). "Denaturing Nature, Dissolving the Self: An Analysis of Kurahashi Yumiko's *Popoi*," in K. Isuruta (ed.) *Nature and the Self: Proceedings*. Vancouver: University of British Columbia.

Sato, Ikuya (1991). *Kamikaze Biker: Parody and Anomy in Affluent Japan*. Chicago, Ill.: Chicago University Press.

Sato, Tadao (1982). *Currents in Japanese Cinema*. Tokyo: Kodansha International.

Shively, Donald (1971). "The Japanization of the Mid Meiji," in Donald Shively (ed.) *Tradition and Modernization in Japanese Culture*. Princeton, NJ.: Princeton University Press.

Shirane, Haruo (1987). *The Bridge of Dreams: Poetics in the Tale of Genji*. Stanford, Calif.: Stanford University Press.

Siebers, Tobin (1984). *The Romantic Fantastic*. Ithaca, NY.: Cornell University Press.

Silverberg, Miriam (1990). "Marxism Addresses the Modern: Nakano Shigeharu's Reproduction of Taisho Culture," in Thomas Rimer (ed.) *Culture and Identity: Japanese Intellectuals during the Interwar Years*. Princeton, NJ.: Princeton University Press, pp. 133–153.

Slusser, George, Rabkin, Eric, and Scholes, Robert (eds.) (1983). *Coordinates: Placing Science Fiction and Fantasy*. Carbondale, Ill.: Southern Illinois University Press.

Swinfen, Anne (1984). *In Defence of Fantasy*. London: Routledge & Kegan Paul.

Todorov, Tzvetan (1975). *The Fantastic: A Structural Approach to a Literary Genre*. Ithaca, NY.: Cornell University Press.

Tolman Mori, Mary Ellen (1994). "The Subversive Role of Fantasy in the Fiction of Takahashi Takako," *Journal of the Association of Teachers of Japanese*, Vol. 28, No. 1, pp. 29–56.

Tudor, Andrew (1989). *Monsters and Mad Scientists: A Cultural History of the Horror Movie*. Oxford: Basil Blackwell.

Turner, Victor (1969). *The Ritual Process: Structure and Anti-structure*. Ithaca, NY.: Cornell University Press.

Tyler, William Jefferson (1990). "Introduction" to Ishikawa Jun *The Bodhisatt-va*. New York: Columbia University Press.

Ueda, Makoto (1983). *Modern Japanese Poets and the Nature of Literature*. Stanford, Calif.: Stanford University Press.

Vogel, Ezra (1978). *Japan as Number One*. Cambridge, Mass.: Harvard University Press.

Vohra, S.K. (1987). *Negative Utopian Fiction*. Meerut: Shalabh Prakshan.

Waugh, Patricia (1989). *Feminine Fictions: Revisiting the Postmodern*. London: Routledge.

Wilson, Michiko (1986). *The Marginal Worlds of Oe Kenzaburo*, White Plains, NY.: M. E. Sharpe Inc.

Yu, Beongcheon (1972). *Akutagawa*. Detroit, Mich.: Wayne State University Press.

Zamora, Lois (1995). "Introduction" to Lois Zamora and Wendy Faris (eds.) *Magic Realism: History, Theory, Community*. Durham, NC.: Duke University Press.

Zamora, Lois and Faris, Wendy (eds.) (1996). *Magic Realism: History, Theory, Community*. Durham: Duke University Press.

SECONDARY WORKS CONSULTED IN JAPANESE

Egusa, Mitsuko and Urushida, Kazuyo (eds.) (1992). *Onna ga yomu Nihon kindai bungaku*. Tokyo: Shinchōsa.

Etō, Jun (1974). *Natsume Sōseki*. Tokyo: Shinchōsa.

Fujimoto, Tokuaki (1980). "Bodai no roman: Kyōka bungaku ni okeru seikai," in *Nihon bungaku kenkū shiryogosho: Izumi Kyōka*, Tokyo: Yūseido.

Hino, Tatsuo (1977). *Edojin to yūtopia*. Tokyo: Asahi shimbunsha.

Imaizumi, Fumiko (1991). "Yumeno Kyūsaku no anchiyūtopia," *Koku-bungaku*, Vol. 36, No. 9 (March), pp. 78–85.

Imamura, Tadazumi (1982). "Inoue Hisashi," *Kokubungaku*, Vol. 27, No. 11 (August), pp. 126–7.

Isoda, Kōichi (1974). "Mukokusekisha no shiten: Abe Kōbō ron," in *Nihon bungaku kenkyū shiryōgōsho: Abe Kōbō Ōe Kenzaburō*, Tokyo: Yūseido.

Kasai, Kiyoshi (1988). *Monogatari no uroboros*. Tokyo: Chikuma Shobo.

Kawamura, Jiro (1985). *Ginga to jigoku: Gensō bungakuron*. Tokyo: Kodansha Gakujutsubunko.

Kawamura, Minato (1988). "Mizu to bōmei: Shifuku sennen no sekai," *Yurika*, Vol. 20, No. 8 (July), pp. 213–221.

—— (1989). "'Shinsekai' no owari to haatobureiku wandaarando," *Yurika*, Vol. 21, No. 4 (June), pp. 174–181.

Kawano, Tsuneaki (1975). "Taisho no roman to fuantaji: Miyazawa Kenji, sono hoka ni tsuite," *Kokubungaku*, Vol. 20, No. 4 (March), pp. 154–156.

Kurihara, Akira (1983). "Sokō to saisei: Aidenchichi seiji," *Yurika*, Vol. 20, No. 8 (July), pp. 52–56.

Kuroko, Kazuo (1990). *Murakami Haruki to dōjidai no bungaku*. Tokyo: Iwade Shuppan.

Kuwahara, Tetsuo (1987). "Ijigensekai o byōshō shite miseta: Ginga tetsudō no yoru," in *Miyazawa Kenji*, No. 7, Tokyo: Yoyosha.

Maeda, Ai (in discussion with Yamaguchi Masao) (1985). "Kyokaisenjo no bungaku: Kyōka sekai no genkyō," *Kokubungaku*, Vol. 30, No. 7, pp. 8–24.

Matsuda, Osamu (in discussion with Yura Kimiyoshi) (1974). "Yurei kanwa: Sono genshō sono ronri," *Kokubungku*, Vol. 19, No. 9 (August), pp. 7–32.

Mishima, Yukio (1981). "Izumi Kyōka," in *Bungei dokuhon: Izumi Kyōka*. Tokyo: Iwade Shuppan.

Miyasaka, Satoru (1985). "Kappa," *Kokubungaku*, Vol. 30, No. 5 (May), pp. 110–111.

Nakamura, Shinichiro (in discussion with Yura Kimoyoshi) (1984). "Gensō no sakiwau kuni ni," *Kokubungaku*, Vol. 10, No. 29, pp. 10–30.

Oka, Yasuo, Kasahara, Nobuo and Soya, Shinpei (in discussion) (1979). "Gensō bungaku sono honshitsu to hirogari," *Kokubungaku*, Vol. 44, No. 10 (September), pp. 14–38.

Suzumura, Kazunari (1987). *Terefuon.* Tokyo: Yozumisha.

Tatsumi, Takayuki (1988). "Kyōmen hōkai," *Yurika*, Vol. 20, No. 5, pp. 76–85.

Teruhiko, Tsuge (1984). "Ōe Kenzaburō to Tsutsui Yasutaka: Gensō no genzai". *Kokubungaku*, Vol. 29, No. 10 (August), pp. 120–124.

Togo, Katsumi (1980). "Kōya hijiri no suichimu," in *Nihon bungaku kenkyū shiryōsōsho*, Tokyo: Yuseido.

Torigoe, Makoto (1975). "Unno Juza no shōnen SF shōsetsu," *Kokubungaku*, Vol. 20, No. 4, pp. 157–160.

Yahashi, Ichiro (1985). *Hyōden: Tsutsui Yasutaka*. Tokyo: Shinchōsha.

Yamada, Yusaku (1988). "Inoue Hisashi: Kirikirijin," *Kokubungaku*, Vol. 28, No. 4, pp. 88–91.

Yoshimura, Hirotō (1983). *Izumi Kyōka no sekai: Gensō no byōri*. Tokyo: Bokuya Shuppan.

Yura, Kimiyoshi (in discussion with Inoue Hisashi) (1982). "Gendai bungaku wa SF o mezasu," *Kokubungaku*, Vol. 27, No. 11 (August), pp. 6–27.

Biographical reference

This is a highly selective reference list. I discuss the writers largely in relation to their contributions to the fantastic genre, give examples of some of their major fantasy works, and mention any English translations, if available.

Abe Kōbō (1924–1993)   One of the major writers of modern Japan, Abe Kōbō is perhaps the most consistently "fantastic" in his use of avant-garde and surrealist themes. He could also be termed "the master of dystopia," since his visions, although original and fascinating, are almost relentlessly bleak. Along with Murakami Haruki, Abe is one of the most "international" of modern Japanese fantasists, frequently placing his characters in anonymous and bizarre situations that could potentially occur in any generic industrialized society, although, as I suggest with *Tomodachi* (1967) (trans. *Friends* (1977)), they can also be related to distinctively Japanese social structures. Perhaps not surprisingly, Abe is highly regarded in both the West and the former Eastern bloc countries and is one of the most widely translated of any of the writers discussed here. Important works include: *Suna no onna* (1962) (trans. *The Woman in the Dunes* (1972)), *Dai yon Kampyō-ki* (1958) (trans. *Inter Ice Age 4* (1970)) and *Mikai* (1977) (trans. *Secret Rendezvous* (1980)).

Akutagawa Ryūnosuke (1892–1927)   Like the postwar Abe Kōbō, the early-twentieth-century writer Akutagawa is one of the most frequently translated of the authors treated in this volume, but for almost opposite reasons. While the grey post-industrial tones of Abe Kōbō's dystopias evoke the postwar world of almost anywhere, Akutagawa's prewar colorful and vibrant fantasies, often with a distinctive ironic twist, communicate vividly across international borders. Akutagawa's fictional territory, frequently drawn from premodern Japanese literature, as in his short story "Jigokuhen" (1918) (trans. "The Hell Screen" (1956)), sometimes evokes an almost Oriental (in Said's sense of the term) atmosphere. In other works, however, as the fantasies discussed in this book suggest, he was also a passionate and powerful critic of newly industrial, newly urban Japan.

Enchi Fumiko (1905–1986) Arguably the greatest female writer of the twentieth century, Enchi was the daughter of a distinguished scholar of Japanese and she herself often reworked classical themes in modern-day guise in her own writings. Although not primarily a fantasist, Enchi often evoked a mysterious and eerie atmosphere in stories such as "Nisei no en shūi" (1957) (trans. "Love in Two Lives: The Remnant," in Noriko Mizuta Lippit (ed.) (1991), *Japanese Women Writers*. Armonk, NY.: M.E. Sharpe. Also trans. "A Bond for Two Lifetimes: Gleanings," in Phyllis Birnbaum (ed.) (1982), *Rabbits, Crabs, etc.* Honolulu: University of Hawaii Press). Her novel *Onnamen* (1958) (trans. *Masks* (1983)) brilliantly interweaves the theme of female revenge from the classic *Tale of Genji* within a structure closely resembling Todorov's definition of the fantastic as the hesitation between natural and supernatural explanations.

Endō Shūsaku (1923–) One of the most well known of Japanese writers in the West, with at least seven novels in translation, Endō is unusual among Japanese writers for his frequent treatment of Christian themes. His works are often historical in nature, such as *Chinmoku* (1966) (trans. *Silence* (1961)) and *Samurai* (1980) (trans. *The Samurai* (1982)). Although many of his writings deal with the miraculous in terms of questions of faith, *Sukyandaru* (1986) (trans. *Scandal* (1988)) is perhaps the most explicitly "fantastic" of all his writings.

Inoue Hisashi (1934–) Belonging to the same postwar generation of writers as Ōe Kenzaburō and Tsutsui Yasutaka, Inoue shares with Ōe a rural background and a belief in what might be termed "Utopian humanism," while he shares with Tsutsui a love of language and parody. His long Utopian trilogy *Kirikirijin* (The People of Kirikiri) (1980) discussed here weaves all the above elements into a fantasy of rural regeneration. His novel *Boon to Phoon* (Boon and Phoon) (1970), a fantastic satire on the modern world, has been called a "nonsense masterpiece." A major playwright as well, Inoue has also written the popular play, "Ii hatōbo no gekiesha" (The Dramatic Train of Iihatoo-bo) (1980), an homage to the turn-of-the-century fantasist Miyazawa Kenji.

Ishikawa Jun (1899–1987) This brilliant and multi-faceted writer was born in Tokyo and initially studied French literature, but was also heavily influenced by the "floating world" literature of the Edo period. One of the greatest and most powerful fantasists discussed in this book, Ishikawa produced a large number of brilliant fantastic novels, many of which incorporate extensive political satire. One of Ishikawa's great themes is the paradoxical appeal and fearsomeness of power and he deals with this in such works as the dystopian *Taka* (The Hawk) (1953) and the fantastic *Aratama* (The Wild Spirit) (1963). Regrettably undertranslated, only one novel, *Fugen* (1936) (trans. *The Boddhisatva* (1990)), is available in English.

Izumi Kyōka (1873–1939)   In terms of his mastery of such traditional supernatural elements as ghosts, monsters, and demonic females, all set within an appropriately eerie atmosphere, Izumi Kyōka is the greatest of twentieth-century Japanese fantasists. The enormous amount of critical literature about him by Japanese scholars over the last two decades bears witness to his extraordinary ability to evoke such archetypal tropes as the demonic/nurturing female and the supernatural yet familiar landscape. Unfortunately, however, translations of Kyōka are at this point few and hard to come by. The extraordinary richness of Kyōka's language does make him difficult to read even in Japanese, let alone to render his work into English, but the sheer beauty of his imagery alone makes any effort worthwhile. It is surely no accident that a number of Kyōka stories have been made into evocative and memorable films.

Kanai Mieko (1947–)   A complex and sometimes shocking writer, as her short story "Usagi" (1976) (trans. "Rabbits" (1982)) powerfully indicates, Kanai is also a major poet. Her short stories often combine a poetic and dreamlike atmosphere with bizarre occurrences to create an eerie, unsettling atmosphere where nothing is as it seems.

Kawabata Yasunari (1899–1972)   One of the greatest of Japan's writers of any century and Japan's first Nobel Prize winner, Kawabata combined a sensitivity for past Japanese traditions with a surprisingly modern, even avant-garde sensibility. His major theme was the loneliness of relationships between men and women, and his surreal fantasy "Kataude" (1965) (trans. "One Arm" (1970)) is a memorable example of this theme. Although most of his many novels available in translation are more realistic, almost all share a mysterious and evocative atmosphere in which nature, dreams, and human lives intermingle.

Komatsu Sakyō (1931–)   One of Japan's leading science fiction writers, Komatsu's bestselling novel *Nippon Chimbotsu* (1973) (trans. *Japan Sinks* (1976)), describing the Japanese islands' destruction by a series of earthquakes, also became an immensely popular movie. A conservative, who often uses writing to lament the destruction of traditional culture, Komatsu also stresses the dangers of scientific experimentation on the environment.

Kōda Rohan (1867–1947) Discussed here largely as a transitional figure, Kōda Rohan was particularly popular during the Meiji period, when Japan began to explore a new identity as a modernizing nation. Rohan initially made a name for himself as a "modern" writer, but his most influential stories such as "Fūryūbutsu" (Love Boddhisatva) (1889) and "Taidokuro" (Encounter With a Skull) (1890) blend traditional elements such as Buddhist miracles and Nō play structure to create a supernatural atmosphere.

Kurahashi Yumiko (1935–) Perhaps one of the most interesting and sophisticated of contemporary women writers, Kurahashi studied French literature while at university and her study of the existentialists influenced both her politics and her anti-realist style. Her works include political satire, reworkings of classical literature, and a variety of fantasies such as her collection *Otona no tame no zankou dōwa* (Cruel Fairy Tales for Adults) (1984), which are parodies of traditional fairy tales.

Mishima Yukio (1925–1970) Mishima's writing, including short stories, modern Nō plays, and a variety of novels, has been widely translated in the West. Although I do not discuss Mishima's writing at great length in this volume, his tetralogy *Hojo no umi* (The Sea of Fertility, widely available in English as *Spring Snow, Runaway Horses, Temple of the Dawn*, and *The Decay of the Angel*) is based on the premise of using a series of reincarnations to show the decay of modern Japan. As I have discussed in my previous work (Napier, 1991), Mishima ultimately questions the validity of his own fantasy as a means of problematizing Japanese history and the tetralogy thus becomes an almost Todorovian example of fantasy's subversive capabilities.

Miyazawa Kenji (1896–1933) is one of Japan's most beloved fantasy writers. Readers appreciate his simple pastoral visions, his faith in Buddhism and his clever and lyrical fantastic tales. Written primarily for children and often using animals as the main characters, the stories can still be appreciated by adults. They frequently express concerns for the environment and other wholesome values such as education and living in peace with one's natural surroundings.

Murakami Haruki (1949–) was born in Kobe the son of a teacher of Japanese literature, but he rejected Japanese literature in favor of studying Greek drama at Waseda University. Disappointed by what he saw as the defeat of committed politics in the 1960s, Murakami began managing a jazz coffee shop in Tokyo in the late 1970s during which time he began to write stories that ranged from the realistic to the classically fantastic. One of the most international of modern Japan's fantasists, Murakami's novels have been criticized for being "too atmospheric" and lacking a strong political vision. His often perversely funny and skewed visions of contemporary humans in quest of something (perhaps themselves?) that they have almost forgotten, have made him one of Japan's most popular writers as well as making him known in the West, where he now chooses to live.

Nakagami Kenji (1946–1993)   The prolific and talented Nakagami's early death was a tragic loss to the postwar generation of writers. Noted for his brutal confessional realism, Nakagami often set his works in the *buraku* or "outcast" district of Shingū in the Kumano region where he was born. But Nakagami also used the otherworldly myths and legends of the mysterious Kumano region as another major source of inspiration, combining them with a provocative and powerful style to produce the kind of unique and unsettling vision which permeates "Fushi" (1984) (trans. "The Immortal" (1985)) discussed in this book.

Natsume Sōseki (1867–1916)   Sōseki is still considered by many Japanese to be their greatest twentieth-century writer. Although most well known for the series of dark psychological novels he produced in later years, Sōseki was also a unique and creative writer of fantasy. His fantastic works range from the Swiftian satire of *Wagahai wa neko de aru* (1905/6) (trans. *I Am a Cat* (1986)) through the sentimental lyricism "Maboroshi no tate" (The Shield of Illusion) (1907) to his surreally exquisite masterpiece *Yume jūya* (1908) (trans. *Ten Nights of Dream* (1970)). In this last work, discussed at length in this book, Soseki's major realistic themes, such as the problems of modernization and Westernization and the suffocating power of the past are powerfully expressed within a uniquely fantastic framework.

Ōba Minako (1930–)   Ōba Minako's writings are full of aliens who are not necessarily fantastic but simply foreigners. An unusually international writer, her first short story, "Sanbiki no kani" (1968) (trans. "The Three Crabs" (1982)), dealt with a group of cosmopolitan friends in Alaska and brought up themes of women's loneliness, frustration, and search for identity. These themes are important in her fantasy literature as well, as "Yamauba no bisho" (1976) (trans. "The Smile of a Mountain Witch" (1982)) discussed in this volume, superbly attests.

Ōe Kenzaburō (1935–)   When the Nobel Committee awarded Ōe Kenzaburō the Nobel Prize for Literature in 1994 they cited his political commitment, his concern for the ongoing effects of the Second World War on Japan, and the grotesque realism that is a stylistic hallmark of his stories. Ōe uses fantasy brilliantly and highly idiosyncratically, as the works discussed in this volume attest. *Dōjidai gēmu* (The Game of Contemporaneity) (1979) draws from folk tales and legends to create an alternate mythic world somewhat on the lines of the Macondo of Gabriel Garcia Marquez. "Sora no Kaibutsu Aguii" (1964) (trans. "Aghwee the Sky Monster" (1977)) is an almost textbook example of Todorovian fantasy which is still able to deliver a deeply moral message concerning the need for belief in a chaotic contemporary world.

Satō Haruo (1892–1964) A poet and Utopianist, Sato Haruo is included here because of his lovely short fantasy "Supein inu no ie" (trans. "The House of the Spanish Dog" (1962)). Although Satō considered the story to be a modern example of the traditional "hermit literature" of both China and Japan, the story is also interesting as an example of using Western architecture and accoutrements to create a defamiliarized, "fantastic" atmosphere.

Tanizaki Junichirō (1866–1965) A superb writer, many of whose works have been ably translated into English, Tanizaki's major preoccupation was with the female character, preferably in demonic but arguably realistic form. His works range from the clearly fantastic, such as "Shisei" (1910) (trans. "Tattoo" (1910)), which has been translated a number of times, to radically experimental studies of male–female obsessions such as *Kagi* (1956) (trans. *The Key* (1961)). Born in Tokyo, Tanizaki eventually retreated to the Kyoto–Osaka area where he could combine his obsession with women with an obsession with the Japanese past.

Tsutsui Yasutaka (1934–) Irreverent, black-humored, and extraordinarily imaginative, Tsutsui clearly enjoys offending the Japanese literary establishment. At the same time he is an exceptionally popular writer whose science fiction stories, mysteries, and social satires have made him something of a cult figure among the younger Japanese. Even critics who do not appreciate his outrageous lack of political correctness are willing to recognize his exceptional ability to weave complex and often supremely funny variations on the Japanese language. Regrettably, it is precisely this linguistic facility which makes Tsutsui so hard to translate, although one dystopian science fiction story, "Standing Woman", is available in Apostolou and Greenberg's anthology, and a "psychic novel" *Kazoku hakkei* (What the Maid Saw) appeared in translation in 1990.

Uchida Hyakken (1889–1971) Like Yumeno Kyūsaku, Uchida is a fantasist who is virtually untranslated in the West but has a strong following in Japan. Less weird and convoluted than Kyūsaku, Uchida's fantasies often center around such traditional fantastic tropes as metamorphoses and bewitchments.

Yumeno Kyūsaku (1889–1936)   Virtually untranslated in the West, I mention Kyūsaku because he has recently been rediscovered in Japan. An international cast of androgynes and hermaphrodites involved with family curses and love beyond death populate Yumeno's sinister but entertaining fantasies. His most well-known and critically respected work *Dogura magura* has recently been reissued in Japan in comicbook (*manga*) form.

Index